What people are

365 Blessings to Heal My...

What a labor of love your newest book is. Wow! Thank you for offering this to a hungering planet. Pierre's life, and this precious book, are an invitation to abide in an affectional consciousness. He leaves no situation or relationship unblessed, modeling for us a devotional practice that embraces our world in grace. Anyone who yearns to feel the presence of Love will find it in the application of each blessing offered.

Sanford (Sandy) C. Wilder, Founder, the Educare Unlearning Institute and author of *Listening to Grace: Unlearning Insights and Poems*

Anyone working to heal personal, societal, world situations, no matter what religious or spiritual path they follow, will benefit immensely from Pierre's compilation of blessings. There is so much that needs healing in our world, and this is a book that will touch many because it speaks to the heart and gently reminds us of our oneness with the Divine.

Fr. Richard Rohr, OFM, Founder of the Center for Action and Contemplation, Albuquerque, New Mexico. Fr. Rohr is the author of numerous books, including *The Divine Dance*.

Pierre's first book, *The Gentle Art of Blessing* (now in seven languages), helped readers discover a completely new vision of blessing and a simple practice which has changed the lives of thousands all around the world. This second book offers you a means of truly participating in the healing of the world – not to mention of yourself. It will enable you to raise your level of inspiration at the start of every new day and will slowly start changing even your relations to others.

Steve Farrell, Worldwide Executive Director, Humanity's Team

I couldn't stop reading. From one page to the next, it filled me with such love!

What a total blessing it is! On every page you will know what it is to feel deeply blessed and to experience the power and beauty of this to lift you into a great light of love! Pierre Pradervand is a master teacher of the spiritual art of blessing! Your heart will be full! You will feel it! If all those who long for love would learn the art of blessing, it would end loneliness, sadness, and depression forever. And hearts everywhere would feel comforted and connected, lit with love!

Shannon Peck, Spiritual Life Coach, author, *Love Heals – How to Heal Everything with Love*, and several other books co-authored with Dr. Scott Peck

If we are on an evolving path to realize everything is Consciousness we may well be on an evolving path to also understand that nothing in the world of the Heart is really impossible. These 365 daily challenges remind us of the sheer breadth of the worlds that can be brought into Love by The Gentle Art of Blessing.

Kurt Johnson PhD, co-author *The Coming Interspiritual Age*

This is a very special book! A beautifully distinct follow-up to your Gentle Art of Blessing. I'm relishing your pages for so many reasons. For example:
- Because you've included blessings for specific groups of people – nurses, homeless, politicians, etc. It stirs awareness and care. It draws us closer together and widens the circle of compassion.
- Including not only blessings composed by you but also some that come from other individuals and cultural groups provides a variety of voices that enliven the book and encourage me with the idea that the practice of blessing is coming from many corners. That is mighty comforting.
- The intros you provide for each blessing orient and guide in ways that shed light on the blessings without thwarting a reader's own

creative interpretation and application.

- The instances where you link the blessor to the blessee bring the practice full circle, reminding us how we are all inextricably intertwined, that we find our own in another's good, that "what blesses one blesses all."

Bunny McBride

365 Blessings to Heal Myself and the World

Really living one's spirituality
in everyday life

365 Blessings to Heal Myself and the World

Really living one's spirituality
in everyday life

Pierre Pradervand

BOOKS

Winchester, UK
Washington, USA

First published by O-Books, 2018
O-Books is an imprint of John Hunt Publishing Ltd., No. 3 East Street,
Alresford, Hampshire SO24 9EE, UK
office1@jhpbooks.net
www.johnhuntpublishing.com

For distributor details and how to order please visit the 'Ordering' section on our website.

Text copyright: Pierre Pradervand 2017

ISBN: 978 1 78535 729 9
978 1 78535 730 5 (ebook)
Library of Congress Control Number: 2017940724

A CIP catalogue record for this book is available from the British Library.

Design: Stuart Davies

Printed and bound by CPI Group (UK) Ltd, Croydon, CR0 4YY, UK

We operate a distinctive and ethical publishing philosophy in
all areas of our business, from our global network of authors to
production and worldwide distribution.

Contents

Previous books in English by the author

The Gentle Art of Blessing, ISBN 978-1-58270-242-1, 978-1-43915-363-5 (ebook), Atria Paperbacks, Simon and Schuster, 2009. Winner of the 2010 Gold Nautilus Book Award for Spirituality. English editions also in Great Britain (Cygnus Books) and India (St. Paul's, Mumbai). The book originally appeared in French (Jouvence, 1998) and has also appeared in Spanish, German, Dutch, Danish and Slovene.

Messages of Life from Death Row, ISBN 10: 095493265X, ISBN 13: 9780954932657, BookSurge Publishing, 1999 (originally in French, and also Dutch).

Listening to Africa, ISBN-13: 978-0275933890, ISBN-10: 027593389X (a 14,000km trip through over 100 villages of the Sahel, Kenya and Zimbabwe I undertook in 1987, talking with around 1,300 peasant farmers at the grass roots, published in 6 languages including Japanese), Praeger Publishers, NY, 1989.

I dedicate this book to my very special friends Robin and Ron Radford who are a living incarnation of the truest friendship I could ever imagine. Thank you for being the very bright light you are in my life – and that of so many others.

Special Thanks: I wish to thank my dear friend Manuela, who is coeditor of the blessing website, for her exceptional assistance in cleaning up my manuscript, suggesting a variety of blessings from various sources and finding a publisher. Without her assistance, I'm not sure the book would have been published.

Foreword

The author of this remarkable compendium of unusual blessings writes that he hopes that the blessings he proposes could serve not only those who emit them, and not only those to whom they are addressed, but all people in the human community. I think he may be right.

Let me recall Einstein's famous words: we cannot solve the significant problems of our time with the kind of consciousness that gave birth to them. Our world is beset by significant problems, and we seem unable to solve them – perhaps because we try to do so with the same consciousness that framed them. We need a new consciousness, and achieving it calls for a leap – a leap of faith as well as of courage. The author of this book offers a shining example of that leap, thanks to a deep and initially traumatic experience he had. Now we, his readers, can accomplish this leap without undergoing a traumatic experience, simply by reading his book and following his example: offering blessings in at least as many of the 365 days of the year as we can.

A blessing a day is one way to shift to the consciousness we need, and there are others. Whatever the way we choose, we know that the result must be a serious shift in the way we think and the way we are – a shift in consciousness. It is this shift that the author of this book has experienced, and the blessings he offers are a consequence of that shift. This is an important offer, because it could shift the way we think and act. And only a major, indeed radical shift is of use in the critical situation in which we find ourselves.

The actual substance of the blessing committed to paper in this book is not new: it has been known to all right-thinking and well-meaning people today and throughout history. But this substance needs emphasis, and being followed up. We need a new consciousness, and we need to act differently. Instead of revenge we need to practice forgiveness, instead of all-out competition, we need embracing love, and in place of looking for our own advantage in

1

every situation, we need to embrace everyone concerned – and do so unconditionally.

Such a shift in acting needs to be underpinned by a shift in our view of ourselves and of the world – a new paradigm. The root cause of the crisis in which we find ourselves is the narrow, self-centered view we inherited from the mechanistic-reductionist paradigm adopted by the followers of Newton. That view justifies taking only ourselves and our immediate interests into account. Together with the Darwinian idea – one that likewise was not the idea of its originator but of his followers, namely that the world is a jungle where only the strongest survive – it justifies that we, our country or our company alone, count. That is what comes first, and the devil can take the rest.

To overcome crises we face we need to abandon this view, and the behavior it justifies. We need not become saints and martyrs, sacrificing ourselves for the greater good. Serving the greater good does not call for sacrifice. Our own good is intimately bound up with the good of others – ultimately, with the good of all. We share the same boat, the same spaceship in this galaxy. We have been exploiting our shared ship unthinkingly and selfishly for centuries. And now our shortsightedness is taking its toll.

We need to embrace the planet and its inhabitants with the same care and concern we feel for ourselves. There are no "others" on this planet, no strangers. We are all partners, fellow explorers of the realms of life on a small and already overpopulated and overexploited planet. We are together, for better or for worse. If we bless those around us rather than trying to outcompete and eliminate them, we can be together for the better. This is the lesson we need to learn. It is a lesson we can all learn – and we can all benefit from.

A Chinese saying has it that even the longest voyage begins with the first step. In changing our views and our behavior the first step is to change our view of the world. We can then explore what our new worldview would mean for our behavior in the world – what we could accomplish by projecting love instead of scheming for revenge, by practicing cooperation with friends and partners rather than fighting desperate and embittered competitors. And neglecting everything and anyone who is not of direct relevance to our immediate concerns.

Given that our world is one and that we are part of it, the answer as to what we can accomplish by coming together and feeling and acting together is clear. We can create a better world – more fair and equitable, and more caring. And, at the same time, more sustainable, because caring for the planet is part of our caring for everything and everyone around us. With a new view of the world supporting a new consciousness, we could transcend the quagmire of the current crisis and set out on the path we were meant to follow: a path of cooperation and harmony, leading to the flourishing of one and all.

It is time to get started. Everyone can offer blessings every day – perhaps not as eloquently as the author of this book, but with the same intention. Try to bless the author: that should not be difficult. Then try blessing your partners, your friends, your acquaintances, and then your competitors and your enemies. Going that far will be difficult – more and more difficult. But it should not be impossible. And it would be important. If your example would catch on and help create a sort of blessing-epidemic in the world, the effort would pay off. It would realize not only the intention of the author of this book, but the intention of well-thinking and ethical people everywhere. Realizing that intention could be our best hope for the future – perhaps our only realistic hope.

Read this book and offer your blessings today. It could well be worth your effort.

Ervin Laszlo

April 2017

Founder-Director of the Laszlo Institute of New Paradigm Research and of The Club of Budapest. His latest publications are *What Is Reality: The New Map of Cosmos and Consciousness*, and *The Intelligence of the Cosmos: Why Are We Here – New Answers from the Frontiers of Science*.

Introduction

In 1986, a very powerful experience enabled me to discover a much deeper and more meaningful dimension of blessing than the rather sweet, often ritualized and stereotyped practice it usually is.

I was employed by a group of Swiss non-governmental organizations working in Switzerland in the field of public education on North-South issues (and involved in development programs in the Third World). I loved my work which was essentially in schools and was so committed I even had a camp bed at the office for late nights. I had invested a very sizeable portion of my savings to organize a roving exhibit on hunger for schools, as there was no money in our budget for this. It was written up in the press, and my employers spoke very highly of my initiative.

However, one gentleman among them simply detested me and decided he would get rid of me. After a great deal of manipulation and underhand scheming, he managed to convince his colleagues in the different organizations that they needed to get rid of me, despite the undeniable success of my work.

So I was summoned to a business meeting. No minutes of any sort were taken, and I was put in an impossible situation where I had to choose between doing something that went totally against my deepest convictions – or quitting my job. As I did not wish to commit a moral hara-kiri, I quit.

In the following weeks, I started being literally eaten up by the most tremendous resentment against my former employers. It became literally, in psychological terminology, an obsession. I was thinking about it from morning to night. Resentment is a particularly horrible emotion, as it is almost like a rat eating up your entrails – it gnaws at you constantly. I was doing all the right things, meditating, studying spiritual texts, praying, repeating affirmations and mantras – but absolutely nothing changed.

Then one day, reading the Sermon on the Mount, one sentence just blew my mind: "Bless those who curse you." Well *of course!* It was so simple. I just had to bless them! And then and there I started blessing them in their joy, their peace, their family life, their abundance and health, their deep contentment and their work... I started doing it day in, day out, to dispel all that resentment.

And suddenly, one day, I started doing it in the street, on the bus, at the post office and the supermarket, everywhere. I just couldn't stop. I would travel the whole length of trains both ways to be sure not to miss anyone, just blessing them. And I started having amazing things happening, with situations of conflict being reversed or resolved sometimes instantaneously, sometimes in a matter of days.

A few months later into this practice, I was preparing a talk I had been asked to give at an international youth meeting in Zürich, and while writing my text on the theme *Healing the World*, I received an influx of inspiration such as never before (or since) in my life. I was literally like a scribe under orders taking dictation from some unknown but infinitely loving source. The result was the following text:

The Gentle Art of Blessing

On awaking, bless this day, for it is already full of unseen good which your blessings will call forth; for to bless is to acknowledge the unlimited good that is embedded in the very texture of the universe and awaiting each and all.

On passing people in the street, on the bus, in places of work and play, bless them. The peace of your blessing will companion them on their way, and the aura of its gentle fragrance will be a light on their path.

On meeting people and talking to them, bless them in their health, their work, their joy, their relationship to the universe, themselves and others. Bless them in their abundance and their finances... bless them in every conceivable way, for such blessings not only sow seeds of healing but one day will spring forth as flowers in the waste places of your own life.

As you walk, bless the city in which you live, its government and teachers, its nurses and street sweepers, its children and bankers, its priests and prostitutes. The minute anyone expresses the least aggression or unkindness to you, respond with a blessing: bless them totally, sincerely, joyfully, for such blessings are a shield which protects you from the ignorance of their misdeed, and deflects the arrow that was aimed at you.

To bless means to wish, unconditionally, total, unrestricted good for others and events from the deepest chamber of your heart: it means to hallow, to hold in reverence, to behold with utter awe that which is always a gift from the Creator. He who is hallowed by your blessing is set aside, consecrated, holy, whole. To bless is yet to invoke divine care upon, to speak or think gratefully for, to confer happiness upon – although we ourselves are never the bestower, but simply the joyful witnesses of Life's abundance.

To bless all without discrimination of any sort is the ultimate form of giving, because those you bless will never know from whence came the sudden ray that burst through the clouds of their skies, and you will rarely be a witness to the sunlight in their lives.

When something goes completely askew in your day, some unexpected event knocks down your plans and you too also, burst into blessing: for life is teaching you a lesson, and the very event you believe to be unwanted, you yourself called forth, so as to learn the lesson you might balk against were you not to bless it. Trials are blessings in disguise, and hosts of angels follow in their path.

To bless is to acknowledge the omnipresent, universal beauty hidden to material eyes; it is to activate the law of attraction which, from the furthest reaches of the universe, will bring into your life exactly what you need to experience and enjoy.

When you pass a prison, mentally bless its inmates in their innocence and freedom, their gentleness, pure essence and unconditional forgiveness; for one can only be a prisoner of one's self-image, and a free man can walk unshackled in the courtyard of a jail, just as citizens of countries where freedom reigns can be prisoners when fear lurks in their thoughts.

When you pass a hospital, bless its patients in their present wholeness, for even in their suffering, their wholeness awaits in them to be discovered. When your eyes behold a man in tears, or seemingly broken by life, bless him in his vitality and joy: for the material senses present but the inverted image of the ultimate splendor and perfection which only the inner eye beholds.

It is impossible to bless and judge at the same time. So hold constantly as a deep, hallowed, intoned thought the desire to bless, for truly then shall you become a peacemaker, and one day you shall behold, everywhere, the very face of God.

PS: And of course, above all, do not forget to bless the utterly beautiful person YOU are.

(Source: *The Gentle Art of Blessing*, by Pierre Pradervand, Simon and Schuster, NY, 2010)

Ten years later I unexpectedly met my former tormentor who had organized the plot to fire me from my job and I was suddenly overwhelmed by the most incredible joy one can imagine. I felt like taking him in my arms and hugging him!

We had dinner together and for days my heart was ringing with the purest joy. And it took me another ten years (speak of being a slow learner!) to understand the reason of this joy – which was explained carefully in the above text on blessing. (See the paragraph, "When something goes completely askew in your day...") I now believe we both distributed our mutual roles in this situation to each other before incarnating on earth so that I could have the opportunity of discovering and explaining this wonderful spiritual tool which has since helped so many.

As I understand it now, and after many years of practice, in its initial stages blessing is a way of sending unconditional love, peace, healing, goodness to a person or a situation, or simply seeing them bathed in that love. Blessing isn't associated with any religious denominations. It can be practiced by anyone, and I have an atheist friend who purchased the first edition of *The Gentle Art of Blessing*, and even gave copies away!

The heart of the practice is reversing the material appearances, as described in the two paragraphs on prisons and hospitals above. For it is becoming more and more apparent to a growing number of us on this planet that the material world we live in is, in some manner, a total dream (even though it can often be a nightmare!) and that we are here on earth to learn much-needed lessons (that we ourselves possibly chose before coming on earth).

After (usually) considerable practice, it may simply transform itself into a constant state of consciousness and also a deepened sense of sensitivity to and awareness of the suffering of others. Personally, I cannot see any form of suffering anywhere without immediately blessing the person, being or situation concerned. It could also develop into an immense and deep yearning for the happiness of all mankind.

Blessing has an immense healing potential, not only on the individual level, but also for the world, hence the title of the book. For this reason, healings of personal and interpersonal problems and situations can be found all through the book, taken from the blessing website managed by two dear friends (www.gentleartofblessing.org). They are all in italics.

Because this book wishes to be an instrument of world healing, it also attempts the not always easy task of calling a cat a cat and addressing numerous social, economic, environmental and other problems – some extremely challenging and disturbing – without ever attacking groups, companies or individuals. As the old medieval saying goes, condemn the sin but not the sinner. Not always an easy task but I have done my best and warmly welcome any corrections from readers on this point. I believe with many others that the number one issue, challenge and need in the world today is *raising world consciousness*, because the solution of every single problem ultimately depends on that. And here our collective blessings have an immense and perhaps decisive role to play.

I also wish to stress that blessing is a wonderful practice for living one's spirituality in everyday life, and readers will find blessings for innumerable real life situations, from raising children to gardening, from driving, teaching, making love, from being a taxi driver to nursing and so many others and various qualities such as compassion, trust, love, etc.

I do not believe there is any "right" way of blessing. The *intention* and *sincerity of the heart* are infinitely more important than any so-called correct way of giving a blessing, and any formulas or rigid forms in this field are a direct route to failure. A blessing that is just on the level of the mind has no healing power whatsoever. One can never stress too much that blessing is one hundred percent heart energy. I believe it has to be felt in the heart to heal.

Finally, a third quality in addition to intention and sincerity is of course perseverance. But then that is true of almost any honest human endeavor.

And how better to conclude this introduction than by sharing this e-mail I received while writing these lines from Sabine, a German-speaking reader of *The Gentle Art of Blessing*:

I just finished reading your book The Gentle Art of Blessing. *It is the best book I have ever read! It should be taught in every school on this planet! It touches my heart and soul, gives me hope for a better life and world.*

Until today I only practiced it once, and it worked! It is so wonderful. My words can't describe my feelings. Here is my experience.

For a long time, my husband and I have had a hard time managing our bills. Plus I am unemployed and my husband's contractor doesn't pay on time. I even tried to sell some of my belongings over the Internet for almost a year, with no result. Last week, when everything got really bad (we could no longer afford to pay the rent) I went to bed at night and started blessing. I thought about our landlord, blessed him in his kindness and understanding, his family and his joy.

And this happened the next day:

- I had a phone call with the Social Security Office and the most kind clerk told me they would pay a part of our rent

- I got invitations for two different job interviews

- my husband's contractor paid

- my ex-husband wrote me a message that he would pay his debt in cash the following day (which he did)

- I sold my designer purse on the Internet

Nothing had directly to do with the landlord. But we were able to pay the rent!

This really overwhelmed us and made us cry. So many good things happened in just a few hours.

What a blessing! I'm so grateful! I will definitely make it my way of life. Everyday!

I want to bless everybody in this world in their loving kindness, wholeness and inner peace! WE ARE ALL ONE.

It is important, however, to stress that blessing is not a "trick" to make things happen on the material level. It is an acknowledgment of, and a rejoicing in, the perfection of the infinite unseen. It just happens that this acknowledgment does often result in the solving of various situations and challenges on the human level. When a gift comes with an added bonus, we are not going to say "no" to the bonus. However, we never forget that the Real Thing is the rejoicing in, and the contemplation of, the reality behind the veil. The green pastures already surround us. We just have to open our spiritual eyes and see.

I have added a certain number of blessings from other sources so that the reader can be exposed to a variety of ways of blessing other than mine. Some themes appear more than once, because they are themes that touch me in a special way or that I consider especially important. And from time to time you will encounter a healing reached through blessing taken from my blessing website: www.gentleartofblessing.org.

A last comment: it goes without saying that I still consider myself a beginner on the spiritual path and the practice of blessing, and someone who is almost daily learning from the people who write to him. As the French philosopher Jean Guitton once wrote, "There are no educators, only people who teach others how they educate themselves." That is my only claim – to share with you how I have been (so joyfully) educating myself in the practice of blessing – which thankfully puts me at the antipode of being any authority on the topic.

My deepest hope, dear reader, is that you will find in the following lines inspiration that will open up new vistas for you and especially a practice that could deeply transform your life, as it has done for so many others around the world.

Day 1
For the Fullness of This Day

May these blessings bring you peace, inspiration, courage... whatever your need may be. These blessings will take many forms, and some will be from other sources and cultures so that they may meet different needs. Many are concerned with world problems, as I believe blessing can be an important tool in healing the world by healing our own vision of the world, so that rather than despairing over the number of problems facing our planet and its inhabitants, we rejoice in having a tool to help solve them.

I bless this day in the fullness of good it already contains, in the many occasions it offers to listen deeply, to be of service to others, to express gratitude moment by moment and to keep my mind so filled with love, beauty and joy that no negativity can find even the tiniest crack in which to set foot.

I bless this day in the infinite opportunities it gives me to love: to love and bless every human I meet, every beast or bird I pass by, every plant I behold, for all are but the manifold expressions of the infinite Life that undergirds all.

Truly, I bless this day for the wonderful adventure it can become as I walk through it with the eyes of wonder rather than boredom, use every opportunity to express peace rather than irritation, and chose love over fear.

Thank you, Life, for this day.

Day 2
Blessing Myself

The PS of my text on The Gentle Art of Blessing *that you will find in the introduction to this book says: "And above all, bless the utterly beautiful child of God you are." So today, we are going to bless ourselves, for it is very difficult to really love and bless others from the heart if we do not start with loving ourselves. As the great Irish poet*

John O'Donohue said so beautifully, "May there be kindness in your gaze when you look within."

I bless myself sincerely and joyfully for being the utterly beautiful divine creature I am, at one with the Source of infinite Love.

I bless myself as a child of the universe, a child of the light in which there is not a speck or residue of darkness or self-condemnation.

I bless myself in my sinless joy, boundless bliss and total contentment, my ageless, tireless being.

I bless myself as divine Mind's expression of constant wisdom, enlightenment, discernment and understanding.

I bless myself as Spirit's manifestation of glorious liberty, total freedom and unlimited innocence – and this is true of all humanity.

I bless myself in my perfect oneness with the Ground of Being, the unconditional cosmic Love force called the Creator, which sustains every cell and atom of my being in perfect health.

I bless myself as my sister's and my brother's keeper, overflowing with compassion, a fount of unending tenderness for every suffering heart.

And finally, I bless myself in my constant enjoyment of the Green Pastures of the Kingdom within which I share with all humanity.

Day 3
A Cherokee Blessing

Today, we will borrow from that very rich, deep and varied lore of Native American blessings, one of the most precious cultural heritages of the USA. You may, if so moved, replace "Great Spirit" with "divine Love" and "Rainbow" with "Grace." What counts is that these daily blessings speak to you, wherever you may be on your spiritual path. So feel free to make any adaptations that are meaningful for you, be it in

this blessing or any other you encounter in this book.
　　May the warm winds of heaven
　　blow softly upon your house.
　　May the Great Spirit
　　bless all those who enter there.
　　May your moccasins
　　make many happy tracks
　　in many snows,
　　and may the Rainbow
　　always touch your shoulder.

Day 4
Seeing with the Eyes of the Heart

Marianne Williamson writes: "Nothing about your material circumstances has the power to stop the engine of cosmic intention that you be blessed. And you are blessed 'eternally' which means moment after moment after moment. In any instant, regardless of what has happened in the past, the universe has arranged and is continuing to arrange infinite possibilities for you to prosper." Her words offer a lovely introduction to today's blessing.

I bless this day in the infinite beauty that will unfold as I learn to see with the eyes of the heart: the beauty of my neighbor, whatever the material appearances – glorious or grumpy; the resplendent beauty of creation, of nature bedecked in so many constantly changing forms and colors; the infinite opportunities to express thanks – to the cashier for her radiant smile, the local baker for his delicious bread, my journalist neighbor for a positive article, the public transport company for an efficient service, for an especially kind receptionist or the friendly nurse at my doctor's, the food which blesses my table three times a day.

And I say yes, yes, yes for the innumerable opportunities to bless, knowing that each sincere blessing returns to bless me too:

the water I drink for its cleanliness and those that produce it, the clothes I wear and their convenience or beauty, my amazing body for its 24-hour performance.

Truly, blessing enables me to discover Love's perfect plan for me moment after moment after moment.

Day 5
A Psalm to Bless This Day

Did you know that blessing is probably one of the oldest cultural expressions of human religious activity, dating back many thousands of years? One of the many things I love about blessing is that it is expressed in a great variety of forms. Take for instance Ps 23, attributed to King David, which is one of the most universal and beautiful spiritual texts in world literature. Whatever a person's religious or spiritual background, they can nearly always find something that speaks to them in this text. Today, with minor modifications of its form, we are going to use it as a blessing. So here is:

May divine Love be your shepherd today.

May you not lack any good.

May it make you to lie down in green pastures,

and lead you besides still waters.

May Love restore your soul (your spiritual sense).

May it lead you on the paths of right action for Love's sake.

When you walk in the valley of the shadow of death,

May you fear no evil, for truly Love's rod and Love's staff are there to comfort you.

May divine Love lay a table in front of your enemies – all the challenges you are facing.

May divine Love anoint your head with oil and may your cup overflow.

May goodness and mercy accompany you all the days of your life,

And may you live in the Presence of divine Love for evermore.

Have a peaceful day in the trusted company of this Love, my friend, and be assured that it will never let you down, ever.

Day 6
A Blessing for Teachers

From time to time, we shall give a blessing for a specific profession or job. Today, we will start with one of the most important activities on the planet – that of teacher. There are so many stories of children whose lives were turned around by a remarkable teacher. So if you have teacher friends who do their best in their challenging job, please share this blessing with them.

I bless this day for the constant opportunities that it offers me to share wisdom and truth, to broaden my circle of compassion and my understanding, and to manifest patience and love toward all the children or students entrusted to my care.

I bless myself in my ability to assume full responsibility for all I do and to face any situation that could develop in the classroom, to handle tensions with nonviolence and to generate productive relations with the students, their parents and my colleagues.

I bless myself in my ability to discern the divine in each student, however contrary or aggressive outward appearances, to manifest constant calm whatever breaches to discipline may occur and to encourage serene discussions and debates.

I bless my students in their desire to learn and progress, in their ability to contribute positively to the atmosphere of the class, to cooperate with and help fellow-students and to resist group pressure when this pressure would attempt to lead them to the use of drugs, alcohol or sex emptied of all beauty and norms.

Finally, I bless myself in my ability to produce exciting and stimulating courses which challenge the intellect of my students, reinforce their sense of values and offer them also a meaningful morality freed from dusty, guilt-producing norms. And I also bless myself in my ability to open them up to a high and noble vision of their lives and a deep desire to serve usefully both their community and all humanity and our planet.

Day 7
The Invisible Divine Order Behind Everything

In her book The Healing Secrets of the Ages, *Catherine Ponder writes: "Bless the world around you unselfishly with divine order. As you do so, you release the power of order into the atmosphere to do its perfect work. Look for, expect and give thanks for divine order, often. By doing so, you release one of your most important mind powers to work for you and through you to bless yourself and mankind." So today our blessing will be for the invisible divine order behind everything, despite the aggressive material claims of disharmony on the human plane.*

I bless the amazing divine order in nature, from the tiniest molecule to the rolling of the galaxies in our stupendous universe.

I bless the divine order in my life and that of my neighbor, even when to the human sense of things this order is all but apparent.

I bless the exquisite, stunning order that runs the over 37 trillion cells that make up my body and the hundreds of millions of chemical reactions occurring every second.

I bless the divine order in the universe that is constantly arranging innumerable possibilities for me and all to progress in life if only we will listen to its quiet whispers.

I bless the same divine order which forms the foundation of my spiritual GPS – God Positioning System – that gently corrects me when I stray out of ignorance or willfulness.

And finally, I bless the divine order that is leading the whole of humanity through the many upheavals present and probably to come to the win-win paradigm which will finally give birth to that world which works for all, which is our divine destiny.

Day 8
A Blessing by John O'Donohue

Our blessing for this day comes from that great Irish writer John O'Donohue's book, Anam Cara. *We owe him many beautiful and deeply meaningful blessings. He says that: "a blessing is a circle of light drawn around a person to protect, heal and strengthen." I love that metaphor, especially if one extends it to all one blesses, including events. He also speaks of the sacredness of our work. And remember that what makes work sacred is the love you put into it, be you a cashier or simple street sweeper. Sweeping a street with love or smiling to your clients as a cashier does more to save the world than running the most successful business with avidity and pride. So here is his blessing for work.*

May the light of your soul guide you.

May the light of your soul bless the work you do with the secret love and warmth of your heart.

May you see in what you do the beauty of your own soul.

May the sacredness of your work bring healing, light and renewal to those who work with you and to those who see and receive your work.

May work never weary you.

May it release within you wellsprings of refreshment, inspiration and excitement.

May you be present in what you do.

May you never become lost in the bland absences.

May the day never burden.

May dawn find you alert and awake, approaching your new day with dreams, possibilities and promises.

May evening find you gracious and fulfilled.

May you go into the night blessed, sheltered and protected.

May your soul calm, console and renew you.

Day 9
A Blessing for Political Leaders

Hatsat Abiola, a Nigerian activist, says to us: "Guard your light and protect it. Move it forward into the world and be fully confident that if we connect light to light to light, and join the lights together of the one billion young people in our world today, we will be enough to set our whole planet aglow." Blessing is a way of joining our lights together. I personally believe that the number needed to move the world is much smaller – maybe a few million really committed spiritual thinkers. So today, our blessings will be for those who still believe themselves to be the world movers, the political leaders of the world.

We bless our leaders that wisdom rather than narrow interests or fear may guide their decisions.

We bless them in their ability to move beyond the narrow confines of nation, class, creed, race or narrow financial or economic concerns.

We bless them in their desire to put the service of mankind and their nations before their thirst for prestige or power. We bless them in their ability to put the care of Mother Earth and the environment before short-term planning and purely economic motives.

We bless them in their authentic compassion that they may be sensitive to the needs of the downtrodden and the marginalized.

We bless them that, despite all the judgments, the prejudices concerning them with which we too often hold them captives, they may be sensitive to the winds of grace which blow freely for all those who hoist their sails.

And finally, we bless ourselves in our ability to hold on to their divine image that too often remains cloistered in their hearts that it may find expression in political courage, deep caring for the outcasts of society and decisive action for the reconciliation of man and nature.

PS: To help you make this blessing more real, may I suggest that you think of three politicians who are your favorite scapegoats and that you visualize and bless them in three qualities they express. And even if you can only think of a single quality, congratulations, that is a good start.

Day 10
Blessing My Body

Have you ever thought about, given thanks for, and talked to that quite extraordinary instrument called the human body, your body, which enables you to function day after day, year after year, decade after decade with incredible versatility? And that despite the rather rough treatment with which so many of us too often handle it!

Today, I bless my body in its perfect functioning and the gift and tool it is for me to live and play, work and serve.

I bless my heart which beats over 84,000 times a day without me ever giving it a second thought, or my lungs which inhale and exhale effortlessly and smoothly well over 20,000 times a day also.

I bless the trillions of cells which constantly communicate with an intricacy and perfection we have barely started understanding.

I bless the hundreds of millions of chemical reactions happening every second which keep the whole system functioning and that utter marvel called the immune system and the green and red lights it is constantly switching on and off.

I bless my eyes that allow me to absorb the faintest nuances of nature's beauty and all shades of color and which enable me to fall in love and, hopefully, one day rise in love with the object of my desire.

I bless my ears which enable me to vibrate to the slightest variations of sounds and music or listen to my neighbors' woes with patience and compassion...

I bless my body in all its innumerable functions which defy

my wildest imagination…

All that and so much more, with not one day's vacation in 60, 70, 80 years or more.

Truly, I bless this unbelievable marvel called my body.

May I never forget to daily thank it and the universe for that without which I would not exist here on earth.

Day 11
Apache Blessing for Newlyweds

If you have acquaintances who are thinking of marrying or moving in together, or if you yourself wish to renew the bond that links you to your companion or spouse, you will be deeply touched by the beautiful Native American Apache blessing that follows which has inspired so many couples.

Now you will feel no rain

for each of you will be the shelter for each other.

And now you will feel no cold,

for each will be warmth to the other.

Now there will be no loneliness,

for each of you will be a companion to the other.

And now you are two persons,

but there are three lives before you:

his life, her life and your life together.

Go now to your dwelling to enter the days of your life

together.

May beauty surround you,

both in your journey ahead and through the years.

May happiness be your companion

to the place where the river meets the sun.

And may your days be good and long upon the earth.

(Many different sources)

Day 12

A Blessing for the Homeless in the World

Blessing, as I have stated time and again, is 100% heart energy. For that reason, most people can compose a blessing for a great variety of situations. All you have to do is just open up to, and listen to, your heart. While composing the first of these blessings for this book during a brief retreat, one evening I just opened my heart and listened. This is what came to me.

I bless those whom the circumstances of life have driven to live in the streets or in derelict basements and other abandoned places.

I bless them in their courage to hang in there until the circumstances of their life take an upturn for the better – knowing that I may be part of that improvement.

I bless the authorities of this city or small town that they may provide shelters for the homeless.

I bless restaurants and those stores which sell food, that they may donate what they no longer need to the homeless and destitute.

I bless those with open hearts who search the streets and alleys for those who need assistance and help them find places where they can stay.

I bless those employers and others who have jobs to offer that they may think also of the destitute when providing work.

And above all, I bless the homeless that they may see themselves, not as poor victims needing assistance, but as children of the universe here to move the hearts of their fellow humans to deeper compassion and more active love.

Day 13

A letter from Zimbabwe (Testimony)

"I feel I must write to tell you how much your wonderful book The

Gentle Art of Blessing *has helped me.*

I live in Zimbabwe and read your book with great interest some months ago. Shortly after this my house was broken into in the early morning by four men armed with knives. I am a widow 84 years old, but they tied me up and gagged me and proceeded to look for money. I lay on the bed quite helpless and wondered what I could do. And the teachings in your book flooded my mind and enabled me to overcome my fear and to bless the inner core of their being.

This brought much peace to my being, almost beyond description, and enabled me to handle the aftermath of the situation without hysteria or too much stress. Everyone remarked on my poise and serenity in such a situation but I knew it was due entirely to the wonderful teachings of your book.

The men left having found the money they wanted – which was also replaced anonymously that very same day!

As you can imagine life here in Zimbabwe enables me to demonstrate every day the law of unconditional love, especially just now with the elections!! Many people here have your book and we all find it a wonderful support and comfort. They quickly realize the only way to live is by this fundamental law of unconditional love."

(Pauline)

Day 14
For Mindfulness in the Present Moment

There is a lovely Sanskrit poem which goes thus:

Look to this day, for it is life, the very life of life.
In its brief course lie all the realities and the varieties of existence,
The bliss of growth, the splendor of action, the glory of power,
For yesterday is but a dream, and tomorrow is only a vision.
But today well lived makes every yesterday a dream of happiness
And tomorrow a vision of hope.
Look well, therefore, to this day.

I bless this splendid day which extends before me for every second it offers me to be present to the present, to be really alert to where I am, totally attentive to what I am pondering or doing right now.

When in public transport, I bless myself in my ability to bless those around me with total attention rather than letting my mind drift aimlessly from ad to ad.

When doing household duties, or shopping, or whatever I may be undertaking, I bless myself in my ability to rest in my total presence to what I am doing with serenity, rather than fret over what I did not do right yesterday and could do wrong tomorrow.

I bless myself in the gift of total mindfulness which is one of the greatest riches I can bestow on myself and others:

- mindfulness in eating

- mindfulness in walking and moving,

- total mindfulness in listening to others which is the most basic expression of my love for them,

- mindfulness in every single moment of this wonderful day which Life has gifted me.

Day 15
To Love God More

The First Commandment is extremely powerful when one ponders its deeper meaning – to love Her with ALL one's heart, soul, strength and mind – not 95%, but all. May this blessing encourage us on the way to this goal.

May my love for You become the center-current of my life – fresh, inspired, serene and strong.

May it be so steadfast that it cuts right through the muddied waters of indecision and compromise, hesitation and doubt. May its full, vibrating and clear intent dissolve the mortal triplets of apathy, indifference and humdrum habit that would stifle

24

Love's bugle call.

May my love be so strong that in the burning heat of deserts I need but pause a while in my inner secret place to stand inspired and refreshed; or in the biting chill of a world that does not care, pause once more and feel its warm and steady inner glow.

May this love become brother, mother, husband or wife to me, my constant companion of every hour, that I may choose to love because I know no other path. And may I bless with its healing touch every being I meet – person, plant or beast.

Day 16
A Blessing for Nurses

For 25 years, I have been receiving feedback from all round the world from people telling me that blessing works. In my little book on blessing called The Gentle Art of Blessing, *I give some examples and you will find many others on the website: www.gentleartofblessing.org – some of them amazingly powerful, many of them reproduced in this book. Here is a blessing for nurses.*

I am aware from speaking to nurse friends that the blessing outlined below is often extremely difficult to apply in understaffed wards. So I will just say: do your best. No decent human being will ask more of you.

I bless this day as a series of opportunities to serve with love.

May each branch of my tree be for the healing of every patient that I meet. I especially bless the opportunities:

- to do all I undertake with mindfulness and care rather than haste or neglect,
- to smile rather than carry a grim face or look indifferent,
- to express the tender interest of love to all I meet,
- to make a pause and listen rather than rush on to the next activity.

I bless the hospital (clinic, private practice) where I work as a temple of love rather than a source of profit that it may function with a true spirit of service rather than for the bottom line. And I bless all the personnel serving there in their diligence, humor and authentic spirit of service.

Day 17
A Blessing to See the Divine Everywhere

In his profound and illuminating book Practicing the Presence, *spiritual teacher and healer Joel Goldsmith goes as far as saying that in the 2nd Commandment, "Love thy neighbor as thyself," the term neighbor refers not only to people but to the whole of creation – animals, plants, even the inanimate world. This agrees fully with the explanation of blessing in my book* The Gentle Art of Blessing. *So today we will bless ourselves in our capacity to see the divine in everyone and everything.*

Today, I bless myself in my ability to see the true spiritual reality behind the veil of material appearances.

- When I behold the beauty of a flower, I will see divine Love smiling at me.

- When I see a flock of sheep, I will remember that the divine Shepherd, infinite Love, is constantly guiding me and all.

- When I see my neighbor, I will remember that I am looking at myself in disguise, and joyfully bless what I see from the deepest wellspring of my soul.

- When I look at the sun, I will rejoice in the reminder that I am the light of the world, as a great spiritual teacher taught 2,000 years ago.

- When I look at a loaf of bread at the baker's or fruit at the supermarket, this will be a reminder that I live not by bread alone but also of what the Spirit whispers to me in the secret of my heart. Am I listening?

- When I see a person in tears or deeply afflicted by some woe, I will silently bless them in the divine joy that waits in their heart to spring forth and lift their pain.

- When I pass a prison, I will bless its inmates in their true freedom which none can take away,

- and when I pass a hospital, I will bless its patients in the fullness of their health that awaits in them to be discovered.

- Finally, when I pass a mirror I will exceedingly rejoice in and joyfully bless the daughter or son of infinite divine Love I behold there.

Day 18
A Wish for You

This is a very slightly abbreviated version of a blessing that you can find as a beautiful video on the website:

http://play.simpletruths.com/movie/may-you-be-blessed/

As it is rather long, we have divided it in two. The second part follows tomorrow.

Part I

May you be blessed by all things good.

May your joys, like the stars at night, be too numerous to count...

May lack and struggle only serve to make you stronger, and may beauty, order and abundance be your constant companions.

May every pathway that you choose lead to that which is pure and good and lovely.

May every doubt and fear be replaced by an abiding trust as you behold the evidence of a higher power all around you.

And when there is only darkness and the storms of life are closing in, may the light at the core of your being illuminate the world.

May you always be aware that you are loved beyond measure and may you be willing to love unconditionally in return.

(To be continued.)

Day 19
A Wish for You, Part II

I love what David Steindl-Rast says in his book A Listening Heart, *"The more alert we become to the blessings that flow into us, the more our own touch will bring blessing."*

This is a continuation of yesterday's blessing from the site:
http://play.simpletruths.com/movie/may-you-be-blessed/

May you always feel protected and cradled in the arms of God like the cherished child you are.

And when you are tempted to judge, may you be reminded that we are all one and that every thought you think reverberates across the universe, touching everyone and everything.

And when you are tempted to hold back, may you remember that love flows best when it flows freely and that it is in giving that we receive the greatest gift.

May you always have music and laughter and may a rainbow follow every storm.

May gladness wash away every disappointment, may joy dissolve every sorrow and may love ease every pain.

May every wound bring wisdom, may every trial bring triumph and with each passing day may you live more abundantly than the day before.

May you be blessed and may others be blessed by you.

This is my heartfelt wish for you: may you be blessed.

Day 20
Understanding the Impact of My Blessings

It is so important to understand – especially for one who practices blessing – the impact of our thoughts, blessings, meditation and prayers. They can (and will) change the world.

We bless ourselves in our understanding that every one of our thoughts, blessings and prayers can reach to the end of the world.

May we really grasp that an ocean is made up of hundreds of billions of drops, just as the present and future of humanity is made up of the addition of billions of thoughts and intentions.

May we get it that every single minute we are, albeit minutely, impacting the level of consciousness of the whole planet, that every thought of love and light, every heartfelt blessing, is having an impact some place, helping meet a need, allay a fear, bring inspiration, awaken in someone, somewhere, that vision which will meet their need – just as every negative thought or feeling can delay our progress as a race to the wider horizons of grace awaiting us all.

May we humbly realize that a sincere blessing of ours can help a desperate mother in a shanty town the other side of the planet find the assistance that will save her sick child or uplift the prisoner who has been for 35 years in solitary confinement to avoid suicide – and will meet some need, somewhere, for such is the law of love.

Finally, we bless ourselves in our understanding that we are world healers, however unaware we have been of that fact until now.

May we truly feel deep gratitude for this powerful realization and joyfully buckle down to the task of incarnating it every day, in every way we can, in any place we are, in each mental space we inhabit.

Thank you, Infinite One, whoever/whatever You may be, that You love us so much and are guiding us all to this perfect understanding.

Day 21
A Blessing for Trials

It has been often said that trials – and I would add weaknesses – are blessings in disguise and for those who have discovered the unerring truth of this statement, life changes completely, and from frequent cursing passes to constant blessing.

I bless myself in my shortcomings, that they may be opportunities to learn and grow.

I bless myself in my fears, that I may see through their hollowness and falseness and learn to manifest the courage that is my natural endowment as a child of the Universe.

I bless myself in the challenges I face in life, for they are the most precious tools of my inner growth.

I bless myself for what seem to be insurmountable problems, for they enable me to discover hidden resources in me.

I bless myself for moments of solitude for they enable me to discover divine Love as a never-failing friend and Presence.

I bless myself when faced with the challenge of disease, because it is an opportunity to discover that perfect health is our natural, divine endowment always available to each of us.

I bless myself when faced with betrayal, heartbreak, what may appear as irreplaceable loss, hatred, rejection, doubt… and so many other challenges because they are the ultimate way of discovering that "trials are proofs of Love's care" and hence that I can even then discover the silver lining in the storm cloud.

Day 22
A Blessing for Terrorists, Part I

We are all aware that terrorism is one of the great challenges of our world. Can you imagine the tormented, deeply sick state of mind needed to perform a terrorist attack? Cursing such people will not heal this plague. Only blessing can do that. Let us feel only the most immense compassion for such people who remain our brothers and sisters, whatever somber motives may be theirs.

I bless those who are tempted to commit terrorist acts, be it out of despair, hatred, fear, lust for power or any other tormented human motive.

I bless them in their integrity, so they discover that the wholeness in themselves cannot be reached at the cost of the wholeness in others.

I bless them in their realization that Love is the ultimate law governing the universe and mankind, and that their deepest honest longings can only be reached through the law of love.

I bless them in their awareness that right deep down, they are children of the light, and that terrorist schemes are but an inversion of the light with no true cause, substance or law behind them.

I bless them in their understanding that the darkness they see or imagine can only be dispelled by light, not by more darkness.

(To be continued.)

Day 23
A Blessing for Terrorists, Part II

This is a continuation of yesterday's blessing for terrorists. Get into contact with the deepest level of compassion in your heart. That terrorist remains your brother, whatever he may have wrought.

I bless terrorists in their unlimited goodness, kindness, compassion and caring which, as children of God, is awaiting in them to be kindled and brought to full fruition.

I bless them in their grasp of the law of right returns, that they may understand that the good or evil they do to another, they ultimately do to themselves.

I bless them in their hunger and thirst for righteousness, that they may be fulfilled.

I bless them that any sense of lack in them may be healed by a clearer consciousness of infinite abundance now; that any restlessness may give way to Your peace; that any feeling of insecurity with its attendant aggressiveness or fear may be healed by the sense of Your comforting presence; that any sense of separation, clannishness and loneliness way be assuaged by

31

the understanding that WE ARE ALL ONE.

And I bless myself in my awareness that divine Love sees no terrorists, only its perfect reflection and that this same consciousness can be mine as I understand that, behind the veil of appearances, all men and women have ONE MIND, the divine Mind.

Day 24
For Victims of Terrorist Attacks

From the activity of a few wild anarchists in the 19th and early 20th centuries aimed essentially at celebrities, terrorism has become a world plague that hits at random, usually groups or gatherings, almost anywhere on the planet.

I bless the victims of terrorist attacks everywhere, including those of random, totally senseless mass killings, that they may ultimately find meaning in what appears as a meaningless, crazy act of insanity or cruelty.

I bless them that they may find, deep down inside themselves, the strength and courage to forgive, as they understand that resentment is first of all an attack against themselves, just as forgiveness is a gift to themselves.

I bless them in their ability to avoid demonizing their attackers, be it as individuals or groups, and to avoid any desire for revenge, understanding that violence always begets violence on whichever side it may be practiced – the victims or the perpetrators.

Finally, I bless those who have been physically wounded in their rapid healing and those who have lost family members or friends in their finding that deep inner peace that heals.

Day 25
A Blessing for Mother Earth

Finally humanity is just beginning to perceive that our planet is a living being which has been infinitely patient with the abuse we have wrought upon it.

We bless Mother Earth in its infinite abundance and stunning beauty, the wealth of its fauna and flora, the infinite subtlety of its growth and survival mechanisms and its mission of supporting the human race.

We bless it in its ability to protect itself against the chemical and physical abuses of which it is a victim. And we bless ourselves in our ability to use fewer pollutants and to simplify our lifestyles.

We bless Mother Earth in the purity of its water resources and their sane management by human communities and we bless ourselves in our ability to use them wisely and discerningly.

We bless our Earth in its soils everywhere and their ability to recover their original integrity.

We bless the numerous animal and plant species – be they in the seas, the skies, the soil or on land – and their ability to resist all attacks on their habitat, be it through overgrazing, overfishing, deforestation, etc.

And finally, we bless the human race in its ability to exercise wise stewardship in all areas of the environment.

Day 26
Healing of a Work Relationship After 12 Years (Testimony)

Anne was a participant of one of my workshops on blessing. A schoolteacher in an average-sized school, she had a colleague who stubbornly ignored her very existence. Anne had not the foggiest idea why. When they would cross in the school corridor, the other teacher

*would simply look the other way, conveying the clear message: you
don't exist for me. Six months of such behavior would be bad enough,
but 12 years... So Anne decided to try blessing. She just showered
blessings on her colleague day in day out, and shortly after, just before
the school break, this woman came up to her with a wonderful smile
and, shaking her hand, wished her a wonderful vacation!*

(Anne, Switzerland)

Day 27
For Our Brethren of the Animal Kingdom

*Humankind is making amazing discoveries concerning our partners
from the animal kingdom. More and more observers believe animals
have a conscience akin to ours and daily we are discovering their
amazing abilities – while at the same time continuing to slaughter
them on an increasing scale!*

We bless ourselves in our ability as a race to honor and respect
our animal neighbors as an end in themselves and no longer just
as means to cater to our needs and wants.

We bless our health industry in its ability to find alternatives
to laboratory testing which costs monthly millions of innocent
animal lives.

We bless the world food industry in its ability to devise
creative alternatives to the mass-slaughter of billions of cattle
worldwide.

We bless our schools and families in their ability to open
the minds of the young to the awesome splendor of the animal
kingdom.

Finally, we bless ourselves in our ability to grasp that loving
our neighbor includes all living creatures of whatever form or
species.

Day 28
My Wish for You

A precious friend sent me this anonymous text I have slightly adapted as a blessing. Enjoy!

This is my blessing for you.

May you have comfort on difficult days and smiles when sadness intrudes.

May rainbows follow your clouds and laughter kiss your lips.

May sunsets warm your heart and hugs when spirits sag.

May beauty open up for your eyes to see.

May friendships brighten your being and faith abound that you can believe.

May confidence appear when you doubt and may you have the courage to know yourself, patience to accept the truth and love to complete your life.

Day 29
A Blessing to Celebrate the Divine Presence in My Life

From that gem of Western spiritual literature, The Practice of the Presence of God, *by Brother Lawrence, a 16th century French Carmelite monk who worked as a cook, to numerous more modern authors, this simple practice of the divine presence has been seen as a royal path to the inner Kingdom we all carry in ourselves. Joel Goldsmith writes for instance that: "the degree of your own unfoldment depends upon how much you practice the Presence of God each day."*

I bless myself in my desire and innate ability to enter the inner chamber of my soul to commune with the mystical divine Presence, the great Heart of Love.

May I be increasingly aware that this Presence accompanies me wherever I go, be it in the pleasantness of the green pastures or the terrors of hell on earth.

Wherever I may be, may I learn to feel Your Presence as the most gentle and powerful companion I could ever have.

Whatever I may be doing, may I feel that Presence at my side, beneath me, around me, above me. May I always remember that there is not a place on earth where Your insistent Presence does not accompany me, that even "if I make my bed in hell" You are with me and Your Presence hugs me close, tenderly enfolding me at all times.

Whenever I enter a home, a place of work or a shop, a restaurant or any new space, may I consciously pause just seconds to let Your Presence precede me.

When I awake in the morning, lying in my bed, may my first thought be for the Presence which already fills my room and my home, every second of every hour, and may I rejoice that I am privileged to consciously and once more spend a whole day in the blessed companionship of Love.

Day 30
Blessing for the World's Street Children, Part I

*Today I am asking you to open your heart very wide and deep to welcome the street children of the world who are around 150 million according to some UN sources. It is one of the world's greatest scandals on a planet of such incredible abundance. Around 2 million of them are forced to prostitute their young bodies to survive. What heals in a blessing is **feeling** the words, not saying them. So let your compassion pour forth like a torrent.*

From the bottom of my heart, I bless the world's street children in their peace and their rest. I bless them in their consciousness of their own value and their self-respect, that they may transcend the innumerable obstacles of which they are victims.

I bless them in the gift of the divine creativity that resides in each one of them, that they may find their right place in life despite all hurdles.

I bless them in the beauty and the light that resides in them despite all appearances to the contrary. I bless them in their consciousness of abundance that they may transcend all the socially imposed beliefs of lack.

I bless the numerous children that poverty, cupidity or indifference has pressed into selling their own bodies that their innocence and purity never be harmed, and I bless them in their perfect health that they may not be victim of AIDS or other sexually transmitted diseases.

(Continued tomorrow.)

Day 31
Blessing for Street Children, Part II

Today we continue our blessings for those street children forced into prostitution.

I bless these children in their consciousness of their divine nature that it may eliminate all sense of self-condemnation, of despair, fear or impotence.

I bless them when they walk in the valley of the shadow of death. May they feel Your rod and Your staff protecting and comforting them.

I bless them in their infinite possibilities of growth that they may free themselves from their condition and one day walk upright and free as useful and confident citizens of their societies.

I bless the adults who abuse of them sexually or otherwise that they may awaken to their own divine nature and be brought to repentance and repairing the harm they committed.

And finally, I bless myself that I may never indulge in thought or in deed in the type of sensuality that reinforces the very existence of this exploitation and slavery.

Day 32
For the Fount of Goodness We Are

We are endless founts of abundant goodness awaiting simply to be expressed. As usual with all these blessings, read them first slowly to really grasp their deeper meaning, and then say them from the heart, feeling the words rather than thinking them.

May my joy be a geyser springing towards the sky,
A lark soaring to the heavens with its crystalline song,
A bush of spring blossoms bursting into flower.
May my love be a deep ocean resting in its endless depth,
An open heart whose unjudging welcome embraces all,
A cataract whose boundless giving is freely available to every living being.
May my peace be a deep pool where all may come to rest,
A forest bed of moss where those who are tired can lay down with their burdens and rise refreshed and free,
An open sanctuary that no cruel trial nor screaming tempest can disturb.
May my presence be as open arms to all seeking support, companionship or comfort in any form.
May my life be an endless source of giving, sharing, caring, trusting and a source of constant inspiration and happiness to all I meet, human or plant, bird or beast.

Day 33
A Taxi Driver's Blessing

Today, we will share a blessing for taxi drivers, such a useful and important activity in our towns and cities.

Spirit of Truth and Love, I bless this day for all the goodness it includes. I bless this cab as a rolling temple of Your presence.

I bless the roads I shall travel on and all those whose paths I cross. I bless every person who enters this cab. I bless them in their coming and going, in their perfect path and sense of guidance.

I bless the space of this cab that all those who enter it may find therein peace and a moment's haven from the pressures of life.

I bless myself in my patience, humor and joy that I may uplift the downhearted, console the sad, rejoice with those who rejoice, and be for each one the mirror of the infinite Mother-Love's caring for them.

And I bless myself in my calm that I may stay poised in the stress of urban traffic, smile at those who curse me and end the day with a song in my heart and cash in abundance to cover all my expenses.

Day 34
A Blessing for Parents

Here is a blessing for one of the most challenging jobs in the world – that of parent!

We bless ourselves in this sacred trust of raising children and in our ability to meet all challenges as they arise. We bless the garden of our home in its ability to produce strong and beautiful plants from the rich soil of tested values which constitute the true nourishment of our children.

We bless You, infinite Love, for the sacred privilege of raising these children of the stars. May their light shine ever brighter and may we and others be receptive to their brilliance. We bless ourselves in our ability to express boundless patience and unconditional love toward each other.

We bless ourselves in our wisdom in transmitting to our children that inner sense of integrity that will enable them to resist with grace and humor undue peer pressure – be it in the fields of sex, drugs, clothing, success, popularity, drinking or whatever – and be loved all the more for it.

We bless ourselves in our ability to share with our offspring that true wealth has little if anything to do with material possessions and a great deal to do with qualities such as love, compassion and giving. May we express such qualities so unselfconsciously that our star-children will reflect them.

Finally, we bless ourselves in our ability to stick together as a family through thick and thin, to do unto others as we would have them do unto us, and to be open to the world's problems and any heart in need.

Day 35
The Beatitudes Revisited

The Beatitudes found in the book of Matthew, chapter 5, are possibly the most well-known blessing on earth. I have adapted them slightly so that they may speak more directly to you.

Blessed am I when I am without any guile, for it will access the inner Kingdom of heaven for me.

Blessed am I when I mourn, for You will comfort me, infinite Love.

Blessed am I in my choice to express meekness, for it is the portal to inheriting immense good.

Blessed am I when I hunger and thirst for righteousness and justice, for much good will come to me.

Blessed am I when I express mercy and compassion, for they will return to bless me.

Blessed am I when my heart is pure, for it enables me to see the divine everywhere.

Blessed am I when I make peace for it awakens the divine in me.

Blessed am I when I am persecuted for pursuing the path of integrity, for it will lead me to the Kingdom of heaven.

Finally, blessed am I when men revile, persecute or slander me for pursuing that which is right, for I shall be rewarded with an abundance of good.

Day 36
A Scottish Blessing

Today, we will share a Scottish blessing sent to me by a precious friend.

May the blessed sunlight shine on you like a great peat fire, so that stranger and friend may come and warm himself at it. And may light shine out of the two eyes of you like a candle set in the window of a house, bidding the wanderer come in out of the storm.

And may the blessing of the rain be on you, may it beat upon your Spirit and wash it fair and clean, and leave there a shining pool where the blue of Heaven shines, and sometimes a star.

And may the blessing of the earth be on you, soft under your feet as you pass along the roads, soft on you as you lie out on it, tired at the end of the day; and may it rest easy over you when you at last lie out under it.

May it rest so lightly over you that your soul may be out from under you quickly, up and off on its way to God.

And now may the Lord bless you and bless you kindly.

(Source: http://www.faithandworship.com/Celtic_Blessings_and_Prayers.htm)

Day 37
A Blessing for Single Mothers

In Western societies, due to numerous social changes, there are a growing number of single mothers. Today's blessing addresses their challenges.

I bless myself in my ability to raise my children with intelligence, unconditional love and wisdom.

I bless myself in having amply sufficient resources to offer my child the best available and to cover her/his needs if not always her/his wants.

I bless myself in my wise discernment that I may find the

right balance of discipline and freedom enabling her or him to grow as they should.

I bless myself in my ability to create a home environment that fosters her/his growth for the best, where lightness and joy find a perfect blending with spiritual and human depth and deep peace.

I bless myself in my ability to nourish a space of such deep mutual trust that my child may always feel free to share needs and challenges as they present themselves, whatever they may be.

I bless myself in my balanced expression of masculine strength and feminine gentleness so as to foster my child's balanced development.

I bless myself in my capacity to be completely non-possessive in raising this precious plant Life has entrusted to me for a while, that I may never be tempted to cling to her or him in any way, remembering as the poet says that I am simply the bow from which the arrow will spring forth to find its own unique goal.

Day 38
For Seeing the Perfection in My Life

For many years, I have been corresponding with a former death row inmate who has spent over 25 years on death row in Texas (the worst in the US) for a crime he never committed. This man has reached such a level of enlightenment that he has stated that divine Love has a perfect plan for his life. Paul Ferrini, in one of his beautiful daily meditations, writes that our suffering results from our refusal to accept and bless our lives exactly as they are now. He adds, "The truth is that there is nothing broken or missing in your life. Your life is perfect the way it is." So let us learn to discern this perfection.

May I learn to discern the perfect plan behind all events of my life. May I see that every single thing that happens in my life is a gift from Providence to enable me to grow and flourish and expand. May I bless those who curse or harm me, those who gossip or spread lies about me, as Life's tools to enable me to grow in integrity, detachment and strength.

May I see that behind the disease or accident that assails me there is a loving plan leading me to discover the ultimate source of true health and the GPS – God Positioning System – that really runs my existence. May I discern in the most distressing or challenging situations divine Love's means of forwarding my growth Spirit-ward.

May I bless every single encounter, event or unplanned situation as a clarion call to greater steadfastness and ever deeper trust in Love's provision for my good. May I trust that there is "nothing broken or missing in my life... (which) is perfect the way it is."

And as I learn in faith to discern this perfection, may it shine forth a little more every day.

Day 39
Addiction to Drugs, Alcohol and Violence Healed (Testimony)

My friend Mamadou of Mali (West Africa) is one of the most wonderful persons I have met in my life. A devoted and tolerant Muslim, he has adopted blessing as a way of life and witnessed amazing healings among the people he recommends it to. He met in the street an acquaintance of his, Fatoumata, whose son was going really wild with drugs and alcohol. He also had a knife with which he threatened people and she had to more than once go and fetch him at the police station. She was really desperate. Mamadou told her quietly about blessing and to simply bless her son throughout the day in those qualities which he did not seem to express. Sometime later, he came up to his mother and told her he was tired of the life he was living and was going to change. From one day to another, he just dropped the alcohol, drugs, knife toting and the rest and even started going daily to the mosque to pray.

Day 40
For the Healing of Being a Control Freak

Wanting to control everything is a very strong tendency among many people in our Western culture (and possibly others too). From my early adolescence, I was a total control freak and it was only many years later, when I went through the major crash of my life, that it really dawned upon me how unloving this had been – not only for my partner, but still more for me. Living in a straightjacket is not the most pleasant experience.

We (I) bless all those who live in the shadow of constant control in their ability to look at what they are doing – to themselves as well as to others.

We bless them in their ability to unveil the deep, hidden fear that is behind all such forms of behavior – a fear that things will get out of hand, will escape their control.

May they see that to control something as incredibly complex, moving, rich and unpredictable as life is a wild, unrealistic fantasy.

We bless them in their understanding that in a universe where the most stupendous, loving Mind is running the show and governing all "from mental molecule to infinity" the best attitude is to leave all in the hands of this infinite power.

May they understand that the ability to respond to every situation with unconditional love is the ultimate guarantee that things will work out for their good in all situations, and the ultimate insurance policy against the most unpredictable circumstances and insane forms of behavior.

May they learn to enjoy the unexpected and to look forward to entering unknown territory – both inside and outside themselves.

And may they even learn to welcome when things get "out of control" as a precious lesson from the universe to learn, to let go and TRUST the infinitely loving law of good that ultimately runs the show, whatever the material appearances may be.

Day 41
For the Militants of ISIL

We have all heard of or been witnesses to the horrendous executions exposed on the Internet and done by the more extreme Islamic militants of the organization called ISIL (Islamic State of Iraq and the Levant), who aim at setting up what would become a new Islamic caliphate in the Middle East. Today, our hearts go out to those who, despite all, still remain our precious brothers and sisters.

Today, we bless the militants of this network in the divinity that resides in them, despite all outward material appearances to the contrary. We bless them in their deep humanity and compassion, that they may awaken to the fact that what they are doing to others, they are doing to themselves.

We bless the populations of the areas involved, that they may be spared the suffering engendered by the fighting taking place in the region. We bless the hundreds of Yezidi women kidnapped to become sex slaves or forcibly married to Islamic militants in their courage and determination to never give in or give up.

We bless the political leaders in the West involved in this challenge that they may receive the wisdom needed to face this situation. And finally, we bless ourselves that in the comfort of our homes we may never forget our less fortunate brothers and sisters around the world and be active in whatever way is right for us to alleviate their suffering.

Day 42
Inspired by the Prophet Muhammad

As a follow-up to yesterday's blessing for the militants of ISIL, I wish to stress that the sense of brotherhood is very strong in Islam.

The following brief blessing is adapted from a text by the prophet Muhammad who, asked which actions were most excellent, gave the following answers I have turned into a blessing:

May I gladden the heart of every human being,

May I feed the hungry and help the afflicted,

May I light the sorrow of the sorrowful and remove the wrongs of the injured.

And here is a blessing based on the opening words of the first verse of the Koran, "Bismillahir Rahmani Raheem" ("In the name of Allah, the most gracious and most merciful") which is the most famous of all Muslim affirmations.

I bless this day, in the name of Allah, for all the goodness He bestows on us,

I bless this day, in the name of Allah, for the countless opportunities to serve and praise Him,

I bless this day, in the name of Allah, the most gracious and merciful, for the numerous opportunities to honor His holy name.

Day 43
Standing Strong

Joel Goldsmith, in his book The Infinite Way, *states that: "We are a law of love unto all with whom we come into contact. We should remember that all who come within our range of thought and activity must be blessed by the contact, because we are a law of love: we are the light of the world." Really understanding this gives added power to our blessings.*

Today, I am sharing one by Duncan Tuck from Wales taken from the book 600 Blessings and Prayers from Around the World.

May you know, like the oak, how to stand

Rooted in truth, reaching for light, patiently enduring and learning;

Sheltering without favor all who come into your shade; and becoming part of the rock on which you rest.

Day 44

A Blessing for Inmates in Prison and Their Guards, Part I

As one who has been a prison visitor for 20 years, I feel like sharing with you this blessing for inmates and their guards. This blessing will cover two days, the first one for inmates, the second for guards or wardens.

I bless inmates everywhere in their ability to forgive, starting with themselves.

I bless them in their perseverance and steadfastness, their hope and their patience when days, months and years draw out endlessly.

I bless them in their capacity to find deep down in their hearts the ability to return good for evil, including when abused by guards or other inmates.

I bless them in their trust in divine justice which always triumphs in the end and redresses wrongs, including those of a human penal system with its imperfections, outright abuses and miscarriages of justice.

I bless them in their ability to find rest and peace in their bodies in spite of the tensions of the prison system and, for many of them, their famished sexuality.

I bless the tens of thousands in solitary detention 24 hours a day, that they may find in themselves the inner resources to hold on, despite everything.

And finally, I bless the inmates in their ability to unite with that space of total integrity which resides deep down in themselves and which has never been touched by crime, fear, hatred, darkness or lack of any sort and their ability to reignite the flame of their true being which has always remained pure, generous, upright and free.

Day 45

A Blessing for Inmates in Prison and Their Guards, Part II

This is a continuation of yesterday's blessing for inmates of prisons.

I bless the guards in their desire and ability to treat inmates as equal human beings and to see through the human label to the soul aspiring to brotherhood or sisterhood.

I bless them in their ability to be generous rather than mean and to apply the spirit of the rules that can appease rather than the letter which so often stifles.

I bless them in the demanding ability to reinvent their work every day rather than fall into a soul-killing routine which harms them as much as the inmates entrusted to them.

I bless them in their ability to counter the often extreme violence of the system with quiet, nonviolent power.

I bless them in their deep compassion for the sufferings of inmates that they may never give in to the belief that that's just how things are and that they may accomplish their challenging work in a spirit of true service.

Finally, I bless the inhabitants of our countries that they may understand that as long as a single one of them is behind bars, part of them resides there too and that if they accept to keep inmates in conditions which constitute an affront to human dignity, they are denying the divine in themselves and the invisible spiritual unity that binds all people.

Day 46

Putting First Things First

The psychotherapist and philosopher Piero Ferrucci tells the striking story of the follower of an Indian guru who comes to his teacher, saying, "Master, I so want to reach illumination. How do I get there?" The master tells his disciple to follow him and they go down to the river. The teacher orders his student to kneel by the river and put his head just above the water. He then pushes his disciple's head under the water and holds it there firmly. After a moment, the shocked student manages to free himself from his master's grip and looks at his teacher with an air of total disbelief, spouting water from nose and mouth. "The day you want illumination with the same intensity with which you wanted to breathe, you will get it" was the terse comment.

I bless myself in my desire and ability to put order in my life that I may really make room for what matters most to me.

May my priorities be so clear that I prune my existence of all inessentials and all activities and contacts not aligned with my life's goal.

May my vision be so vibrant and strong that it instantaneously eradicates all clutter, all halfhearted efforts, all unnecessary daydreaming, all foggy thinking and diluted action.

May my concern for my fellow humans and my love of true good so nourish my goal that it may withstand all storms and hurricanes that would attempt to destroy it.

And may I ultimately rest in the quiet assurance that a deep sincerity is assured of succeeding, for the universe takes unfailing care of it.

Day 47
Blessing My Food

Most of us do not realize that the food we find on our plates comes from all round the world. Most if not all Western countries import food from well over a 100, often 150 countries. So blessing your meal can enable you to reach all over the world – to Colombian banana-pickers through Swiss cheesemakers to Indian or Chinese producers of spices, North African date producers... you name them. This blessing of producers, transporters and others who deal with them while you eat is also a wonderful means of staying centered rather than letting your mind stray left and right, and of realizing we are linked to the whole world in our simplest, most mundane activities. I have done it here just for bananas and have fun doing it for anything else. Be aware that this blessing only mentions a very few of the activities concerned with getting that banana on your plate!

I bless the plantation workers from Colombia who produced my bananas, often poorly paid and working long hours in torrid heat.

I bless the drivers who took them to the port, the dock hands who loaded them, the motley crew of sailors from many countries who transported them and their wives who stayed at home to take care of their children.

I bless the Polish naval yard workers who built the ship, the German technicians who created the boat's guidance system and so many others who participated in its construction.

I bless the customs officers who inspected the produce, the merchants or supermarkets who purchased them, the drivers who transported them for long hours on monotonous highways from the port of arrival to the supermarkets and shops all over the country.

I bless the shop personnel and the salesgirls and cashiers who sell them.

And finally, I bless myself in my constant gratitude for the infinite abundance of good that is constantly pouring down on me.

Day 48
An Irish Blessing for Times of Sorrow

May you see God's light on the path ahead
when the road you walk is dark.
May you always hear, even in your hour of sorrow,
the gentle singing of the lark.
When times are hard, may hardness never turn your heart to stone.

May you always remember, when the shadows fall,
you do not walk alone.
(Source: islandireland.com/Pages/folk/sets/bless.html)

Day 49
A Blessing on Service

The famous Indian writer Rabindranath Tagore, a friend of Gandhi and the first writer from the Third World to receive the Nobel Prize for literature in 1913, wrote the following poem which is the inspiration of our blessing for the day:

I slept and dreamed that life was joy,

I awoke and saw that life was service,

I acted and behold service was joy.

We bless ourselves in our ability to discover the profound joy, deep contentment and lasting peace born of unselfed service. We bless ourselves in our ability to serve with no strings ever attached to our activity, as a simple gift of our love we lay on the altar of divine Love.

We bless ourselves in our ability to serve, never counting the hours or minding a possible inconvenience, truly treasuring the gift it is to be able to put our modest qualities in the service of others.

We bless ourselves in the incredible privilege it is to be counted among those who constitute the invisible "servant nation" of world servers working towards *a win-win world that works for all.*

And may we perform the most humble or menial task in the same spirit as if we were serving at the court of a queen – for truly that is exactly what we are doing.

Day 50
For Unselfed Being

Maybe our only true challenge in life is letting go of the human ego. Only the ego – not the divine Self which deep in us is the foundation of our authentic being – can feel fear or anger, hatred or doubt. As we learn to gently let go of this imposition we no doubt needed in our formative years but no longer need now, we will discover the glorious sense of freedom that comes as we feel a growing sense of oneness with our true Source.

I joyously bless myself in my unfailing ability to let go of the human ego and its continuous pandering for attention.

May You, infinite Love, shine as me, that I may be so You that all those whom I encounter may experience me as Your radiant presence, Your unconditional Love and forgiveness.

May they no longer see me, but only, only, only You.

I bless myself in my desire to do good in secret, that my good deeds may remain ignored of others, and to give generously and anonymously.

May I never seek honors or first places, still less human approval, but find my deep joy in serving in the shade even if others receive the human applause.

May I so clearly see that truly I can of my own self do nothing – 'tis the Love in me that doeth the works.

Day 51
Harmony Restored in a Polygamous Household (Testimony)

Here is a second healing story of my friend Mamadou. You will find the first one, Addiction to Drugs, Alcohol and Violence Healed, *above.*

One day, Mamadou met in the street the first wife of a polygamous marriage he knew well. Assiatou was well in her fifties. As is frequent *in this culture, the husband had taken a much younger and sexier second wife and was making life for his first wife impossible, beating her up, insulting her. The young bride followed suit very quickly, and Assiatou's life became a daily hell. She poured out her woes to Mamadou who told her to simply bless them both from the bottom of her heart.*

People in Africa who are not members of the Westernized elite are often extremely receptive to new ideas. Assiatou went home and started blessing her husband and co-wife that very evening. The very next morning, he came to her and presented his apologies for the way he had been behaving. The new bride followed suit soon after, and now in their neighborhood the two women are given as models of understanding in a polygamous household.

Day 52
For Inner Peace

In a world of growing agitation and accelerating change no one on the human scene controls any longer, peace of heart becomes a most precious privilege. As thousands and thousands learn to enlarge their inner circles of peace, they will expand more and more on an energetic level until one of these days they will all join and encompass the whole of mankind.

I bless myself in my ability to feel and express the "peace that passes all understanding."

I joyfully bless myself in the deep peace that flows from feeling my complete oneness with my Source, the infinite divine Love that engenders and supports all beings.

I bless myself in my capacity to exude this peace amidst the greatest storms and tsunamis of life. May I be a lake of unruffled calm and serenity to all those who cross my path, that they may pour out their woes in my open hands and heart and leave hopeful and restored.

As I learn to still the thousand and one noises of the outer world, may I feel deep inside me the still small voice of Truth whispering its message that "all is well, all is well, all is very, very well" and may I learn to rest in this unshakeable assurance which is the foundation of my existence.

Day 53
A Buddhist Blessing

We borrow this blessing from the book Chanting from the Heart: Buddhist Ceremonies and Daily Practices, *by Thich Nhat Hanh, one of the great Buddhist teachers of the end of the last century and the beginning of this one. His village Les Pruniers in South West France attracts students of Buddhism from all round the world.*

May everyone be happy and safe, and may their hearts be filled with joy.

May all living beings live in security and in peace:
beings who are frail or strong, tall or short,
big or small, visible or not visible,
near or far away, already born or yet to be born.
May all of them dwell in perfect tranquility.
May no one do harm to anyone.
May no one put the life of anyone in danger.
May no one, out of anger or ill will,
wish anyone any harm.

Day 54
A Blessing for Abundance

Abundance is not something material "out there" awaiting to be discovered, or something that we have to "attract" to ourselves from another source. Abundance is first and foremost a way of meeting life – either we come from lack or we come from abundance. And it is a choice each of us makes moment after moment after moment.

I bless myself in my ability to see the infinite riches life has in store for each one of its children,

Where there appears to be disease, may I see the health just waiting to be expressed.

Where someone seems sad, may I see the consolation and joy just ready to well up from the depths of their being.

Where hatred is manifested, may I sense the love hidden in the wings that is just awaiting to be expressed.

Where material lack and intense need seem to prevail, may I hold on to the five thousand fed with two loaves and five fish, or the widow's jar which endlessly poured forth the good oil.

Where loneliness and solitude weigh a person down, may I know that as a child of infinite Love he/she will be companioned.

Where blatant, cold indifference seems to reign, may I be an instrument to offer the deepest compassion and tender caring needed.

So be it now and forever.

Day 55
On Stewardship of My Life

One of the secrets of an unburdened and happy life is to realize that absolutely everything we believe is ours is actually simply lent to us by life, by the universe so as to grow in love, service and joy.

Thank You for the gift of the years You have lent me – may I use them to forward the coming of a world that works for all.

Thank You for the many talents which You have entrusted to me – may I make them grow and multiply in your service.

Thank You for the money You have put into my account – may I use it to relieve the widow and the orphan and support those causes I truly believe in.

Thank You for the possessions You have poured upon me – may I be as generous in sharing them as You in giving them.

Thank You for the wonderful friends You have blessed me with – may I do unto them as I would have them do unto me.

Thank You for the trials You have sent my way – may I transform them into tools for my inner growth.

And thank You for the numerous joys You have strewn upon my path – may they increase my determination to become a faithful servant of the New World to come.

Day 56
A Blessing by Steve Jobs

Today, our inspiration comes from a no lesser source than Steve Jobs, the genial founder of Apple Corporation. I have transformed a simple text of prose into a blessing by adding "May I" and replacing "you" with "I." The dogma he speaks about may be interpreted to mean any form of rigid thinking.

Because my time is limited, may I not waste it living someone else's life.

May I not be trapped by dogma – which is living with the results of other people's thinking.

May I not let the noise of others' opinions drown out my own inner voice.

And most important, may I have the courage to follow my heart and intuition. They somehow already know what I truly want to become. Everything else is secondary.

(Source: www.weforum.org/agenda/2016/05/your-time-is-limited-don-t-waste-it-living-someone-else-s-life-6-inspiring-graduation-speeches/)

Day 57
A Blessing for Financial Speculators

In this rather strange world we live in, thousands of people are involved daily in financial speculation – trying to make more money with money. One figure says it all: less than 3 percent of all daily financial transactions are for real goods and services. All the rest is speculation.

Often at the cost of the poorest of the poor. The desire to accumulate still more when all one's basic needs are more than abundantly met usually comes from one source: a repressed fear of lack. You and I can help change this situation.

We bless all those who channel their divinely bestowed precious life energy into financial speculation, in the hope of immediate financial returns.

We bless them in their understanding that no real gains can ever be made at the cost of others and that, because of the law of right returns, i.e. that one reaps what one sows, they will one day have to come face to face with the results of their activities.

We bless them so that, despite the frantic rush and electric atmosphere of trading rooms, the discreet but persistent voice of truth may eventually reach them and lead them to ask: but what on earth am I really doing? And what am I doing to my soul?

We bless them in their true sense of wealth that they may come to grasp that all true abundance comes from within, not without, and that what they give to others, not what they take, constitutes their true wealth.

We bless them in the courage needed to denounce illegal activities, be they even in favor of the group or bank they work for, and to resist the resulting pressure on themselves to just keep quiet.

We bless them in their grasp of the new win-win paradigm percolating through the nooks and crannies of The System which, one day, will overturn the tired, old, win-lose, me first model which has run a great part of the world for so long.

Above all, we bless them in their consciousness of their perfect divine identity and indissoluble oneness with their divine Source.

And we bless ourselves in our own financial integrity, that we may aim at our highest sense of what is right in all our own financial affairs, from what we pay a student working his way through college for tending our garden to purchasing and selling stocks and other financial transactions.

Day 58
Native American Blessings: Holding on to Good

Today, here are three Native American blessings which express such simple beauty. First a Pueblo exhortation to which I have added "May you..."

May you hold on to what is good,
even if it's a handful of earth.
May you hold on to what you believe,
even if it's a tree that stands by itself.
May you hold on to what you must do,
Even if it's a long way from here.
May you hold on to your life,
Even if it's easier to let go.
May you hold on to my hand,
Even if I've gone away from you.
https://sunshineandchaos.wordpress.com/2014/12/31/a-pueblo-indian-prayer-for-the-new-year/

The second one is by Chief Dan George
May the stars carry your sadness away,
May the flowers fill your heart with beauty,
May hope forever wipe away your tears,
And above all, may silence make you strong.
(http://www.goodreads.com/quotes/72132-may-the-stars-carry-your-sadness-away-may-the-flowers)

A Navajo prayer which I have transformed into a blessing
May there be happiness before us. May there be happiness behind us. May there be happiness above us. May there be happiness below us. May there be happiness all around us.

May words of happiness extend from our mouths for we are the essence of life, the source of happiness. All is finished in beauty. All is finished in beauty. All is finished in beauty.

(Source: https://episcopalarchives.org/cgi-bin/ENS/ENSpress_release.pl?pr_number=73141)

Day 59
For an "Anonymous" Clerk or Cleaning Woman

There are many activities in our societies that seem of little significance or "unimportant," but that is such a superficial view of things. It bears repeating that the humblest activity performed with love certainly uplifts the human race more than a high prestige or "important" job performed out of self-interest. Love is the key indispensable ingredient of true progress and the most powerful healing agent on the planet.

I bless myself in my ability to perform my humanly modest task with the greatest love and sense of perfection.

May I even delight in the anonymity of the job, knowing that for infinite Love, nothing is anonymous, because every single one of its creations, from the tiniest micro-molecule to the rolling of the galaxies, has its perfect place, function, purpose and aim in the divine Plan which encompasses all things.

May I enjoy the privilege of performing every single activity, from cleaning a dusty cupboard in the basement to filing documents no one may ever use again with true care, knowing that the fundamental attitude I manifest in my work uplifts or depresses, however minutely, the energy field around me.

May I rise above the lack of appreciation for my activity and the authentic care I bring to performing it and bless those who withhold such appreciation, knowing that the withholding impoverishes them, not myself, and may I bless them in their sensitivity to the hidden good they will one day rejoice in discovering.

Day 60
A Blessing Psalm

Stephen Mitchell, author of The Gospel According to Jesus, *has given us some beautiful translations of the psalms. Here is his version of Psalm 1 which reads as a blessing. You may easily change it into a more personal blessing by adding "May I..."*

Blessed are the man and the woman
who have grown beyond their greed and have put an end to
their hatred
and no longer nourish illusions.
But they delight in the way things are
and keep their hearts open, day and night.
They are like trees planted near flowing rivers,
which bear fruit when they are ready.
Their leaves will not fall or wither.
Everything they do will succeed.

Day 61
A Blessing by Peace Pilgrim

Mildred Lisette Norman was a well-known pacifist, nondenominational spiritual teacher and activist of the last century, who crisscrossed the US many times on foot promoting her message of love and peace. Here is a blessing of hers.

Blessed are they who give without expecting even thanks in return, for they shall be abundantly rewarded.

Blessed are they who translate every good thing that they know into action, for even higher truths shall be revealed unto them.

Blessed are they who love and trust their fellow beings, for they shall reach the good in people and receive a loving response.

Blessed are they who have seen reality, for they know that not the garment of clay but that which activated the garment of clay is real and indestructible.

Blessed are they who after dedicating their lives and thereby receiving a blessing have the courage and faith to surmount the difficulties of the path ahead, for they shall receive a second blessing.

Blessed are they who advance towards the spiritual path without the selfish motive of seeking inner peace, for they shall find it.

In this world you are given as you give
And you are forgiven as you forgive –
While you go your way
Through each lovely day
You create your future as you live.

Day 62
Seeing Through the Eyes of Love

At every single moment of our lives, we choose our thoughts, hence our vision of reality. It is in that sense that one can say that we truly do create our reality. So what if the most productive and helpful way was in seeing all through the eyes of Love?

I bless myself in the supreme freedom we have – to choose how we view life.

I bless myself in my ability, today, to see all through the eyes of Love.

I bless myself in seeing that my neighbor is myself, hence as worthy of love as I am.

When I see someone worn out by life or buried in grief or sadness, may I embrace them with the eyes of love and be for them a reflection of Life's tender, loving care.

When I see someone torn by resentment or hatred, may my deepest compassion surround them in its warmth as a cloak.

When I see someone struggling with fear, may the eyes of love give me the inspiration to meet their need in the best way available to me at that moment.

When faced with any appearance of lack in any form or guise, may I be graced with the vision that will alleviate that lack and replace it with the peace of true abundance and an abundance of true peace.

Day 63
A Blessing for Silence

The great Sufi poet Rumi once made this remarkable statement: "Silence is the language of God. All else is poor translation." I believe the highest form of prayer is listening to God who, being omniscient, already knows of any meaningful request we could make and which She has already granted us in advance, before the request was even made.

May I enter the deep silence of Your Presence and just sit in quiet adoration, listening to You.

May I so quiet my mind that the roar of passing thoughts be stilled.

May I appease my heart so that the noise of desires and wishes calms down until it resembles the peaceful lake down yonder, where Love's smile is reflected on its serene, unruffled surface.

May I put all my plans aside, knowing Yours are so much better – if only I allow myself to hear them.

May I create such a receptive space that I am ready to welcome suggestions or requests from You that totally brush aside and dissolve any views of what I thought possible or impossible, knowing that miracles are Your normal way of addressing Your children.

May I so still my emotions and even hopes that I may hear in the deepest recess of my soul and *feel* the truth of Your most amazing statement of all times, of any belief system, "My child, you are ever with me and ALL that I have is yours." (Luke 15:31)

And in the stunned silence of my listening soul, may I hear Your last comment: "And that is how much I love you all."

Day 64

Gives Away Hundreds of Copies of The Gentle Art of Blessing *(Testimony)*

A couple of years ago I was contacted by a Spanish woman from Barcelona who told me that her husband, a great admirer and practitioner of blessing, was going to be celebrating his 60th birthday. She wanted to prepare something special for him and asked me if I would be ready to come and give a surprise talk on blessing to his family, friends and acquaintances and that she would pay all expenses. I was only too happy to agree. At the last minute she told her husband I was coming to Barcelona to give a talk and would he like her to invite me to dinner. Of course he was delighted, and I told him about the talk on blessing I was giving the next day and invited him to come along.

The next evening, all the guests were there punctually at 8pm in the conference hall and he arrived around 8:30. I will never ever forget the air of total amazement and joy when he turned around and saw over 150 of his friends and family assembled to honor him.

The next day, I went to the bookstore where he purchased all his copies of the book on blessing, and the owner of the store confirmed that he had purchased over six hundred (600) copies of the book over the years! It was his daily practice, the foundation of his spiritual life. He always had copies of the book with him and would give it spontaneously whenever he met a heart receptive to its message.

Counting, counting…

Day 65

Waiting in a Café

I am in the restaurant of the Geneva train station with an unoccupied hour in front of me. What a blessing!

Infinite One, I bless this space of Your omnipresence – every nook and cranny filled to overflowing with Your tender, caring, compassionate Love for all who are here.

I bless every single person in this space in the feeling of their oneness with You and of their divine identity.

I bless this forlorn looking person opposite me in her quiet joy and contentment.

I bless this ever-friendly server F. in his peace and good humor in what is often a stressful job with rarely even a brief pause.

I bless this person with an apparently challenging physical problem in her perfect health, her wholeness and deep trust that divine Love *is* taking care of her.

I bless all those who enter here that they may feel the touch of Your grace in just the form they need now.

And I thank You that rather than letting myself be constantly distracted by ads and the constant hustle-and-bustle of urban life, I can rest in the gentle practice of sending out blessings to all at all times.

Day 66
John O'Donohue

Today, I again borrow a blessing from that magical crafter of blessings, the Irish poet John O'Donohue, which he wrote for his mother, Josie.

On the day when the weight deadens on your shoulders and you stumble, may the clay dance to balance you. And when your eyes freeze behind the grey window and the ghost of loss gets into you, may a flock of colours, indigo, red, green and azure blue, come to awaken in you a meadow of delight.

When the canvas frays in the currach of thought and a stain of ocean blackens beneath you, may there come across the waters a path of yellow moonlight to bring you safely home. May the nourishment of the earth be yours, may the clarity of light be yours, may the protection of the ancestors be yours.

And so may a slow mind work these words of love around you, an invisible cloak to mind your life.

(Source: http://www.scottishpoetrylibrary.org.uk/poetry/poem
s/beannacht-blessing)

Day 67
A Blessing for Time

No civilization in history has ever been as subjected to what has become
the slavery of time as ours. It struck me so forcibly when a dear friend
of mine quoted her daughter, a high-level university trained employee
in an environmental organization, who told her: "Mother, I don't have
the time to live." So today, we will address this issue.

I bless my ability to slow down and start really living. I bless
myself in my firm intention to master my use of time rather than
letting the clock run my existence. I bless myself in my desire
to home in on a clear goal in life and hence to establish clear
priorities – that I may avoid dispersing my energy here and
there in useless consumption and superficial distractions.

I bless myself in my ability to realize that every second is
filled with unlimited possibilities of good if only I allow myself
to slow down sufficiently to become aware of them.

And I bless myself in my ability to see that time is a gift divine
Love has entrusted to me that I may use it to forward my inner
growth, create trustful relationships and any task that I feel the
universe is inviting me to accomplish.

Day 68
To Heal Violence in Homes

Are you aware of the extent of domestic violence around the world,
including countries like Bolivia where in over 70 percent of homes
the woman is subjected to violent punishment (sometimes leading to
death), the proportion for children being still greater? Home should be
a place of rest and peace, not a battleground. So your help is so needed
in this area – as in so many others.

I bless the women submitted to the brutal violence of husbands who deep down despise themselves so terribly they exteriorize their self-hatred on often defenseless partners. I bless them in their courage in facing the storms and their inspiration in seeking constructive solutions.

I bless them in their self-image that they may resist the temptation of loss of self-esteem or of victimhood.

I bless the partners who unleash this violence that they may heal the deep dissatisfaction, possible self-loathing and lack of empathy which can only lead them into a dead-end road and the vicious circle of more violence.

I bless the neighbors who are aware of such situations in their honest concern and wisdom in seeking help and potential solutions as well as the social services and possibly the police in the sensitivity and wisdom of their interventions.

And above all I bless both partners in their discovery of the incredible divine beauty and perfection hidden in their own souls which will enable them to see the same wholeness in their partners, children, and all those surrounding them.

Day 69
Gregg Braden: On the Practice of Blessing

Today we will ponder this very simple practice on how to bless from an interview with Gregg Braden.

If we can embrace the experiences when someone or an event hurts us in life, not that we like the experience or want to have it again, but the ancients say that we should bless the experience. This sounds very strange: to bless the things that hurt you? But here's what happens. When we begin to bless the things that cause us the pain, the blessing is simply the acknowledgment.

For example, "I bless the person who has just been dishonest with me." "I bless the person who violated my trust, betrayed my confidence." And you say that again and again. And you say it out loud. What begins to happen is that the verbal expression brings the physical energy up from the heart and into the body. Soon, your body becomes warm and you have tears in your eyes. And you say, "I bless this person, I bless this person." That's all we need, for because for just a moment when the charge is relieved, we can replace the hurt with something else.

So rather than judging the experiences when they come to us, we can look to each experience as a blessing. And, when we find ourselves hurt, say again, "Yes, I feel hurt." So acknowledge it first. Secondly, what is this hurt saying to me. What voice am I hearing? What does it tell me about my life? And bless the hurt that is giving us information about ourselves.

(Source: Consciouslifenews.com in August 2012)

Day 70
A Blessing for the Homeless

Today we will take the homeless deep into our hearts. As I write this blessing here in Geneva, Switzerland, where I live, we are in an exceptionally cold spell with temperatures plunging far below freezing. In a few hours I will be meeting with a former convict recently out of prison who has no family, no home, no job, no friends. This wonderful young man has had a life of such incredible toughness – and there are millions like him around the world, some probably not too far from where you live.

From the bottom of my heart, I bless the homeless of this planet, my country and neighborhood.

May they discover that Your abundance is available to every single one of thy children at all times.

May they find a warm place to rest and nourish their tired bodies.

May they find an activity that enables them to restore their sense of dignity.

May they find the contacts that will bring them out of their often desperate solitude.

Despite the huge challenges facing them daily, may they keep a strong sense of their self-worth and discover that their ultimate home is in omnipresent divine Love of which they can never be deprived.

I bless the authorities and concerned private organizations of my region that they may undertake the maximum they can do to find the solutions to start alleviating this challenge.

And may I be led to undertake what I can to help solve this challenge, if such is my calling, for each homeless I meet is myself.

Day 71

For Accepting the *Total* Responsibility of My Life

Accepting the total responsibility of everything that happens to us is one of the most fundamental steps any individual can take. It marks the passage from child to adult. This does not mean one has caused a specific situation, but that one accepts one's ability to respond with creativity, intelligence and love to every single event in our lives. It is a gateway to great freedom and quiet joy.

I bless myself in my ability to feel the deep empowerment growing from accepting my responsibility for all that enters my life.

I bless myself in my ability to finally say good-by to every single victim attitude:

- complaint which I choose to replace with gratitude
- refusal of all timorous "NOs" which I choose to replace with acceptance and a powerful "YES"
- fear which I learn to replace by trust

I bless myself in accepting the immense inner liberation that comes from being master in my own home rather than letting events and people shuffle around my inner mental furniture.

Above all, I bless myself in my sincere desire and deep yearning to hold on to seeing all others as free, to hold on to the true reality of their grandeur and majesty as children of God rather than the poor stumbling mortals they sometimes appear to be.

Day 72
Drive with Love Along the Way!

There has been an increase in road rage incidents lately, including one where a mother of four was followed and shot dead in her driveway in Arizona. A friend of mine composed the following one on this theme.

Today I bless the millions of drivers who will be on our highways and roads. I bless them in their desire to obey speed limits, their alertness to driving conditions, and their courtesy to other drivers.

I bless them in their wisdom to focus on the task at hand and their refusal to be distracted by the use of cell phones and other devices.

I bless them in their patience in heavy or slow traffic and in their trust that they'll arrive at their destination in good time. May they use these moments to send loving thoughts and blessings to all those in the same situation.

I bless those drivers prone to anger in their recognition that road rage will not only endanger others but also hurt themselves. I bless them in their peace and their acknowledgment that a car is to be used as a tool, not a weapon.

I bless the driver in front of me and the driver behind me, and I especially bless myself as a competent, respectful, law-abiding, and alert driver.

Day 73
Homework!!!

Some of you have been reading these blessings for quite a while and I trust you have gotten the gist of how blessings can be structured and written. So rather than composing a new blessing, today I am going to suggest that you start blessing some neighborhood, national or world issue. The topics are certainly not missing!

There is a lovely African proverb that states: "When the mouths of the ants join together, they can carry an elephant!" You may feel that your blessing is not moving much, but joined with millions doing the same thing, it will help move the world.

Here are a few suggested topics just to get you launched. In the area of world issues, many aspects of the world environment need support: the rapidly shrinking forest coverage, pollution of water resources and oceans everywhere, decrease of wildlife and biodiversity. Conflicts all around the world are not missing, especially in the Middle East. Close to 800 million go to bed hungry every evening, millions of children have to prostitute themselves to survive – the list is endless. I am not going to mention national or local issues, as readers of these blessings come from many countries. But with an open heart, you will never, ever lack an issue to bless. And I bless you in your caring endeavor.

Day 74
Taking Time for the Important Things

This can easily be changed to the first person, "may I."

May you take time to smile at a stranger – he or she is YOU
May you take time to love, unconditionally – it is who you are
May you take a little time for silence – it refreshes your soul
And may you take time to be grateful and count your blessings!

(From an anonymous poem)

Day 75
A Poem by US Poetess Doris Peel

A friend sent me the other day the loveliest e-mail in which she wrote: "God is so happy to live in you" (and I would add: as you, dear reader). So today my blessing for you will be in the form of a poem by American writer Doris Peel. You can conclude the poem by saying: "I bless myself as this wonder."

Daily I am His delight
Daily He rejoices in His handiwork – all fresh, all bright,
    all wrought from elemental life
    to be what He beholds as me.
His song sung out in world this day!
His theme in play! His act of joy!
Love laughs. And I – O, it is laughter that I am!
His poem, His psalm!
In sight of Him,
    How fashioned of gladness I must be!
    How lark-on-wing, a thing that
That He daily should thus delight in me:
His poem, His song sung out, His theme!
His everlasting act of joy.
So bless yourself as this wonder, most precious reader friend.
(Source: http://sanctuaryofangelsblog.blogspot.com.es/2009/08
/his-delight-is-you-x.html)

Day 76
A Blessing for Perseverance

Succeeding in a spiritual quest demands at least four basic qualities: a strong motivation, total sincerity, a lucid and firm intention and, as in most other endeavors in life, great (and sometimes immense) perseverance, as the seeker will almost invariably encounter important trials (which are necessary to test us). Grit will be helpful in such moments!

I bless myself in my ability to stay firmly on course when tested and never fall into the easy trap of feeling a victim.

May I never fall prey to the temptation to take the easy superhighway where I will meet the crowds... and mental chloroform, rather than follow the rugged and oft mountainous terrain of my own inner calling.

May I muster the inner determination to face the insidious doubts and outright taunts slyly suggested by error as my own thoughts or thrown at me in derision, or even coming through the well-intentioned words of friends – and just continue my allotted path, whatever the cost and however lonely the journey.

Be the temptation disease or injustice, unending dryness on the spiritual path, utter confusion over choices facing me, or the sneaky desire to just give up, may I, in the poet's great metaphor, "hitch my chariot to a star," rather than to the lamppost in the street.

And finally, may I trust Divine Love sufficiently to know that ultimately *all is very, very well* in the unfolding of the incredible divine Plan already written into the destiny of the universe for me and all.

Day 77
Blessing Uplifts a Dying Patient (Testimony)

"I am a Christian Science nurse and when I first began to practice blessing there was a certain bedridden patient with whom every nurse seemed to have a difficult time and I was no exception. I would go in her room when assigned to it and she would (seemingly) bark orders in a tone that was like fingernails on a chalkboard. Screeching and unending... It was miserable.

I began to bless. At first it seemed crazy to be blessing as she was barking orders. But I silently blessed her in her gratitude, her contentment, her peace of mind, her love. No matter how difficult at first (and believe me at first it seemed quite difficult) I did not stop my silent blessing.

Within a few days, and unexpectedly, my view changed. Suddenly I felt myself in her position and realized the honor of my own. It became a joy to hold a cup of water to her mouth so she could sip, to wash and clean her and to do the smallest of duties. Suddenly, what once felt like a dictatorship had become a friendship.

Soon demands turned into expressions of gratitude. I would sit and read to her, we would hold hands and laugh. In those moments she would enrich me with her own life experiences and I would come to better know our Father-Mother God. I was thrilled on the days I would come to work and find I had been assigned to her room. For our relation had truly become one of harmony. One in Love!

A month or so later, I was working in another hall of the facility. I was moved by Spirit to go and enter her room, and as I did, she looked up at me, placed her hands on my cheek and smiled. "I love you," she said and I mirrored her words back as I kissed her brow and turned to walk out. In that moment, she died. And I was blessed, yet again, in knowing her."

(Susan, USA)

PS: The most wonderful thing about blessing is that it can apply to practically any situation. As a matter of fact, I could not think of a single situation one could not enrich, uplift or transform through blessing. *(PP)*

Day 78
A Blessing for Forgiveness

I believe it is impossible to live a happy life if one nourishes resentment for some harm done to oneself, or guilt or repressed anger for an error of omission or commission we caused. On the other hand, we become incapable of resentment when we have understood that everyone is at every moment at their highest level of consciousness. We then live in deep peace and quiet joy.

I bless myself in my ability to understand that forgiveness is one of the greatest gifts I could ever make to myself and to the world.

I bless myself in my understanding that when I refuse to forgive, I make an unconscious choice to suffer.

I bless myself in the understanding that the prisoner I am freeing when I forgive is myself.

May I understand that when I forgive, or request forgiveness, I not only free myself but help free all others in the world struggling to forgive, and will also elevate world consciousness.

Above all, I bless myself in my ability to forgive myself for any and every mistake or harm I ever occasioned – to myself or to others – so as to walk free, head high and my heart singing.

Day 79
Dreaming the Impossible

Miracles are happening every day, everywhere, to those who believe in their possibility. "Impossible" healings are happening all round the world. "Impossible" business, technical or scientific challenges are solved by people who welcome the unknown and the unconventional as a testing ground for new happenings. "Impossible" spiritual breakthroughs are actually experienced daily by people who are suddenly overwhelmed by grace or who have had a NDE. Jesus said: "To my Father all things are possible." That is our measuring rod.

NB: you can replace "myself" with "us" ("my" with "our") as in all the blessings in this book.

Spirit of truth and love, I bless myself and all humans in our ability to roll back our little human limits. I bless myself in my understanding that absolutely ALL things are possible to You. I bless myself in my willingness to let go of the comfort of my mental harbor and set sail in the direction of the limitless horizons of the ocean of Love.

May I understand that so-called "miracles" are built into the very structure of the universe. I bless myself in my readiness to love and embrace the unknown as a seedbed of infinite possibilities. May those who work with so-called "unredeemable" humans, in whatever field of activity it may be – health or social institutions, prisons, schools – actively prepare for miracles.

And I bless the people of this planet in their vision of a win-win world that works for all and their trust that we WILL bring it about – soon.

Day 80
May Love Make a Bridge

It is such a privilege for me to be sharing these blessings with you. So I am the one who thanks you – for really "listening" to their message and sharing them further. Today's blessing is adapted from Singing the Living Tradition *by the Unitarian Universalist Association and is called "Love Makes a Bridge."*

May love make a bridge from heart to heart, and hand to hand.

May love find a way when laws are blind, and freedom banned.

May love lift the hopes that force and fear have beaten down.

May love break the chains and give us strength to stand our ground.

May love make a bridge that winds may shake, yet not destroy.

May love carry faith through life and death to endless joy.

Day 81
Love's Perfect Guidance of All

Mary Baker Eddy once wrote that: "Infinite Mind creates and governs all, from the mental molecule to infinity," which resonates with Jesus' statement that even the hairs of our head are numbered. If the universe is totally and perfectly governed by the law of unconditional Love – despite all that our senses scream to the contrary – then everything in our lives has meaning.

Dear Love, may I see Your hand in absolutely everything that enters my life.

May the thrush so gaily singing in the tree remind me of Your endless joy.

May I see the person who screams at me today as an opportunity to develop my tender compassion and may I silently bless them in their peace and contentment.

May the kindness I discern in a passerby's eyes remind me that You inhabit every single heart and may I thus be led to bless those I pass in their divine essence.

May I understand that our huge environmental predicament is a wake-up call for humanity to treat Mother Earth with the deepest respect and this or that regional war a call to us all that we may build the necessary economic, social, cultural and political structures so as to enable us to grasp our oneness as a race and act accordingly.

May I understand that any upset in my life, any major challenge, is simply a clarion call urging me to grasp that absolutely everything in my life happens to forward my growth and my good, and hence bless it and even give thanks for it.

Day 82
A Blessing for Journalists

Blessing functions on the level of the invisible spiritual reality hidden behind the veil of material appearances. Some of the journalists you are blessing may appear to be devoid of any scruples or be completely ego-driven. That is the very reason you are blessing them: that they may reconnect with their original integrity.

I bless the journalists of… (here you can name a newspaper, TV or radio station, etc.) in their deep love for truth, their sensitivity to beauty and what is good. I bless them in their ability to resist any force which would impel them to report on what is superficial, or unnecessary, or would press them to dissimulate the truth.

I bless them in their ability to denounce evil with the sole aim of correcting it. I bless them in the total integrity of their being which enables them to avoid all sensationalism and an unhealthy curiosity with the private life of others.

May they evoke with exactitude, integrity and true impartiality all that they have to present to their listeners or readers and resist any undue pressure which would attempt to dilute their highest sense of truth for the benefit of financial or other motives such as prestige and power.

Day 83
A Mutual Blessing

This blessing by Ann Palmer from 600 Blessings and Prayers, *edited by Geoffrey Duncan, is slightly adapted and followed by a very brief Quero Apache affirmation I have turned into a blessing.* (http://www. greenhearted.org/mutual-blessing.html)

May the energy emanating from every step I take,

May the energy emanating from every breath I take,

May the energy emanating from every action I take,

May the energy from every thought, action, word and deed of all humanity re-sanctify the Earth.

And so, by this exchange of blessings may grow, in symbiosis, the consciousness of Oneness.

QUERO APACHE BLESSING

Looking behind may I be filled with gratitude,

Looking forward may I be filled with vision,

Looking upwards may I be filled with strength,
Looking within may I find peace.

Day 84
Tagore and Wesley

Today I have taken two brief pieces from Indian writer Rabindranath Tagore and John Wesley, founder of the Methodist movement, and turned them into blessings.

TAGORE
May I not pray to be sheltered from dangers but to be fearless in facing them.

May I not beg for the stilling of my pain but for the heart to conquer it.

May I not crave in anxious fear to be saved but hope for the patience to win my freedom.

WESLEY
May I do all the good I ever can

By all the means I can, in all the ways I can, in all the places I can, to all the people I can, as long as I ever can.

Day 85
For Love as the "I" of My Being

Who would not one day wish to attain that state where they express nothing but love, in whatever situation they may find themselves, facing whatever or whomever it may be, from a tiger to a troglodyte. May this blessing help you on the way, dear friend.

May I learn to just live love in every moment of my life, just be it, express it, and love, love, love. May I not know anything else but love and may my whole being just radiate love to the exclusion of all else.

And may I grasp deeply that on the true plane of being there IS nothing else.

Love will accomplish all I need to do, it will heal everything and anything, it will raise the dead – especially the dead in spirit. May I be nothing but love.

May love inspire my every thought, dream, desire, intention, motive, my visualizing, my speaking and my acting.

When people meet me may they experience only a sea of love surrounding them and carrying them.

And may I in turn see only through the eyes of love, till, everywhere, I behold the very face of God and feel only the gentle Presence of Love.

Day 86
A Blessing for the United Nations

Our world is more and more unified in its structures, exchanges and communications yet politically there are well over 200 independent nations. Some people are highly critical of the activity of the UN, but it is our major human opportunity and structure for moving toward world peace and collaboration. So it is more helpful to bless than to criticize.

I bless the United Nations as a positive meeting ground for all nations. I bless the UN in its capacity to encourage authentic dialogue between nations.

I bless the UN in its essential role of mediation between conflicting parties and I bless the UN soldiers that they may face with wisdom and integrity the very demanding challenges often facing them.

I bless the numerous UN agencies in their attempts to develop efficient solutions to the problems of a totally interdependent world, be it in the field of the environment, health, employment, development, communications and many others.

I bless the UN personnel that they may develop both a strong feeling of being world servants and a deep personal commitment to the aims of the UN.

Finally, I bless the UN as a promoter and defender of human rights, that through an awareness of these rights we may develop a keener sense of the dignity and worth of every single human being on earth.

Day 87
What/Who Is God?

It might behoove a book which is constantly speaking about a deity to ask a question or two about this mysterious being. So today's blessing will be in the form of a story, which, I hope, will bless its readers in their deeper understanding.

It takes place in Dakar, Senegal, where I lived for seven years in the seventies. I had a small bungalow on the beach between two shanty towns, and on Saturdays a group of teenage boys would occasionally come and drink Moroccan-style green tea at my home. One of them was the son of the local kind Muslim imam, Imam Sall by name, and I would occasionally go and talk with him. At the time I was a follower of a spiritual teaching that claimed to be the ultimate revelation of truth, a very heavy claim to carry through life! This teaching had a very carefully crafted definition of God, and for me of course that was the highest definition possible. So one Sunday I strolled over to his little shack in the small shanty town where he lived with the idea of asking him how Islam defined God. I was so cocksure that I had the best definition, and my frame of mind was that of the Japanese proverb which states that it's very difficult to describe the vast horizons of the ocean to the frog sitting at the bottom of his well. How comfortable and secure I felt at the bottom of my well!

After receiving me with his usual kindness, we sat down on his modest carpet on the sand on which his hut was built, and I asked him, "Imam Sall, how does Islam define God?" And the little frog in me had the surprise of its life when he replied in his gentle voice, "Pierre, if you took all the branches of all the trees in the world as pens, and the water of all the rivers, lakes, oceans and seas as ink, you could not write out all the names (the qualities) of God." In the moment of stunned silence that followed, he added, "You know, Pierre, you are a better Muslim than most of those who live around me," by which he meant that I did not run after the girls, that I did not drink or swear and gave generously (Islam prescribes tithing).

American poet Ed Markham once wrote a lovely little ditty which goes:

He drew a circle that closed me out
Heretic, rebel, a thing to flout,
Love and I had the wit to win,
We drew a circle that took him in.

I had closed him out with my then sectarian thinking. He had included me with his kindness.

That was one of the great lessons in my life. (I also later left this teaching which nevertheless had some strong redeeming qualities and introduced me to non-dualism.)

"God" is just a word. Great mystics have said that It can only be defined by what It is not. Today, many people use words like "the Source," the Universe, infinite Love, and so on which can be helpful for those who use them but hardly constitute a breakthrough. So hopefully this realization will help us stay modest when we attempt to define the incredible Being or It which presumably created this fabulous place called the universe.

This also explains why great mystics claim that the only way to really enter into communion with this Being is through the deep silence beyond all words.

Thank you, dear Imam Sall, for such an important lesson which will stay with me till the end of my days on earth (at least – afterwards I don't know!).

Day 88

A Blessing for Those Living in Shanty Towns

Hundreds of millions around the world live in slums and shanty towns – over 850 million according to UN-Habitat. Many of them live with small children in insect-infested makeshift shacks which defy every notion of hygiene, living space, comfort, privacy, you name it. Innumerous families have seen their dwellings erased in one morning by government bulldozers. In a world where some pay tens of thousands of dollars per night for private suites in hotels, this has to change. Your blessings will and do help.

I bless the hundreds of millions whose life is a daily, even hourly struggle to survive in the most inhumane conditions. I bless them in their extraordinary courage, especially the mothers who often do not even have the bare minimum for their children.

I bless them in their sense of abundance where lack screams at them day by day. I bless them in their resourcefulness and creativity to invent solutions to survive and find the "impossible" opening which will help them improve their condition.

I bless them in their grit and determination that, as they go through hell, they may have the guts to keep going. I bless them in their ability to create communal pressure groups to improve their situation and break the listless apathy of despair.

And I bless myself in my ability to see that they are not helpless victims of a cruel world, but my sisters and brothers whom divine Love has entrusted to my care.

Day 89

A Blessing for My Mission on Earth

Many teachings and seers claim we each have a mission to perform on this earth, or at least a task, something we were sent here to accomplish. There is of course one basic task for us all: to discover and embody our divine essence – and for some that will be done through a specific plan or accomplishment.

I bless myself in my ability to discern the task I have come here to fulfill. May I silence the noise of the consumer society, or of family and social expectations, or of a heavy sense of duty and so many other suggestions that would attempt to drown the insistent whispering of Love that I unhesitatingly follow my inner calling.

I bless myself in my readiness to be surprised by what may well up from deep inside me as I quietly and persistently listen.

May I give up cultural and social guidelines and the ego's wants for what my life should be so as to follow the clearer and firmer guidelines of infinite Love.

And I bless myself in my deep trust and understanding that true happiness and fulfillment can only come by following this call.

Day 90

Written to the Cygnus book club and magazine (UK) (Testimony)

"Some years ago I bought The Gentle Art of Blessing *from you. The title just touched me. I gave it as a present to a friend and even bought it in Dutch to give as a gift. I was very moved by the content.*

The Power of Blessing is in its essence a true Art, and it has bestowed me with the power that we can respond in a most profound way when faced with adversity, such as a nasty virus that completely invaded my laptop. My "normal" response would have been one of panic and frustration, now I chose to bless the whole situation. I kept my sanity, was able to laugh, and the next day a fantastic neighbor cleaned it all up! Without charging me, but requesting that I pass on my good fortune. So please accept his gift to me for this year's membership.

Thank you, Cygnus, for publishing this book and most of all for

your most beautiful magazine."
(Josie, Ireland)
(See www.cygnusreview.com)

Day 91
For Newlyweds or a Couple Deciding to Live Together

Marriage – and even sharing life with a partner – seems more and more challenged in our contemporary world. However, just because this is such a challenging time, creating a relationship that works can be a most stimulating and exciting experience.

We bless ourselves in our desire to seek above all the real good of our partner, for this is our highest understanding of love.

We bless ourselves in our efforts to be the most authentically ourselves, wherever that may lead us, and to encourage our mutual spiritual growth. May we accompany each other, without ever attempting to possess each other.

My abundance will be your supply, just as my need will be the opportunity for you to share your abundance.

We bless ourselves in our creation of a rhythm of life where there is always space for inner listening and to only accept those structures and forms that help us grow, without ever becoming crutches or barriers.

I bless ourselves in our choice of the spirit of adventure rather than the false security of material comfort, trustful that our universal Father-Mother who adorns the lilies of the valley will provide us with our daily bread in abundance, that we may share it generously.

When your highest visions astonish me, I will listen rather than object, and if life's trials cause you to stumble or fall, I will put your hand in the hand of divine Love, where it will always meet mine. And so shall you do for me.

Day 92
On Counting Your Blessings

Some modern scientific research is showing more and more that there is no objective world "out there" and that we each create our own reality, beyond anything we can imagine. At every moment, we choose what we want to see, as this anonymous blessing I have considerably adapted from The Treasure Chest *stresses.*

May you count your garden by its flowers, not the petals that fall.

May you count your days by their joys rather than their fears and by the hours of sunshine rather than of grey clouds.

May you count your world by the friends you make rather than the strangers who shun you.

May you count your nights by the brightness of the stars rather than the depth of the darkness.

May you count your hours by the love and light you expressed and the good deeds done rather than the time spent in inaction or omission.

May you count your years by the opportunities you fulfilled rather than those you missed and by the projects you succeeded in, rather than the failures we all encounter on our path.

Day 93
A Blessing for the Leaders of the Economy

In a world where the gap between the rich and the poor grows wider and wider (for instance, in the United States, the percentage of wealth of the top 20% of households is 84%, that of the bottom 20% is 0.1%) it is urgent that the leaders of the economy readjust their aims. May this blessing help them.

I bless those who have major responsibilities in the economy and business. I bless them in their spirit of ethical service, that they may offer quality goods and services which correspond to a real need.

I bless them in their understanding that one reaps what one sows, so that they may acquire this deep understanding that whatever they give, sooner or later they receive in return, be it in their relations with their employees, the public or nature.

I bless them in the fundamental integrity of all the contracts they pass and the real value of what they put on the market.

I bless them that their fear may be eradicated by the discernment of the infinite abundance of the universe and their understanding that true wealth resides in ideas and values, compassion and generosity rather than the hollow shell of things and money.

And finally, I sincerely bless them in their comprehension that the economy exists first and foremost to serve human beings and the planet and not as an end in itself, let alone a means to accumulate wealth.

Day 94
For Finding My Right Place

We each have our right place in the grand scheme of things called "the universe," or, more modestly, our existence here on earth. Finding it sooner or later is essential, not only to our happiness, but also to fulfilling what we came here to accomplish and to continuing in a meaningful manner on our spiritual path.

I bless myself in finding my right place in Life's plan for my existence.

I bless myself in my deep listening that I may hear what divine Love is constantly whispering to me if I have ears to hear.

I bless myself in my trust that I may walk fearlessly on the path the Spirit leads me to follow.

May I place total faithfulness in what I feel is my highest calling rather than succumbing to pressures of family, society, workplace, or the siren calls of spiritual conformity or human gurus.

May I always put the courage of following my inner promptings – however challenging or however far they lead me to deviate from the "accepted" or "normal" paths – before all pressures to conform.

Finally, may I rest in the quiet assurance that divine Love is at every single moment and through every single event or trial conspiring for my ultimate good and complete fulfillment.

Day 95
On the Power of Right Thinking/Blessing (Testimony)

Today, instead of a blessing, I am going to share with you a story which shows the power of right thinking, e.g. blessing.

When he was in his early twenties, my friend Mark decided to undertake a trip around the planet. At one moment, he ended in a Buddhist monastery in Thailand. Each morning at 3am one of the monks had to ring a very large gong on a nearby hill. Very soon after his arrival, the abbot of the monastery told my friend: "Mark, as of tomorrow, you will go and ring the bell." At first Mark was very upset at having to get up at 2:15am to go and ring the gong, and pestered all the way up the hill. Suddenly he realized that he had the choice of his thoughts, and rather than making himself miserable, he could do it with joy. So the next day, he got up singing, walked up the hill joyfully, and rang the gong sending peace and blessings to all the neighboring villages.

When he got back to the monastery, there was a lone monk in the courtyard who came to him and asked, "Mark, what did you do differently today? THE GONG HAD ANOTHER SOUND."

Such is the amazing power of right thinking. So, as you go through your days, ask yourself: "Am I having 'gong thoughts' just now?"

Day 96

A Blessing for Migrants in the Mediterranean

One can never insist enough on the fact that blessing is one of the main spiritual tools we have at our disposal for healing the world. Wherever you are, whatever the situation, you can bless. Some people complain that they do not know what to do to heal the world. Well, tell them to just open their daily newspaper or turn on the news and they will have access to a 24-hour program! In recent years, a great drama has been playing itself in the Mediterranean which tens of thousands of often desperate migrants fleeing persecution attempt to cross in overcrowded and often not seaworthy boats and other crafts. Thousands drown. You can help – this very minute!

My heart goes out to these desperate brothers and sisters fleeing persecution and inhumane conditions, often with small children. I bless them in their courage, their wisdom and creativity in plotting their survival and journey.

I bless them in their sensitivity to the plight of their fellow-travelers. I bless them in their health and endurance, their sheer grit and perseverance that they may never give up.

I bless the passers who often mercilessly exploit them and knowingly expose them to major hazards that they may learn to behave with true compassion and caring and become allies rather than exploiters of their fellow humans.

I bless the recipient countries that they may open their frontiers more widely and welcome them more generously.

And I give thanks for all these world problems that are blessings in disguise, awaking us all to the ever more evident fact that there are no more private paradises on this planet and that my neighbor is myself.

Day 97
Reverence for Myself

We can only give to others what we give to ourselves, just as we can only love our neighbor to the extent that we truly and sincerely love ourselves. So today's blessing is an invitation to extend this reverence to that exquisitely beautiful and perfect being in God's eyes – you!

I bless myself in learning to see the infinite wholeness, beauty and perfection that constitute the essence of my being.

I bless myself in my ability to discard all self-condemnation, guilt or self-criticism that I am not good enough, not performing up to family or social standards, that I am inadequate or lacking in any way.

A great teacher told us that ALL that the Divine Entity includes is already ours, i.e. that we are the very same essence as Infinite Love, just as the wave is of the exact same composition as the ocean.

May I learn to see myself beyond the picayune limits of self-imposed fears and doubts and view the stunning, gloriously whole and accomplished, perfect being I am now.

Day 98
May Your Will Be Done

For some major spiritual traditions, following the will of the divine is the most important thing in life. Our readiness to do so is a very clear measure of how much ego we have already dismissed, as the ego is ultimately the cause of all our challenges. However, once we have seen that Love's will is the most beautiful thing on earth, we will yearn for nothing else than to follow it still better.

We bless ourselves in our deep desire to put Your will above all else.

May we not only see but feel that there is no greater peace or joy than the feeling of being aligned with Your will, because that will is conspiring moment after moment for our happiness.

May we abandon our picayune human plans for time and space, for job or income, for our vision of the perfect life, and for all that constitutes a human existence to the higher Intelligence which makes all things work out sooner or later for our good.

May we truly "let go and let God," give up our little human planning and our attempts to outline what we feel would be good for us. May we give thanks in advance that unknown blessings are already on their way and will be manifested increasingly as we give up the insanity of trying to control something we have the ignorance to call "our" life and see that the divine Life is living Itself as us.

May we see that infinite Love creates and governs all, from the tiniest molecule to the rocking galaxies, and that before such a wondrous order and magnificence, which seems to know what It is doing, there can be but one prayer, one cry, one song: may Your perfect, beautiful, stupendous will be done.

Day 99
A Blessing for Bees

Many of us are aware that bees are facing possibly the most critical period of their existence on earth. Some years ago, in one region in China, the excessive use of pesticides had totally eliminated the bees and trees were pollinated by hand. Yet more than 80% of plants – and over ¾ of cultivated plants – in the world owe their existence to bees. They need our support in many ways – political, practical, scientific, environmental and... spiritual.

I bless Your wondrous, amazing creation and our close neighbors called bees. I bless them in their resilience to all forms of aggression menacing them, especially those of chemical origin.

I bless them in the remarkable mission You did appoint for them and in their ability to fulfill their role perfectly. I bless the stupendous organization of beehives and bee colonies which still defy human understanding.

I also bless the producers of contested pesticides and the politicians defending them that they may put the survival of our species and of bees before the bottom line. I bless them in their integrity and true spirit of service.

I bless us, the public, that we may become totally alert to the issue and behave in a way that forwards healing on all levels – zoological, environmental, economic and other.

And above all, I bless us in our ability to develop a relationship of deep caring, unconditional love and authentic reverence towards our sisters the bees and all creation.

Day 100
A Blessing by John O'Donohue

Dear friend, please remember that today God is smiling on the world through you and as you. John O'Donohue is one of my very favorite composers of blessings. Here is another one of his precious texts.

May you listen to your longing to be free.

May the frames of your belonging be large enough for the dreams of your soul.

May you arise each day with a voice of blessing whispering in your heart... something good is going to happen to you.

May you find harmony between your soul and your life.

May the mansion of your soul never become a haunted place.

May you know the eternal longing that lies at the heart of time.

May there be kindness in your gaze when you look within.

May you never place walls between the light and yourself.

May you be set free from the prisons of guilt, fear, disappointment and despair.

May you allow the wild beauty of the invisible world to gather you, mind you, and embrace you in belonging.

(Source: http://noornalini.tumblr.com/post/1984760973/may-you-listen-to-your-longing-to-be-free-may)

Day 101
Love's Protection

If only you knew the joy I am having composing these blessings knowing you will one day read them and hopefully be enriched by them! The following blessing is adapted from hymn 99 by Tate and Brady, itself an adaptation of Psalm 91. I have put it in the feminine tense.

He that hath divine Love his guardian made, shall under Her almighty shade, fearless and undisturbed abide.

Thus to myself of Her I say, She is my fortress, shield and stay, in Her may I confide.

May Her tender love and watchful care free me from the fowler's snare and from every harm and pestilence.

May She over me Her wings spread to cover my unguarded head.

May Her truth be my strong defense.

May She give her angels charge o'er me, that I therefore no evil see.

May my refuge be God most high, and dwelling within Her secret place, may I behold Her power and grace.

And see Her salvation ever nigh.

Day 102
Blessing This Day

As our blessing today, I am borrowing a prayer I have very slightly adapted by well-known writer and speaker Caroline Myss.

May I be committed to staying only in the present time,

To remaining grounded in my world,

To feeling a bond with each person I meet,

To respecting my own integrity and my own honor,

To living within the energy of love and compassion this day,
And returning to that energy when I don't feel it,
To making wise and blessed choices with my will,
To maintaining perceptions of wisdom and non-judgment,
To release the need to know why things happen the way they do,
And to not project expectations over how I want this day to be – and how I want others to be.
And finally my last prayer: to trust the Divine.
With that I bless my day with gratitude and love.

(Source: http://www.spiritualityandpractice.com/practices/practices/view/27122/blessing-this-day)

Day 103
Increased Peace of Heart (Testimony)

"The Gentle Art of Blessing has changed my life already – and I doubt I am anywhere near expert in it. Everything has changed: the reception I receive from my classes, the kind of day I have, etc. Most of all I am loving the peace in my heart and the improvement in my relationship with my younger daughter and the relationship between the two girls. It is still difficult to bless those who have hurt me so much but still I work at it and never forget to bless them."

(From a mail from Angela to my friend Viviane, UK)

Day 104
A Blessing for the Wise Use of Money

Money is one of the most amazing realities. It is used to finance wars and the drug trade, to enrich gang leaders or mafia kings, to break a competitor... that is money as the energy of death. But it also finances good works and charity all round the world, your children's studies and your local spiritual group or hospital, scientific research and innumerable humanitarian causes. That is love-money, or money as love.

I bless myself and humankind in our learning the wise use of money. May we see that true substance is not attached to things, to forms of any kind, be they even words, but that it is in the realm of Spirit. May we see that true wealth is always inside us, and that it is the *consciousness* of this inner abundance (the Kingdom of Heaven within) which produces all other forms of abundance and covers all needs, be it for money, a partner, a job, home, health or whatever the exterior need may be.

May we be constantly aware that every single penny we receive is a gift of love, a form of love-energy to be used for good in all the forms good may take in our lives. May we see that money or any other good the universe may pour into our life is not something we own, but something that Life lends us to manage wisely. And may we rejoice in the extraordinary freedom such a vision bestows upon us.

Day 105
A Prayer for Everyone

Today, we are borrowing our blessing from the Facebook page of Eamon Zicker, a writer from Hawaii.

May your days upon this earth be blessed,
May the poetry of your being be freely expressed.
May the light of compassion always shine in your eyes...
May your heart flow with a tenderness that never dies.
May you hear the universal melody,
May your song sing endlessly,
May the kindness of your spirit never be broken,
And may your heart always be open.
May you awaken each day as if you were born anew.
May you realize the beauty that's in you and all around you.
May you always see a rainbow in the sky above,
And may your heart always burn with the living flame of love.

Day 106
For Raising World Consciousness

Raising the level of world consciousness is certainly the most important thing on the planet today, both for the survival of our race menaced by major challenges and especially for its improvement and breaking through to the higher state of consciousness which alone will enable us to establish the new world that includes all and excludes no one, which is the condition of our very survival as a race.

I bless myself in my ability to constantly devote myself to raising my level of consciousness.

May I be ceaselessly aware that at every moment, I have the choice of my thoughts, which is possibly the greatest freedom I enjoy in life.

May I make the daily commitment to bring my thoughts back constantly to that inner altar of non-dual Love (Buddha-, Christ-, Krishna-consciousness) when they err in the desert of absent-mindedness or lack of mindfulness. And may I do it with great gentleness rather than harsh self-condemnation, as I would correct a little child.

May I cultivate the friendships, activities, readings and spiritual tools that propel me on this path, rather than allowing the consumer-society to foist its cheap, redundant and soul-killing wares down my throat. And may I become aware that I make this choice, actively or passively, moment by moment by moment.

And may I use every opportunity I have – in the street, at work, at home, at rest and in all situations – to redirect the general drift of human thought towards the Green Pastures awaiting us all.

Day 107

For Those Experiencing Constant Physical Pain

A moment ago a friend phoned me who has for months been in constant physical pain. It prompted me to compose this blessing for the people who spend years in sometimes acute pain, if not a lifetime. Many take this harrowing ordeal as a fatality. It doesn't have to be so. Let us take them into the sanctuary of our hearts, the sacred space of our deepest caring.

We bless all those who live in the stress of constant, at times almost unbearable physical pain. We bless them in their courage, grit and perseverance that they may never give in to despair or the temptation to take their own lives.

We bless those who take care of them daily in their forbearance and unconditional support, as well as those who accompany them medically, be they alternative practitioners or regular MDs, that they may never give up looking for new approaches to alleviating the pain of their patients or of healing them completely.

We bless those who suffer that they may discover meaning even in their ordeal. We bless them in their investigation of new and unexplored paths which could lead them to the unfolding of unexpected new horizons of healing, when conventional means have failed.

And above all, we bless them in their consciousness of the support of our friendly universe which, despite all appearances to the contrary, is conspiring day after day for their ultimate freedom and eternal joy.

Day 108

The Oneness of All Things

Marianne Williamson's book of 365 daily devotions and reflections, A Year of Miracles, *is a treasured and trusted companion which I can recommend warmly to any reader, wherever they are on the spiritual path. Here is one of her meditations/blessings.*

Beyond the world of our separate bodies, there is a world of spiritual unity. In the truer realms, there is no place where one of us stops and the other begins.

May I see beyond the veil today, to a world of unity and truth. There are no walls that separate us, no conflicts that are even real. In truth, there is only the love that unites us and makes us one in God.

Dear God

May I see beyond the walls that appear

To separate me from others

May I extend my love

Beyond the illusions of guilt and error.

May nothing hide the truth of my unity with everyone and everything.

Amen.

Day 109
For a Deepening of My Compassion

Love in its special dimension of compassion constitutes one of the foundations of any civilized society. It is compassion that makes me sensitive to suffering, whatever form it may take. It is compassion that enlarges my heart and enables me to be sensitive to a need the other side of the planet, that enables me to recognize a brother or sister in the shoddy bum in the street or the teenage prostitute in the local bar.

May compassion ever deepen my caring for the suffering of the world and still more my desire to heal it.

May my compassion cause me to immediately embrace any suffering I become aware of, not by taking it in and suffering with the other one, but by uplifting it in thought with the inspiration of Grace and depositing it at the feet of the infinite Love which heals all.

Rather than bemoan injustice in the world or catastrophes here or there, may compassion enable me to open my purse, my hands or my heart to relieve the pain others are going through.

And finally, may my compassion be so acute and sensitive that it ultimately learns to pierce the veil of ignorance that makes me see a material world of suffering where true vision discerns only the glorious omnipresence of infinite spiritual Love and its perfect manifestation everywhere.

Day 110
A Blessing for Judges and District Attorneys

The administration of justice is an immense challenge in any society. Biases of class, political ambition, race, personality traits, repressed fears and so many others make authentic justice one of the greatest challenges of human society. The practitioners of the law greatly need our spiritual support.

I bless those in charge of the administration of justice worldwide and in my country in their deepest integrity.

I bless them that they may not be swayed by the temptations of career, of power, of corruption or easy money, of popularity and any other siren song, just as the majestic oak stands unbent by the fiercest gales.

May they grant the same attention and respect to the desperate immigrant and homeless vagrant as to the honored businessman or politician who can afford the most expensive lawyers.

May their sole guide be their highest sense of true justice rather than political or professional ambition or easy popularity which capitalizes on public prejudice or fears. May they learn to lean on divine guidance rather than the subtleties of legal interpretations, and may they have the courage to listen to the urgings of compassion rather than the harshness of the letter of the law.

Day 111
For Living Without Judgment

If everyone is living at their highest sense of consciousness – even the members of mafia gangs and corrupt politicians or businesspeople involved in shady deals – can we ever judge? To live without judging people is a source of such deep inner peace and profound serenity. Still better, when one faces so-called evil persons or "sinners" without judging them, judgment is replaced by the most authentic compassion for the harm they are doing to themselves.

Infinite Love that upholds and blesses all, I bless myself and all fellow humans in our ability to live without judgment and the constant rehashing of opinions about each and all.

May we discover the incredible inner freedom that comes from living without the snake of judgment at the tip of our tongues or in the recesses of our minds and of no longer making the incredible superficial judgments we have been culturally conditioned to make about people's faces and physical appearance.

May we replace judgments and the incredibly fluffy superficiality of mere opinions by an outflowing of the tenderest compassion which embraces our fellow beings and all of creation with the deep caring of unconditional love. And rather than self-righteously judging those who judge, may we have the Christ (Buddha, Krishna...) Mind that not only knows itself as my sisters' or my brothers' keeper, but knows itself to *be* my sister or brother.

Day 112
Buddhist, Jewish, Cheyenne Blessings

Today, to change a little, we have three very brief and very different blessings.

An Ancient Buddhist Blessing
May I be a lamp in the darkness of life,

A home for the homeless,
And a servant to the world.

A Traditional Jewish Prayer
May I:
Believe in the sun even when it is not shining,
Believe in love even when feeling it not,
Believe in God even when He is silent.

Cheyenne (Native American)
May we know peace
For as long as the moon shall rise,
For as long as the rivers shall flow,
For as long as the sun will shine,
For as long as the grass shall grow,
Let us know peace.

Day 113
For Seeing My Sister/Brother as Myself

The Second Commandment – love your neighbor as yourself – is certainly one of the best-known statements on the planet. However, there is an old Aramaic version of that statement (Aramaic was the language spoken by Jesus) which gives an alternative rendering of this commandment: love your neighbor who IS yourself. That great American mystic of the 20th century, Joel Goldsmith, stated that, in God's creation, everything is our neighbor – animals, plants, even so-called inanimate matter like rocks. In non-dual Oneness, ALL is infinite Love and its infinite manifestation.

May I have the vision, the courage, the joy and the desire to see myself in my neighbor, and my neighbor as myself and thus overcome the basic sense of separateness that haunts the human race.

I bless myself in my ability to see that the Life that upholds the tree, the lion or ladybug is the same Life that animates me. To see that, somewhere, the child dying of hunger in a forlorn shanty town of Rio, Nairobi or Calcutta is also me.

May I see that a given office worker who drives me up the walls is myself and Love's special gift to me to develop patience and understanding.

May I see that the drunkard reeling in the bus or streetcar is another me calling for my deep compassion and my blessings.

May I see that everywhere and at all times my neighbor – be he or she, person, plant or thing – is me, and that I am it or she or he, and that we are all the infinite splendor of Her divine Being in disguise.

And finally, may I have such a keen sense of this oneness that I acknowledge the Presence in all things and all beings, including myself.

Day 114
On Bullying in Society

Bullying is an extremely common form of violence. It starts at a very young age and it occurs in daycare centers, on and off school grounds and college campuses, at social and sporting events. This is a worldwide problem, but in the US alone, 2.1 million school children in grades K–12 are bullies, and 2.7 million are victims of bullying. Bullying is linked to 75% of all school shooting incidents and young people suffering from bullying are up to nine times more likely to contemplate or commit suicide, the third largest cause of death among young people. (Abbreviated version of a blessing written by my friend Manuela.)

We bless the children and teenagers who are being bullied by their peers in their peace, their serenity, their strength, and their courage.

We bless them in their understanding of their divine nature as children of the universe entitled to love and respect. We bless them in their recognition that whatever insults and injuries are hurled at them, they are always surrounded by a loving Presence that will guide and protect them and never abandon them.

We bless them in their wisdom to seek help when facing hatred and intolerance from their peers. We bless them in their refusal to accept labels that would demean and humiliate them. We bless them in their courage to resist the temptation to retaliate, feel victimized, or even consider taking their own lives when pressures get too hard.

We bless the witnesses of bullying, no matter what their ages, in their refusal to condone, participate in, or encourage any bullying. We bless them in their ability to take intelligent steps to stop any abusive conduct, and above all, we bless them in their capacity to see the innate goodness in themselves, the victims, and the perpetrators.

And finally, we bless also the ones who bully in their innate goodness as children of God, hidden behind a mask of fear, aggression, negativity, and violence, that they may come to realize their true nature and let love guide their thoughts and actions.

Day 115
A Blessing for Policemen and Policewomen

The police are a frequently maligned group in our societies. However, as guardians of law and order, it is possibly the most indispensable professional group that exists. Society could survive the breakdown of almost all public and private services; it could not survive the disappearance of the police. Let us therefore be deeply grateful to the members of this body which is faced with ever growing challenges.

I bless the police as the cement which helps bind society. I bless them in the courage they manifest in often dangerous situations and their ability to never overreact when faced with potentially harmful contexts.

I bless them in their courage to refuse to bow to the pressures of those who would manipulate them or to give in to media and public pressure in their hatred or condemnation of minority groups of all sorts.

I bless them in their ability to resist the temptation of undue or unnecessary violence in the challenging situations they face daily as well as the temptation of giving in to sexism or mobbing in their own ranks.

I bless them in their ability to resist the pressures of those in power, whatever forms such pressure might take, and to favor truth over deception, integrity over distortion of facts, compassion over indifference or rejection, forgiveness over punishment.

And I bless them above all in the courage they need to express compassion and understanding over the manifestation of toughness and force, however it may be easy to use or justify.

Day 116
The Support of Blessing Palpable (Testimony)

"I am 'living' in The Gentle Art of Blessing. It is my closest companion. A softening is happening. I can 'see' and 'feel' beautiful things happening in me and my two sons. Hope is now a strong foundation, not illusive, not dead. True blessing is the heart expression of (spiritual) Science, this is evident. I have never known such assistance. It is palpable."

(Deborah, Australia)

Day 117
A Lakota Prayer

The Native North American cultural heritage is a never-ending fountain of depth and beauty. This is a Lakota prayer I have adapted with a minor alteration or two as a blessing. It was translated by Lakota Chief Sioux Yellow Lark.

Oh, Great Spirit
Whose voice I hear in the winds,
And whose breath gives life to all the world...
May I walk in beauty and may my eyes ever behold
the red and purple sunset.
May my hands respect the things you have
made and my ears be sharp to hear your voice.
Make me wise so that I may understand the things
you have taught my people.
May I learn the lessons you have
hidden in every leaf and rock.
May I seek strength, not to be greater than my brother,
but to fight my greatest enemy – myself.
May I always be ready to come to you
with clean hands and straight eyes.
So when life fades, as the fading sunset,
My Spirit may come to you without shame.
(Source: http://www.worldprayers.org/archive/prayers/invocat
ions/oh_great_spirit_whose_voice.html)

Day 118
A Traditional Irish Blessing

*Once more, we delve into the quasi endless wealth of Irish blessings,
and we borrow this one from the book* Earth Prayers.

May the blessing of light be upon you, light without and light
within. May the blessed sunshine shine on you and warm your
heart till it glows like a great peat fire, so that the stranger may
come and warm itself at it, and also a friend.

And may the light shine out of the two eyes of you, like a
candle set in the two windows of a house, bidding the wanderer
come in out of the storm, and may the blessings of the rain be on
you – the soft sweet rain. May it fall upon your spirit so that all
the little flowers may spring up and shed their wetness on the

air. And may the blessings of the Great Rains be on you, may they beat upon your spirit and wash it fair and clean, and leave there many a shining pool where the blue of heaven shines, and sometimes a star.

And may the blessing of the Earth be on you – the great round earth; may you ever have a kindly greeting for those you pass as you are going along the roads. May the earth be soft under you when you rest upon it, tired at the end of a day, and may it rest easy over you when at the last you lay out under it; may it rest so lightly over you that your soul may be off from under it quickly and up and off, and on its way to God. And now may the Lord bless you all and bless you kindly.

Day 119
Blessing the Spaces We Enter or Work in

Most of us are moving around considerably, usually every day. Let us realize that we have an incredible opportunity to bless the world simply as we move around. Places, like sponges, absorb energy. A cathedral does not have the same energy as a prison or an emergency medical center. So each time we visit a space, we leave our own energetic imprint – be it positive or negative. We create an energy shift that will impact all those who come there after us, however modest or subtle the shift.

Spirit of Truth, I bless myself in my ability to leave my soul-print in every space I enter.

May I leave a trail of light and goodness that clears out old energies and makes a place for energies of renewal and freshness, of gentle healing and settled peace.

May people benefit from the good energy they feel in my presence and acknowledge it to be the perfume of Your Grace.

In a place where tension and fear reign, may I sow peace and trust.

Where I sense doubt and hesitation, may I leave confidence

and a green light to go ahead.

In a space of depression and sadness, may I send lightness and joy.

And above all, may I walk into any space knowing that despite all material claims to the contrary, Your Presence, infinite Love, reigns supreme over all.

Day 120
A Blessing for Spiritual Seekers

We are in a period of unprecedented, challenging and exciting change. In all areas, old structures are falling away or being challenged, including in the field of religion and spirituality. More and more people are undertaking an individual spiritual quest for their right spiritual niche. This blessing is for them.

I bless all those who are on an honest spiritual quest.

I bless them in their courage to break away from old moorings that keep them in stagnant waters and to embark onto the unchartered territories of their soul and the moving seas of spiritual adventure.

I bless them in their firm determination to continue seeking until they find the pearl of great price and the "peace that passes all understanding."

I bless them, above all else, in their ability to be true to themselves, wherever it may take them and to hold firm to their vision whatever the pressures from family, friends, religious bodies and "authorities" of all sorts to conform.

POST SCRIPTUM: the following quotation is by my dear friend Roger W. McGowen, who found his spiritual path on death row where he spent 25 years for a crime of which many, his lawyer and I included, are absolutely certain he is totally innocent. Roger has become a spiritual guide for many, myself included.

We are what we are looking for. We seek what has not been lost.

When we look too hard, we miss what we seek.
God is all around us, why must we seek Him?
We are what we seek.

Day 121
For Waitresses and Waiters

These words of American poet Amanda Bradley seem a fitting introduction to our blessing: "It takes only one smile to offer welcome... and blessed be the person who will share it. It takes only one moment to be helpful... and blessed be the person who will spare it... It takes only one joy to lift a spirit... and blessed be the person who will give it... It takes only one life to make a difference... And blessed be the person who will live it."

I bless waitresses and waiters everywhere in the important work that is theirs. May the pressures of the job never deprive them of the grace of service to clients offered with love.

May they have hearts wide enough to welcome all with a cheery face and generous enough to offer smiles to all, especially the grumpy, the depressed, the mentally absent, rude or indifferent.

May they serve the homeless bum or penniless widow with as much courtesy and kindness as the rich who leave a generous tip or those who leave none.

May they have the long-suffering forbearance to return the rude or unkind remark with quiet strength and the understanding that the aggressor is making a public confession of their own inner distress.

And when the work gets utterly hectic, may they have the strength and dominion to stay calm and controlled despite everything.

And finally, if they do lose control, snap at others or vociferously complain, may they have the generosity of spirit to forgive themselves on the spot.

Day 122
Another Blessing for Mother Earth

We are all aware that our planet is being greatly challenged by our way of life. So today I will share a very slightly abbreviated blessing for Mother Earth by Helen Weaver.

O our Mother Earth, blessed be your name. Blessed are your fields and forests, your rocks and mountains, your grasses and trees and flowers, and every green and growing thing.

Blessed are your streams and lakes and rivers, the oceans where our life began and all your waters that sustain our bodies and refresh our souls. Blessed is the air we breathe, your atmosphere, that surrounds us and binds us to every living thing.

Blessed are all creatures which walk along on your surface or swim in your waters or fly through your air, for they are all our relatives. Blessed are all the people who share this planet, for we are all one family and the same spirit moves through us all.

Blessed is the sun, our day star, bringer of morning and the heat of summer, giver of light and life.

Blessed are the stars and planets, the time-keepers, who fill our nights with beauty and our hearts with awe.

O Great Spirit whose voice we hear in the wind and whose face we see in the morning sun, blessed is your name.

Help us to remember you are everywhere and teach us the way of peace.

(Source: http://www.gipl.org/interfaith-prayers-for-the-world-day-of-prayer-for-creation/)

Day 123
On the Interconnection of All Things

One of the greatest wonders of this incredible planet and universe we live in is that everything is connected to everything. Amit Ray (Yoga and Vipassana: An Integrated Lifestyle) *has written that: "We are all so deeply interconnected; we have no option but to love all. Be kind and do good to anyone and that will be reflected. The ripples of the kind heart are the highest blessings of the universe."*

I bless this incredible universe of Love's creation where the smallest molecule is connected to the farthest galaxy.

May I realize that I am connected to every single human being and beast on earth, hence that I am inextricably linked to the child dying in a Calcutta shanty town, the worst murderer on death row, the greatest saint or mafia leader, the mayor of my city and the most gifted pianist; to the rhinos being killed to extinction and the fish disappearing from over-fishing – all, somewhere, are linked to my own survival.

May I see that I am totally connected to this planet which offers me freely the air I breathe and the water I drink, the food I eat and the wildlife and flora I admire and hence that our destinies are linked and interlocked.

And may I rejoice that this is because ALL IS INFINITE LOVE AND ITS INFINITE MANIFESTATION. What greater blessing than to be the expression of this Love!

Day 124
Blessing for the Production of Food

On a planet where 30 to 40 percent of food is thrown away or wasted, and where there is enough food produced to feed all decently, some 800 million go to bed hungry every night – almost one person out of nine.

I bless those who produce food worldwide, that they may be motivated by a sense of service rather than profit.

I bless those who run the huge multinationals which monopolize major areas of the markets for seed production and agricultural inputs that they may discern the major responsibility that is theirs and respond in the appropriate manner.

I bless the millions of small farmers everywhere that they

may learn to regroup to defend their interests and innovate intelligently.

I bless the numerous researchers and practitioners of innovative methods of agriculture that they may be listened to as they open up exciting new frontiers in the fields of food production.

I bless the affluent consumers and supermarkets everywhere that they may learn not to waste food but handle it as a divine gift enabling us to live fulfilled lives.

I bless those in government responsible for enacting laws and regulations of all sorts that they may be inspired by divine wisdom rather than narrow interests.

And finally, I bless myself that I may understand my daily bread to be a gift of divine love and a talent to be used with balance and gratitude.

Day 125
For Embracing the Whole World in My Heart

On a mentally, socially and economically shrinking planet, it is not a question of being good, but of survival that we learn to embrace all in our heart. The Kamchatka peninsula in Eastern Siberia is now – mentally speaking – in my backyard. We are all meshed together, nature included, in a web of life that excludes no one and nothing.

May I make my heart broad enough to welcome the whole world! May the understanding that my neighbor is myself enable me to welcome him in my heart, whoever she or he may be, Afghan immigrant or member of a local gang, the drug peddler down the road or the uptight, Victorian spinster.

May I embrace all those I meet today as I learn to see all with the eyes of the heart. May I learn to tear off all labels – social, psychological, ethnic – however resistant they may appear, to see only the manifestation of Life's goodness.

May I embrace the infinite variety of nature's manifestations – from the tiniest insect to the colossal glacier – understanding that my survival is linked to theirs.

May I lift up all those who are suffering and entrust them to the arms of the Love that embraces and cares for every single being.

Day 126
A Blessing for a Child

This blessing is borrowed from A Blessing for a Child – Spiritual Practice *by Edward Searle.*

Welcome dearest child.

Welcome to your two families, rich heritages converging in you. There never has been, there never will be anyone like you.

You are unique!

Welcome to this world... so finely formed and fragile yet amazingly tenacious and abundant. It is shot through with so much beauty. Live in harmony with your world. Freely and gladly accept the bounty it offers.

Welcome to the marvelous era in which you were born. It promises wondrous possibilities. You have before you unimaginable frontiers, great discoveries and new meanings. Seize your days.

Welcome to your age on this earth. May you know a restless yearning to be alive, to know, to reflect and to make meaning. Always be mindful of your place in an awesome universe. It is more than your home. It is in you, even as you are in it. It is your destiny and destination.

Welcome to the greatest journey in the universe, your journey lived through the ongoing gift and graces of your being.

Be hopeful and joyful throughout your days.

In your newness the world is new too. Your mother and father, who brought you into being in love, are so glad and grateful for you. We rejoice with them. We promise to join them in loving nurture... that you may be fulfilled, even as your fulfillment fills us too.

On this day of your birth and forevermore, we give you our love.

(http://www.spiritualityandpractice.com/practices/practices/view/27395/a-blessing-for-a-child)

Day 127
And All Be Made Well

Alan Cohen once wrote: "Wouldn't it be powerful if you fell in love with yourself so deeply that you would do just about anything if you knew it would make you happy? This is precisely how much life loves you and wants you to nurture yourself. The deeper you love yourself the more the universe will affirm your worth. Then you can enjoy a lifelong love affair that brings you the richest fulfillment from inside out." Blessing yourself is an important way of nurturing yourself as in this text by Jan Richardson.

(Source: https://healingsoulstreams.wordpress.com/2015/02/01/and-all-be-made-well-a-healing-blessing/)

And All Be Made Well
That each ill
be released from you
and each sorrow
be shed from you
and each pain
be made comfort for you
and each wound
be made whole in you
that joy will
arise in you
and strength will
take hold of you
and hope will

take wing in you
and all be made well.

Day 128
For Those Condemned by a Medical Diagnosis

A medical diagnosis is too often a closed claim with a veneer of scientific respectability about what could happen in the future based on a very limited understanding of what happened to a certain number of people in the past! However, it remains always an opinion and nothing more than a personal opinion. But anyone who has explored the field of alternative approaches to medicine or spiritual healing knows – as this writer who has had instantaneous healings of medically serious conditions – that the impossible is happening daily. **Hope reigns, not despair.**

I bless those who labor under the heavy weight of a medical diagnosis that condemns them to a somber future and even death.

May they see through the extremely narrow horizons of usually materially based claims to the brighter horizons of another possibility.

May they understand that miracles are happening every day, worldwide, in the most unbelievable situations, because a so-called "miracle" is simply the irruption of other laws unknown to most of humankind.

May they find in their heart the powerful assurance that divine Love supersedes all medical diagnoses, however honest.

May they understand that they are not victims of some bleak fate, and that all trials are truly blessings in disguise.

May they find the blessing awaiting them and may the doors of hope open wide to them, their families and those who care for them.

Day 129

After my visit to a US publisher where I talked to the assembled staff (Testimony)

"I started using blessing the next morning with my daughter. We were both beating heads, so I stopped and started blessing her. You know what she said after about five minutes? 'Mama, I love you and I can feel your love coming to me.' I think my jaw dropped to the floor. And many more times on the road when people have upset me, I've said out loud how I bless them so my daughter could hear.

Today we were driving to work and here is this tree that had been hacked off to make way for power lines. This greatly upsets my daughter. But today she blurted out, 'Mama, I bless those people who did that in their ecology and their wisdom!' I was absolutely astounded. You have made me a believer and my daughter too."

(Rachel, USA)

Day 130

Two Very Brief Blessings from the East

Today, we have two very brief texts, one by the respected spiritual leader Sathya Sai Baba of India (which I have preceded by the words "May we") and the second a few lines from Sufi Blessings of Love and Peace, June 2012, Vol XXV, No 6.

Sathya Sai Baba
May we start the day with Love,
Spend the day with Love,
Fill the day with Love,
End the day with Love:
This is the way to God.

Sufi Blessing
May the blessings of love be upon you

May its peace abide with you
May its essence illuminate your heart,
Now and forever more...

Day 131
To See the Hidden Perfection

That inspired writer of blessing, Kate Nowak, has defined blessing as "an acknowledgment that we live in a perfect universe... While a prayer is usually considered a petition to God asking for intervention, a blessing arises from that inner place of knowing that no intervention is necessary. God already created a perfect world, and it is not the world, but only our viewpoint of it, that needs to be changed." The most outstanding spiritual healers I have known all worked from this basis – not attempting to "correct" reality but seeing what was always there in Her eyes.

I bless You, infinite Spirit, for revealing to me the omnipresent splendor which is all that You ever behold.

May I learn to subdue and still the vociferous voices of the human senses which claim to know what is really going on. May I withdraw to that inner space of deep spiritual listening where the clamor of the world has been silenced and Your gentle whispering, O Spirit, can be heard to my receptive heart.

When an angry human mind shouts, "but how can you be so blind as to deny what is going on?" may I listen to the wisdom of Soul prompting me to sharpen my spiritual senses that I may truly sense what *is* really going on – the unassailable unfolding of Your ever-present perfect creation hidden to the material senses and revealed solely in the humility of my deep yearning for the ultimate true vision of things.

May I have the courage to hold on at all times to my highest sense of what is right for me at the moment, even if that implies refusing to join those hastening to rush in with human solutions, however good and worthy these may be, and however right for those who undertake them.

Finally, may I trust that, anchored to my sincere intention, You will always guide my listening heart and open mind on the path of right endeavor.

Day 132
A Blessing for Trees

It is important that each one of us learns to craft his or her own blessings. You cannot walk around delving into this book each time you face a crisis or situation that needs blessing. Below you will find some information on trees so that you may transform it into your own blessing. Personally, I do not believe there even exists a "right" way of blessing. What counts above all is the sincerity and intention of your blessing. You can simply bless the trees in your yard, or your county or country, or in a threatened area (Amazon basin) in their various functions.

Trees help keep us alive. They provide the oxygen we need to breathe. Without them, our entire existence would crumble. They provide a limited but important part of how planet Earth works. They offer homes and food for many species, including food and medicine for mankind. Wood is a key element for the economy and innumerable human activities, not to mention our homes. Trees clean the soil and control air pollution. Their wood keeps us warm, they save water, prevent soil erosion, sustain climate balance, provide incredible beauty... to name just a few among innumerable services. And finally, they communicate with each other – and it now appears even with animals. So on your next forest walk, why not hug and bless a tree?

Day 133
A Native American Ute Prayer

As with an earlier Lakota prayer, I have slightly amended this Ute prayer and put it in the form of a blessing. It seems such an appropriate follow-up to the blessing on trees, as it stresses the importance of the environment in our lives.

Earth, May You Teach Me

Earth, May you teach me quiet ~ as the grasses are still with new light.

Earth, May you teach me suffering ~ as old stones suffer with memory.

Earth, May you teach me humility ~ as blossoms are humble with beginning.

Earth, May you teach me caring ~ as mothers nurture their young.

Earth, May you teach me courage ~ as the tree that stands alone...

Earth, May you teach me freedom ~ as the eagle that soars in the sky.

Earth, May you teach me acceptance ~ as the leaves that die each fall.

Earth, May you teach me renewal ~ as the seed that rises in the spring.

Earth, May you teach me to forget myself ~ as melted snow forgets its life.

Earth, May you teach me to remember kindness ~ as dry fields weep with rain.

Day 134
A South African Blessing

Do you realize that every single time you send out a blessing or simply one single positive thought you are so-to-speak irrigating the whole mental atmosphere of the planet? Isn't that amazing? Does it not motivate you to abound more and more in blessings?

Walk tall, walk well, walk safe, walk free and
May harm never come to thee.
Walk wise, walk good, walk proud, walk true and

May the sun always smile on you.

Walk prayer, walk hope, walk faith, walk light and

May peace always guide you right.

Walk joy, walk brave, walk love, walk strong and

May life always give you song.

(Source: https://loveletterstograce.wordpress.com/2012/11/12/south-african-blessing/)

Day 135
May the Blessing of God Be Upon You

This text is composed by Reverend Jane R. Dunning.

Because many people have a very narrow understanding of the word "holy" as often referring to saints, it is good to remind readers that it comes from the same Indo-European root as "health" and "whole." It does not describe a sort of plastic "holy man" but someone who is complete and simply good.

May God keep you safe when you are in danger.

May God guide you in the way of Love.

May God support you in danger or hardship.

May God lift up your heart when you are feeling low.

May God comfort you when you are feeling lonely.

May God give you strength when you are weak.

May God bring you home when you are lost.

May God surround you with loving care, always and forever.

You are holy, you are chosen, you are loved and you are blessed.

(Source: http://www.worldprayers.org/archive/prayers/celebrations/may_the_blessing_of_god_be.html)

Day 136
A Blessing for Gardeners

Joel Goldsmith offers us one of the most profound insights into blessing when he writes: "If you truly want to bless a person, you will remember that God animates and God permeates his being, because God is the only being, the life and the soul of individual being." Just remembering that is a major dimension of any blessing. So please remember it when you bless!

I bless amateur or professional gardeners as the keepers of the planet they are and for their loving stewardship of gardens and plants of all sorts.

I bless them in their consciousness that they are the hands of God for beautifying Her own creation. And I bless them in their respect for and nurturing of nature's self-healing abilities rather than running to some chemical product for a quick fix to what nature can do if they are patient enough to collaborate with her.

I bless them in their creativity, intuition and true sense of beauty in imagining new floral arrangements and new grafts.

I bless them in their desire to keep up with the latest discoveries and information in this field they have chosen and to have the curiosity and interest to venture into the exciting field of plant communication and all it can teach us about nature and our relationship to it.

Day 137

A Blessing for Someone about to Undergo a Surgical Operation

I bless...... (name of person) in their clear consciousness that infinite divine Love governs absolutely all from the tiniest molecule to the rolling of the galaxies.

I bless them in their deep trust that nothing will ever take them out of God's hand.

I bless the surgeon and his (her) whole team in their constant alertness, their constant listening for inner guidance and wisdom, and their deep trust in the functioning of the whole surgical team as a harmonious unit in constant intelligent, loving cooperation.

I bless the whole clinic...... (hospital) where the operation is to be held that the energy of the place may be peaceful and serene and all the support personnel in harmonious cooperation and willingness to serve joyfully.

I bless all who are concerned with this situation in their deep grasp that God's law of adjustment is constantly working for the good of every single one of its creatures, and that for this law, no situation could ever be hopeless or even disorganized.

Finally, I bless...... (name of patient) in the perfect functioning of their body, and in its harmonious and rapid recuperation after the intervention. May they feel that a perfectly functioning body is their divine right and the natural outcome of the law of adjustment governing the universe and all things.

Day 138
A Blessing for Life

"Approval may not be the appropriate response in a given situation, but blessing is always appropriate. To fully face reality you have to say Yes. This is the Yes of blessing. It is not necessarily the 'yes' of approval. And blessing in this sense is an inner Yes. It is, as I hope you will see, a worshipful Yes, the essence, in fact, of worship." This statement of Brother David Steindl-Rast perfectly introduces the following brief words by Sathya Sai Baba I have transformed into a blessing by adding simply "may you." (You can alternatively say "May we.")

Life is a song – may you sing it.

Life is a game – may you play it.

Life is a challenge – may you meet it.

Life is dream – may you realize it.

Life is a sacrifice – may you offer it.

Life is love – may you enjoy it.

Day 139
For Walking with Love

I have very slightly adapted (and abbreviated) the beloved hymn by Minnie Ayers so that it can become a blessing for your (our) day. As in many blessings in this book, you may always replace the "I" by "we."

May I walk with Love along the way
that it may be a holy day.
May I no more suffer cruel fear
for I feel God's presence with me here.
May the joy that none can take away
be mine as I walk with Love throughout the day.
May I walk with Love all along the way
that childlike trust be mine today.
May I uplift my thoughts, with courage go
and give my heart's rich overflow.
May peace now crown my joy-filled day
As I walk *as* Love along the way.

Day 140
Learning to Love Yourself

May your blessings be multiplied, you who so faithfully bless others – or have the desire to do so. Henri Nouwen has said that "to give someone a blessing is the most significant affirmation we can offer." Today, your blessing is going to be for a very special person: yourself. As one who has worked a quarter of a century in the field of personal development, I am aware of how many people need to learn to love themselves – sometimes desperately so!

I bless myself as one who is unconditionally cherished by divine Love – with not one single string attached!

I bless myself in my ability to see that my loving others depends in the long run on a very deep acceptance of myself, which no one else can give me.

I bless myself in my total forgiveness of what has not worked in my life – failed relationships, messed up careers, dead-end roads, weaknesses that still challenge me maybe after decades of working on them.

May I see that divine Love does not need to forgive me as it has never held a single thing against me.

As I stand in front of a mirror, may I stand in awe of the amazing beauty that looks at me, the immense kindness, the caring, the goodness and so many other qualities that are simply awaiting my acknowledgment.

As I go into the silence, may I hear the voice in my heart saying: "This is my beloved child in whom I am well pleased" and accept to be pleased, not with the small human, but with divine Love manifesting itself AS me.

Day 141

A Blessing to Overcome the World Belief of Lack

The world belief in lack – lack of resources, of money, ability, time, contacts, health, fresh ideas and creativity, intelligence, food, the right partner, spiritual guidance... – seems omnipresent. And yet we live on a planet of almost limitless resources, as a resource is first and foremost an idea: an idea transformed a stinking, slimy, gooey liquid into gasoline or unlimited free solar energy into electricity.

I bless myself and humankind in our ability to overcome the strange belief of lack.

I bless myself in my understanding that as a wave has the fullness of the ocean it is born of beneath, so do I and all mankind have an unlimited abundance of good at the tip of our creativity and unselfed caring.

Where the world screams "lack, lack, lack... not enough... end of this resource" may I hear the Source whispering "an infinity of good awaits you and all. If you are one with me, the unlimited One, how could you ever lack any good?"

Because ideas originate in infinite Mind, they are infinite and free. I bless myself and all mankind in our ability to be a transparency of this divine Mind so that where there appears to be lack, abundance may appear to bless all, not only a few.

I bless us in our ability to manifest that deep caring and overflowing compassion which prevent that we be sterilized by the beliefs of lack, apathy and indifference and open our hearts to our mission as world healers and interpreters of the infinite abundance ultimately awaiting all.

A post scriptum on creating abundance out of poverty follows:

It was my privilege in the sixties and seventies to live in Africa and be a founding member of what was then the largest grass roots peasant organization of the whole continent, the Six S organization. (See my book Listening to Africa, *Praeger 1989.) One of the experiences that struck me most was that of a self-help women's group in a very poor remote rural area of Burkina Faso to which a Western NGO offered a mechanical grinder to grind grain – a task that easily occupied hours of a peasant woman's daily activities at a time when they had to spend a growing number of hours to fetch water and wood. (In the village of Semari I visited in the Mopti area of Mali the women walked eight hours a day just for the water that was 25 miles away there and back!) The women asked the donor, "Is your gift free?" "Of course," they were told. "Oh, but we have to do our part too. Just wait here a while and we tell you what our contribution will be." An elderly illiterate woman had the following idea: "Every woman who wants to grind her grain will have to give a few cents. It must not be free. We will put part of the payment aside and when we have saved enough, we will purchase another mill we shall call a 'daughter mill' and give to a neighboring friendly village, because in our culture girls marry outside the village. We will continue saving, and when we have saved enough to purchase a second mill, we will keep it in the village as sons in our culture marry into the village. It will replace the original 'father' mill which by then will be ready for retirement." (They were* taken to pieces and used for spare parts.) Thanks to this amazing scheme, not only did hundreds of villages end up getting their own mills and doing the same thing, but the idea was systematized by the Naam movement, which had organized the village groups to begin with, and applied to purchasing trucks and even the creation of a rudimentary social security system.

Ideas are free, and your blessings, if nourished with strong intention and total sincerity, might – for all you know – help a struggling women's self-help group in a Caracas shanty town or a peasant group in Cambodia.

Day 142
Three-Year-Old Blesses His Mother (Testimony)

"I am the busy mother of two young sons and am expecting a third baby in just a few weeks' time. Like many women at this stage of pregnancy, I am not sleeping well at night and am very tired at the end of the day. This means I can be grumpy with my two children and feel very bad about it when I snap at them.

I took a rare five minutes this afternoon to read your article (on blessing) in Cygnus. It was inspiring and echoed many things I have a deep faith in. Alas, the luxury of lengthy meditation is not one a mother of young children can often indulge in, but I sat a few moments, turned my palms up to the sunshine and allowed a sense of well-being to fill me as I blessed the world around me.

A few minutes later I was called into the house by the children. My 3-year-old rushed up to me and put his arms around my neck. He kissed me and looked into my eyes and then said: 'Bless you.' It was an extraordinary moment. Nothing similar has happened before like this but he seemed to know something."

Day 143
A Blessing for Water

75% of the planet's surface and close to 70% of the human adult body is constituted of one of the most amazing substances ever created, possibly the most amazing on our planet – water. Just to list its main properties would easily cover two pages, so I will not even start! Yet humankind has been squandering, privatizing and polluting it at an amazing rate, so much so that at least 36 countries (2014) are under extreme stress in terms of water resources.

I bless myself and humanity in general in our wise use of this incredible gift of Providence.

I bless us in seeing that all life on the planet depends on it – and hence respecting it totally wherever it may be.

I bless us in our firm intention to pool our divine intelligence and immense resources of all sorts to devise ways to avoid squandering or polluting it needlessly.

I bless the multinationals that are privatizing water and often forcing the poorest of the poor to pay for this gift nature offers free to all that their leaders allow Grace to kindle their compassion, that they may reconsider and revise their policies.

And I bless the public in its readiness to change its purchasing habits to support those companies that have a non-exploitative policy towards water use and commercialization.

I bless the scientists and others working to cleanse the oceans, lakes and rivers in their creativity that they may devise ever more efficient ways of protecting this God-given resource.

And I bless politicians everywhere that they awaken to the critical state of world water, choose to put this issue high up on their political agenda – and especially have the courage to exert maximum efforts to achieve this aim, whatever the political cost.

Day 144
Sending Love to Those Who Need It

The blessing below is adapted from a text on love and prayer from John O'Donohue's book Anam Cara *so it may read as a blessing:*

May we offer the warmth of our love as a blessing for those who are damaged and unloved and those who are pushed to the very edge of life.

May we send that love out into the world to people who are desperate, to those who are starving, to those who are trapped in prison, in hospitals, and into all the brutal terrains of bleak and tormented lives.

May we know that when that love is sent out from the bountifulness of our own love, it reaches other people and that this love is the deepest power of prayer – prayer being the act and presence of sending this light to other people to heal, free, and bless them.

Day 145
A Blessing by Eileen Caddy

The following blessing is by one of the spiritual luminaries of the end of the last quarter century, Eileen Caddy, co-founder with her husband Peter of the world's first eco-spiritual community, Findhorn, in Forres, Scotland. It is taken from her book Footprints on the Path *(Findhorn Press). I have very slightly adapted it.*

May you find true happiness and contentment
Wherever you are, whomever you are with, no matter what you are doing.
For true happiness stems from deep within.
May outer conditions never rob you
Of your inner happiness which no one and nothing can disturb.
May joy and happiness fill your heart.

May you realize how mightily blessed you are
And give constant thanks
For those many blessings which are yours.

Day 146
For the Challenges of Climate Change

All round the world, populations are leaving their ancestral lands due to climate change, for instance various populations in the highlands of Nepal. Innovative new measures and policies are urgently needed to face what could with time become huge challenges for hundreds of millions.

I bless the people all round the world who are facing the more challenging aspects of climate change. I bless them in their courage and inner strength when forced to emigrate and resettle elsewhere. I bless them in the vision and wisdom they need to reestablish a new and viable future.

I bless farmers and producers everywhere faced by climate changes that they may devise the innovative new approaches needed to face such situations. I bless the politicians concerned that they have the understanding and caring called for to put the needs of the planet and these populations before narrow party politics.

I bless the journalists called upon to report on these events in their wisdom and farsightedness that they may put the demands of deep, insightful reporting before the temptation of sensationalism and superficiality.

And finally I bless us all in our ability to modify our lifestyles that they may be aligned with the needs of the planet and of enlightened environmental policies.

Day 147
To Witness My Divine Identity

A clear sense of identity is I believe the most important factor for succeeding in life. Deep down, what is really the sense of identity I entertain about myself? Who do I really believe that I am? A poor struggling mortal or the totally divine daughter or son of God? Face this issue fairly and honestly. And remember that the reply must be felt deep down, not just mouthed or believed.

I joyfully bless myself in acknowledging my divine identity – for it is only in recognizing it in myself that I will be able to see it in my neighbor – and vice versa.

May I really understand that truly I am made in the image of the Godhead, that Entity of total, unconditional Love and forgiveness that I reflect fully, not partially.

May I carry myself as the daughter or son of the Spirit of Truth that I am, always have been and always will be, whatever human appearances may scream at times to the contrary.

May I feel deep down the truth of this incredible promise: that as heir/heiress of the Kingdom, the totality of the abundance thereof is mine.

I bless myself in my deep joy, overwhelming compassion and caring, my unshakeable trust and clear sense of direction, my patience and clear-sightedness when faced with error, my perseverance in trials, my inner clarity when faced with the confusion of the world...(*)

And I gratefully rest in this clear sense of who I really am.

(*) qualities are so innumerable and I have just listed a few. You will add those that appeal specially to you.

Day 148
For Seeing the Divine Curriculum of My Existence

Either we live in a universe ruled by chance – or we live in a universe governed by law. If the universe is run by an Entity of infinite, unconditional Love – which is the premise of these blessings – then "all things work together for the good of those who love God" as a certain Paul wrote. All things – not most, and all the time – not sometimes. So, friend, rest on this incredibly comforting assurance.

I bless this day, in which absolutely everything is part of Love's plan for my progress and unfoldment.

I bless myself in my deep trust that absolutely everything that happens today is happening to forward my growth and to broaden my heart and my ability to love.

I bless myself in my ability to face anger with peace, upsets of all sorts with equanimity, hatred with forgiveness, disappointments with confidence that ultimately all will work for the best, fear with the assurance of Love's unfailing presence, negativity with optimism, evil with the understanding that it has no true substance.

I bless myself in accepting all forms of good, the beauty of nature and people and the abundance of life's manifestations with unfailing gratitude. Amen.

Day 149
Why We Bless

There are many reasons to bless. We bless to help heal society. We bless to get out of the shell or cave of our little egos and open up to the world. We bless as a wonderful way of practicing mindfulness and staying present to the present – anywhere. We bless because it is a highly efficient way of solving relationship problems and personal challenges. Ultimately, however, I personally see blessing as an expression of growing in love, which I believe is our ultimate reason for being here, as expressed in the following poem by Sandy Wilder, founder of that amazing place called the Unlearning Institute in Grafton, Illinois (www.educareunlearning.com). You can use it as a blessing for yourself (e.g. "I bless myself in my ability to live on purpose, to use every interaction as a classroom..." etc.). Sandy sends out such texts daily and you can receive them free. For the three years I have been receiving them, they are a major source of inspiration for me.

Living On Purpose
Learning to love
is why we are here.
What if you saw
every interaction
as a classroom
where this was
your primary agenda?
Everything else
was secondary.
What if the Teacher
was resident within
your heart?
Would you learn
to listen to
and heed
that Voice?
Would you enroll
in that school?
Would you be excited
about homework?
Why do anything else
than be a student
of Love?

Day 150
A Blessing for a Meal

Blessing food is possibly the most widespread blessing in the world and history. This is not surprising as, apart from a few thousand people on the planet who live solely off prana, the intake of food is, with breathing, the condition of our survival. But as always in blessing, especially with blessings for meals, never let it become a mechanical ritual or something with no feeling. May it always flow from the heart.

We bless You, Spirit of Love, which so constantly pours its abundance on us, for this meal.

We bless all those round the world who labored to bring it to this table. We bless those who produced it in their sense of mission as producers and farmers.

We bless those who prepared it for their love and caring.

We bless our intake that we may eat mindfully and with deep gratitude.

And finally, we bless ourselves that this food my give us strength to serve You with joy, gratitude and overflowing love for all.

Day 151
A Wigilia Blessing from Poland

I have borrowed this traditional Christmas Eve blessing by Roger Jan Radlowski and John J. Kirvan from the book by Angeles Arrien, The Second Half of Life.

I wish you health
I wish you wealth
That passes not with time.
I wish you long years.
May your heart be as patient as the earth
Your love as warm as the harvest gold.
May your days be full, as the city is full

Your nights as joyful as dancers.
May your arms be as welcoming as home.
May your faith be as enduring as God's love
Your spirit as valiant as your heritage.
May your hand be as sure as a friend
Your dreams as hopeful as a child,
May your soul be as brave as your people
And may you be blessed.

Day 152
A Blessing to Summon Up Courage

Winston Churchill once said, "Success is not final, failure is not fatal: it is the courage to continue that counts." And during the last world war (1939–45), this great statesman illustrated that idea with the following statement made to encourage his fellow citizens, "If you are going through hell, keep going." That's just what the British did. Courage is one of the most fundamental ingredients of life. No one can survive, let alone live the good life, without a large dose of courage. NB: in any blessing for yourself, you can always add: "I bless myself and all humanity."

I bless myself in my ability to face all challenges in life with courage and determination. I bless myself in my courage to never lose heart, however somber the storm clouds on the horizon or the attacks or problems raining on me as so many arrows.

When I feel completely enclosed in the valley of the shadow of death – in an apparently insurmountable situation – may I manifest the courage to keep going, whatever the cost, to just keep going.

When mockery, hate, terrible injustice, illness, betrayal, loss of any kind, financial disaster and all the etc. of the human condition attempt to discourage me or knock me down, may I summon that residue of courage from the very depths of my soul to proclaim: here I stand, and with God's help, here I shall always stand.

Day 153
A Blessing for a New Home

May your reading of this modest book be a great blessing to you and others. Blessing a new home is a very ancient practice that goes back millennia, which can be easily understood given the importance of our homes in our lives.

I bless this space of Love's omnipresence that is to be the home of...... (names of inhabitants).

I bless it in the constant loving protection it has to offer them. I bless it as a holy space of inner and outer restoration. May all those who live or pass through here find their strength restored, their vision refreshed, their courage renewed.

May the deepest rest descend on those who abide here that they may go back into the world as bearers of peace. May its walls represent stability and rest in this world of unceasing change and often turmoil. May its rooms resonate with words of love and its space be filled with gestures of tender caring, joyful service and gentle embrace.

May it also be a place where the rush, clamor and unrest of the world is no longer felt and where reign moments of hushed silence to listen to You, O Infinite One.

May it be a place of warm energy which restores the heart, body and soul of all who partake of its hospitality so that they may return into the world to serve with joy as bearers of all good with constant gratitude in their hearts for their blessed home.

Day 154
An Irish Blessing

We no longer need an introduction to these beautiful folk blessings which touch all hearts in their purity and simplicity.

May the rains sweep gentle across your fields.
May the sun warm the land.

May every good seed you have planted bear fruit, and late summer find you standing in fields of plenty.

And a blessing in each trial for every problem life sends.

A faithful friend to share,

For every sigh a sweet song and an answer for each prayer.

Day 155

My Very Favorite Blessing Story (Testimony)

Just a year after the first French version of the book The Gentle Art of Blessing *(now available in seven languages) I came across an article in one of the leading German-Swiss newspapers (the Tages-Anzeiger of April 15, 1999), concerning a retired nurse, Frieda, who felt led to undertake an amazing task – or mission would be a better word.*

Fourteen hours a day, and for well over ten years (one railway employee who worked at the station said 15 years), Frieda stood in the busiest section of the station... simply blessing people. She refused to grant any interviews explaining simply that she had felt led by God to undertake this task. Her example touched me in a very special way because her definition of blessing was exactly the same as the one in the text on The Gentle Art of Blessing: *wanting the real good for people, events, situations, you name it.*

Over the years, Frieda must have blessed millions of people. Her eyes would constantly move from one person to the other as she rested her arms on her wheelchair. She would only take an occasional brief rest on the chair. Someone brought her to the station in the morning and would fetch her late at night. All one knows is that she lived in a home for the elderly.

Her story made me think of the famous book written in 19th century Russia concerning a pilgrim of modest origin who travels for years seeking a reply to the question of how to pray continually, as the apostle Paul bids his readers. A starets (spiritual leader) teaches him to pray constantly the short prayer, "Lord Christ Jesus have mercy on me." Used as a kind of mantra, the prayer works deeply into the heart of the pilgrim and not only transforms him but touches all those who meet him.

Frieda was a 20th and 21st century pilgrim in her own way, and I am ready to believe that her ultimate impact on the world may have been far beyond those whom the media call "the movers" of today.

You too, friend, can bless anyone or anything, everywhere, at any time, all the time.

(See the extremely brief video of Sister Frieda on the blessing website www.gentleartofblessing.org)

Day 156
For Those Challenged by the Pace of Change

We live in a world of literally mad change. Everything is changing, everywhere, at top speed and at the same time. No wonder many people feel completely overwhelmed by this crazy rhythm of change. However, might it not also have some positive aspects, e.g. letting go of the mental comfort of always doing things the same way? Of opening up to completely new ideas?

I bless all those who feel completely swamped by the rate of change, be it in raising their children, or changes at the workplace, in fashions, social customs, constantly changing administrative practices and above all the speed of change in the field of technology, especially portables and computers, which touch us all.

I bless them in finding practical solutions to immediate needs. I bless them in finding the kind of human assistance that can help ease the change or adapt to it.

I bless them in finding the needed courage to face the fear of being made redundant by new technology such as robots or their fear of the inability to keep up with the pace of change.

And I bless us all in finding that inner space deep inside us which is beyond all change because beyond time and space, where we can always restore ourselves and find that "peace that passes all understanding," is our ultimate home.

Day 157
A Blessing for Humanity's Contact with ETs

More and more, unquestionable examples of contacts with Extraterrestrial beings (ETs) are present in the media and on the Internet. As a matter of fact, the defense departments of various countries have had proof of such visits since soon after the last World War. We need to already now prepare for and embrace these fellow citizens of the universe in our love.

We bless our ability as a race to face our first contacts with our celestial neighbors with warm hospitality, open curiosity and total nonviolence.

We open our minds and hearts to all we certainly have to learn from these beings, to the possibility of totally other modes of relationships, communication and living they represent.

We bless ourselves in our ability to overcome all fear and hesitation and to welcome them literally with open arms, hearts, and minds.

May we be ready to challenge our millennial modes of living, learning and relating and accept all new patterns and ways of being that can enhance the quality of life for all.

And may we rest in the steadfast assurance and trust that, whatever their physical appearances and modes of expression may be, they are, like us, children of the one Creator that guides, governs and upholds all existence.

Day 158

Today's blessing is taken *from* A Blessing for Daily Worship *by Max Lucado.*

Today, may you be aware that worship is a way of life – it's not just a once a week event.

May your worship never cease.

May you continue living in the Father's presence and may you continue being thankful for what he has done.

May the song within you which sings for eternity sing loudly. Heed the songs of heaven. Dismiss the songs of earth.

May the Father quiet the voices around you which tell you to settle for less than what he promises.

May the song within you which sings for eternity sing loudly. Heed the songs of heaven. Dismiss the songs of earth.

Day 159

Blessing for a Priest or a Minister

My father was for many years a minister and then general secretary of the (then) World Presbyterian Alliance, and traveled all over the planet visiting churches in a rapidly evolving world. After running a worldwide movement for a quarter of a century, he became totally disillusioned with traditional church forms and practices, and in his last years he was ardently seeking a mystical experience of the divine. However, others believe in the possible recreation or rejuvenation of their church. This blessing is for them.

Spirit of Truth and Love, I bless myself in my ability to adapt to the immense challenges facing my church in a world of daily accelerating change.

I bless myself in my readiness to transcend outmoded and sometimes archaic structures of all sorts and outdated forms of church service, and welcome the challenge of change as a golden opportunity for renewal.

I bless myself in my ability to face with good humor the impatience for change of younger members and the fears of the elders clinging to the lifeboats of the past.

I bless myself in my ability to see beyond the supposed holiness of specific words, creeds and rituals in the understanding that the essence of all meaningful religion is in fostering the ability to grow in love.

I bless myself in my courage and ability to serenely and firmly hold my ground when faced with angry members or church authorities that I may constantly follow my highest sense of what is right and true in any given situation, knowing that You guide my every step if I seek that guidance.

Day 160
For Friendship

Friendship is unquestionably one of the greatest gifts of life. Family members and close acquaintances may fall away or abandon us in times of trial, never a true friend. So, dear partner for a saner world, I wish you the divine blessing of friendship.

I bless my friendship with...... (name of person or persons) that it may be a blessing not only for me, but through me for all mankind.

I bless us in our ability to always be true to our most authentic selves, whatever the cost, even to our friendship.

I bless us in the complete integrity and limpidity of our communication with each other, at all times and in all circumstances.

I bless us in our ability to make our friendship become a springboard to a more meaningful presence in the world and our neighborhood.

I bless ourselves in our ability to turn our friendship into a deep well where others may refresh themselves rather than a cozy private club, and may we joyfully welcome those without friends into the open circle of our love.

Finally, may we always rejoice in the incredible gift of this friendship and recognize You smiling at us through the face of our friends.

Day 161
When Struggling to Heal a Relationship

Living together seems a growing challenge in our world! In my home town, Geneva, well over 60 percent of marriages end in divorce and more and more couples are choosing to live as companions rather than bonded by marriage – be they hetero or homosexual couples. This is but one minor aspect of the incredible upheavals our world is going through in many areas.

We bless those couples (or: name of a couple you know) struggling to heal or piece together a failing or monotonous relationship that has lost its sense of newness and adventure, its freshness and daily delights.

We first bless them in their intention – the key to the healing. May it be strong and clear so as to face the daily struggles, overcome any sense of weariness, accusation or self-accusation, nitpicking or revolt.

We bless them in their understanding that their partner is at his or her highest level of consciousness which will enable them to free themselves of any temptation to accuse.

We bless them in taking the deeply liberating step of accepting their total responsibility for the state of the relationship, and accepting a hundred percent responsibility for the attitudes they have manifested in all situations, while at the same time avoiding any orgies of guilt.

We bless them in their discovery of the inner resources of patience and perseverance, trust and courage already awaiting to be activated deep down inside their hearts.

We bless them in their ability to "hitch their chariot to a star" so as to constantly renew their vision of their goal and to be guided to the most helpful concrete steps to forward the healing.

And above all, we bless them in their clear sense of their oneness with their divine Source which always responds when appealed to.

Day 162
Scottish and Celtic Blessings

Scottish
May there always be work for your hands to do.
May your purse always hold a coin or two.
May the sun always shine upon your windowpane.
May a rainbow be certain to follow each rain.
May the hand of a friend always be near to you, and
May God fill your heart with gladness to cheer you.

Celtic
May the road rise up to meet you.
May the wind be always at your back.
May the sun shine warm upon your face, the rains fall soft
    upon your fields,
And until we meet again,
May God hold you in the palm of His hand.

Day 163
For a Car Accident in the Street

How do we react when we see a serious car accident in the street? Whether we react with horror or just turn our head in the other direction will not help much. It would be more useful to start quietly blessing.

Spirit of Truth and Love, I bless all those involved in this accident.

I bless the wounded driver/passenger(s) that they may be assisted quickly and efficiently.

I bless the ambulance team that they may take exactly the needed steps to assist the wounded person(s) in the most effective manner possible. And I bless the streets where they will drive to the hospital that they may be clear of traffic jams of any sort and that traffic may flow easily and without impairments.

I bless the reception team at the hospital that they may be guided to take exactly those steps that are needed to be of most use and lead to the best results.

I bless the person(s) involved that they may realize their life is not in blood, bones and other material elements, but that divine Love is their true life and that there can be no obstacle to its perfectly harmonious functioning.

May they be open to miracles which are simply the normal functioning of laws beyond the extremely narrow grasp of our rational understanding and semantic and scientific prisons.

And I bless the person(s) responsible for the accident that they may be lifted to a higher understanding of things rather than embark on a guilt trip which helps or heals no one or a denial of their responsibility.

Day 164
To Increase My Sense of Caring for Others

Surely one of the greatest needs in this world which, seen as a material manifestation, expresses such suffering and sadness, is for the deepest, heartfelt caring for others (whether you call it love, compassion, whatever). This was a key element of the teachings of both Buddha and Jesus, to mention just two of the greatest avatars who came to help the human race progress to a higher consciousness. Each of us can grow in this deep caring if we really put our heart to it.

I bless myself in my ability and desire to express the deepest, most authentic compassion towards all – person, plant or beast.

May I have the deep, burning desire to be that gentle flame of living compassion that embraces all, everywhere, at all times.

May my caring embrace and uplift the most heinous criminal as well as the most dedicated servant of mankind, the stumbling drunkard in the street or the quiet saint, the most tyrannical dictator or greatest pioneer of good, the cruelest sadist or the humblest citizen.

May my compassion tenderly embrace the plant and animal worlds, so endangered by ruthless competition and the race for profit, that I may adapt my lifestyle to the pressing needs of ecology and zoology.

And may my daily newspaper or TV news bulletin become my daily prayer book as I bless and reverse all the dramatic or sad events reported, knowing and feeling that behind the hypnotic material scene there is another Reality of eternal light and universal, unconditional Love awaiting all.

Day 165
A Morning Prayer by Marianne Williamson

We are borrowing today's blessing from Marianne Williamson's book Illuminata: A Return to Prayer.

May my mind stay centered on the things of spirit.

May I not be tempted to stray from love.

May my mind and heart be pure and true, and may I not deviate from the things of goodness.

May I see love and innocence in all mankind behind the masks we all wear.

May I bring Your love and goodness with me, to give to others wherever I may go.

May I become more fully a reflection of Your radiance. May I recognize the good that is available everywhere.

May I be this day an instrument of love and healing.

Day 166
Ultimately, There Is Only Love

There seems to be a growing unspoken consensus among many spiritual thinkers that, on the home run, the only thing that really matters is: have I grown in love? Have I lived love to the best of my ability? Mary Baker Eddy once wrote that, "The Gabriel of His Presence has no contests. To infinite, ever-present Love, all is Love, and there is no error, no sin, sickness nor death." What if this were true?

I bless myself in the understanding that, ultimately, the only thing that really matters is my desire and ability to love all.

May my every thought spring from that deep well of love inside me.

May my every word be inspired by the tenderness of love.

May my every act, every deed be motivated by the fire of love.

May I be driven by a deep yearning to be simply nothing but love.

May I learn to see all with the warm eyes of love and may that same love be the basic feeling of my existence at all times and in all situations.

May I respond to any insult, aggressiveness or hate with the equanimity and calm strength of love.

And may the circle of my love reach to the end of the world, holding all in its tender and strong embrace, now and till the end of time.

Day 167
All Things Work Together for Our Good

The apostle Paul writes that "to those who love God... everything that happens fits into a pattern for good," i.e. a divine plan to bless our lives (Rom. 8:28, JB Phillips translation). If that is so, we can really live the whole of existence, even the apparently most terrible situations, with an expectation of good, or of learning something precious.

I bless myself in my ability to see the hand of Love in every single event of my life.

May I see any attack against me, be it slander, insult, hatred, distortion of my words or deeds or any other form of unkindness, as an opportunity to return good for evil, blessing for cursing.

May I face unemployment as a challenge to express my fortitude and discover hidden talents and creativity.

May I face bereavement or separation as an opportunity to discover that we can never be separated from our true shepherd, divine Love, our ultimate and only true companion, family, friend.

May I face the shrieking grimaces of fear in any form as an encouragement to discover and express a hidden courage and strength I did not know I possessed.

And may I face loss of any kind with the knowledge that the kingdom of infinite endless Love is within me and that it already contains an unlimited abundance of good which no material circumstance could ever endanger.

Day 168

Blessing Acts as a Balm on the Partner (Testimony)

"For a great deal of my life I was centered on myself. Now that you have taught me to apply this practice I ignored, I spend days on end just blessing silently and sincerely all the people who cross my path. As I am the owner of a business, I send blessings and messages of silent love to all my clients as they come in and out of my shop. And even while I am serving them at the counter, I am blessing them.

What a surprise I had at the beginning to see sudden smiles directed at me, to observe faces light up, especially when they came from clients who earlier on had closed, somber faces. They started expressing a warmth they never expressed before.

It is the practice of blessing that taught me what 'living in the present' meant. When one gives out love one can ONLY be in the present moment.

I wish to tell you that I never have any more disputes with my companion. The minute he starts expressing aggressiveness, I just send him a silent blessing and all the love I feel for him in my heart of hearts. And the magic operates! I then ask myself what in my behavior can bring on this kind of reaction, so as to better understand him and improve myself. If his behavior is due to something outside of me, I feel a great compassion for him and let him know it.

Then in less than two minutes we are reconciled. I have changed so deeply that as a result, he also has changed. He is calmer, more tolerant and open.

Our couple has been profoundly transformed."
(Elisabeth)

Day 169
A Blessing for Clean Political Campaigns

The normal functioning of our political systems demands a minimum of integrity and a certain restraint in campaigning. In recent years, these limits have increasingly been overstepped, sometimes in the most distressing manner. However, let us remember that once we have understood that every single person is at their highest level of consciousness, we cannot judge. As the text The Gentle Art of Blessing *states, one cannot at the same time judge and bless. However terrible or disturbing the material picture, blessing always reverses it and claims the innate spiritual perfection of all beings.*

I bless the politicians of my country (state, region, city) in their fundamental honesty and integrity.

I bless them in their consciousness of their divine essence that this essence may be reflected in all they do and say.

I bless them in their understanding that the law of right returns (we reap what we sow) applies to every single one of their words and actions.

I bless the citizens of my country in our grasp that we build this country together and that we are all co-responsible for its future.

I bless us all that instead of reacting with anger or biting judgment we may be led to pour our compassion and love on those who err in word and deed and be made to express still greater kindness and goodness to those who are described by some as unworthy of our citizenship or of residing in our frontiers.

I bless us in our creativity and inspiration that we may respond with humor and uniquely creative actions to those who believe their money, status or power allows them to go against the rules of a clean democracy.

And finally, I bless us all in our understanding that good is ultimately always more powerful than evil, love more healing than hatred and rejection, and that the infinite loving Intelligence that runs this incredible show called The Universe will never allow its plans for our good to be foiled by the illusory power of evil.

Day 170
Blessing for Prisoners in Solitary Confinement

All round the world, there are probably hundreds of thousands of prisoners in solitary confinement. In the United States alone (which houses a quarter of the world's prison population for 5% of the world's population), it is estimated there are around 80,000 to 100,000 inmates in solitary confinement (some for shorter periods, others for decades!) in tiny cells, sometimes with no windows, no human contact of any sort. It is a horrendous, "cruel and unusual" form of punishment which renders many insane. Let your love pour out to them. That grizzly old bear with 12 years of solitary, a former gang leader, is me, is you.

(See: http://solitarywatch.com/2012/02/01/how-many-prisoners-

are-in-solitary-confinement-in-the-united-states/)

Our heart's blessings reach out to the innumerable inmates all round the world often incarcerated in the most trying conditions.

In that darkest of dark hells, may Your light reach them in some magical way.

In the pit of despair, may a ray of hope touch their hearts and lift them out of the well shaft where human revenge and administrative insanity thrust them.

Even in the iceberg of cement walls and clanging metal doors, may a touch of gentleness and divine love find its way to their hearts.

In the mental torture chamber of solitary confinement, may they discover with wonder that an infinitely compassionate Presence always watches over them.

May the politicians and administrators worldwide who conceive of and uphold such inhumane punishment be touched by grace and dismantle "solitary" once and for ever.

And may we never fall asleep in the deceptive comfort of "normal" lives as long as a single one of our sisters or brothers stays one more day in such hell but work, each in our own way, to heal this practice.

Day 171
An Irish Blessing for a Home

Bless this house O Lord we pray,
Make it safe by night and day.
Bless these walls so firm and stout,
Keeping want and trouble out.
Bless the roof and chimney tall,
Let thy peace lie over all.
Bless the doors that they may prove
Ever open to joy and love.
Bless the windows shining bright,

Letting in God's heavenly light.
Bless the earth a-blazing there,
With smoke ascending like a prayer.
Bless the people here within...
Keep them pure and free from sin.
Bless us all, that one day, we
May be fit, o Lord, to dwell with Thee.
(Source: http://islandireland.com/Pages/folk/sets/bless.html)

Day 172
A Blessing for Making Love

For those who see absolutely everything in life as a gift of Providence, and who see themselves as divine Love in expression, blessing the act of making love – which can truly be one of the most sacred, oftentimes ecstatic and profound experiences of existence – is perfectly normal. So please join us in this joyful blessing, especially if you are of the older generation often taught to look down upon, or even feel guilty about, (what can be) such a magical experience.

May our lovemaking be a perfect expression of Your love for us, an experience of ecstatic beauty and profound depth.

May we put our partner's pleasure before our own and be most sensitive to their most subtle wish and hidden desires.

May our bodies become instruments playing music for Your glory and our hearts be filled with the music of soul.

May we, in the rush of busy lives, find refreshment for our souls, a sigh of peaceful rest for our bodies, and a special moment of green pastures for our deeper being.

May it cement our togetherness in the unique way true lovemaking restores both body and soul while at the same time being a gentle playground for the child in us.

And above all may it strengthen our commitment of faithfulness to each other in the understanding that we are both each other's keeper and the keepers of our spoken and unspoken vows.

Day 173
A Healing Blessing at the Unemployment Agency (Testimony)

We will never tire of repeating that blessing is for all times, in all situations (see the above blessing). With time, it becomes as natural and simple as breathing. I love the following blessing by Ophélie from Geneva received by e-mail. It is so simple yet shows how blessing can be used any time, in any setting, in the most spontaneous and natural manner.

"I wanted to share with you a little sparkle that happened in my life. When I went early October to register at the local unemployment agency, for the first time I discovered the large hall where we are all little red numbers silently waiting to be called to one of the numerous little windows facing us. I felt vaguely uneasy and I was thinking of plunging into a book to distract myself when suddenly I read, via an e-mail from a friend, your blog on blessing.

Suddenly it transformed my whole experience. For a long moment I just blessed all the persons present: in their inner and material security, in their self-esteem, in their faith, in their search for a job, in their health... The peace that filled me was so profound that I could no longer stop! Then I started a conversation with the neighbor on my right and we had such an authentic sharing. I was honored that she would share with me her trials and her hopes... I will never cease marveling how our state of being changes reality."

Day 174
A Blessing so as to be Kind Towards Myself

Despite many material claims to the contrary, we live in a gentle universe run by a Source of the most incredible Love which wants our own good more than we could ever desire it ourselves. Hence being gentle toward ourselves is our fundamental right, not a questionable attitude.

I bless myself in my ability to express infinite kindness towards myself as well as towards others.

May I be gentle with myself when I make mistakes or even major errors, however serious they may be.

May I always remind myself that the universe is infinitely good and loving towards all its creations, never accusing, reprimanding and still less punishing, but always encouraging with a "you *can* do better next time."

May I have the wisdom not to push myself to my limits or even beyond, knowing that not I, but infinite Love is the true cause behind all, however needed my efforts are on the human plane.

And finally, may I move from the asceticism of self-sacrifice to the simple joy of giving of my best at all times, remembering that a deep and unwavering sincerity is sure to meet success in all situations, because divine Love takes care of it.

Day 175
For a Life Filled with Opportunities to Bless

I love the Jewish concept of blessing as expressed by Kerry Olitzky and Daniel Judson in their book Jewish Ritual. *"There is a blessing for almost everything in Judaism. There is a blessing for getting up in the morning, for going to sleep, for eating, for seeing wondrous things, for experiencing new things, for the occurrence of good things, for the unfortunate occurrence of bad things, for hearing the news of someone's death, for seeing someone you have not seen for a long time, for going to the bathroom, for studying Torah, for going on a journey, for fulfilling almost any religious commandment, and for just about anything less in life."*

I bless my life (We bless our lives...) for the infinite abundance of good that fills every day, every moment, every nook and cranny of those who have eyes to see.

I bless my 16 hours or more (close to a thousand minutes or

60,000 seconds) of time awake to express gratitude, bless and especially see all with the eyes of love.

I bless my fabulous life for the infinite abundance of Your Presence filling every moment and every space.

I bless this day for every person I meet whom I have the incredible privilege of blessing rather than passing by them with indifference.

I bless the abundance of good You are constantly pouring onto me in the form of food, home and income, nature and beauty in a thousand forms, peace and little moments of silence, the gentle murmur of Your voice within, the angel You do send before me to guide my every step.

How infinitely blessed are those who have eyes to see!

Day 176
A Blessing for a Prison Visitor

For 18 years I worked as a volunteer visitor in the local Geneva jail. Often, the only person the inmate will see who has no official relationship with the State administration is the visitor, which enhances still more his value in the eyes of the inmate. Personally, I have on occasion had deeply moving, even awesome contacts with inmates, such as the young Albanian who told me, "It was worth being sent to jail just to meet you."

We bless volunteer prison visitors in their errand of mercy among those who are rejected by society.

We bless them in their overflowing compassion, that they may give the best of themselves to those they visit, bring a ray of hope to those who despair, the warmth of sister- or brotherhood to the lonely, an open heart to those who have closed their own heart, the tenderness of love to those who may never have encountered true affection.

We bless them in their trust in the innate goodness of those they visit, be it a petty thief or the hardened criminal or murderer, the first offender or one who has spent decades in jail. We bless them in their perceptiveness and wisdom that they may avoid the ploys of those who would trick them or exploit their credulity.

Finally, we bless them that despite all the darkness, quiet desperation and ugliness they encounter, they may keep alive the selfless vision of service that brought them there, the inner flame that nourishes them, the sheer goodness that motivates them.

Day 177
Blessing for a Healing of Resentment

Have you realized that resentment is one of the cruelest forms of suffering one can impose upon... oneself? It literally eats you up – a bit like a rodent gnawing at your guts. It also sends out extremely negative energy into the community, which would no doubt prefer gentler vibes coming from you (not to mention your own immune system which you yourself put under ferocious attack: our immune system is extremely sensitive to changes of mood and feeling).

I bless myself in my deep desire and my ability to give up all resentment towards...... (person or situation) once and for all.

I bless myself in my openness to love's gentle whispering telling me to just let go and be FREE. (Pause here and listen and feel for a moment.)

I bless myself in my desire to experience living in the glorious liberty of total forgiveness towards all, starting with myself.

May I love myself enough to not continue tormenting myself with resentment, not to mention the serious harm I inflict on my own health.

May I love my neighbors and my community enough to not send out the negative vibrations born of resentment but on the contrary radiate the gentle, healing energy of a forgiveness-filled consciousness that uplifts and blesses all.

Day 178
A Walking Meditation

Today's anonymous blessing is called The Blessing Walk, and because it is a walking meditation, you can combine it with your daily walk, so you can get your exercise and improve your spiritual awareness both at the same time.

The technique is very simple: while walking at a moderate pace, take note of all the natural features you pass – the rocks, the plants, the birds, the sky. Direct a feeling of great love and compassion to everything you see around you. Imagine a golden light in your feet as they touch the ground spreading outward as you walk. Imagine golden light streaming from your hands toward everything around you. Leave a blessing on everything you pass.

As you return home, imagine the whole landscape glowing with golden radiance from the blessing you have left. Feel love flowing back into you from everywhere.

A daily practice of this kind will not only develop your compassion – it will connect you at a spiritual level with the natural world.

(Source: borrowed from this website: http://pathstoknowledge. com/954/the-blessing-walk-a-walking-meditation)

Day 179
For the Elderly in Deep Solitude

A few minutes ago, I received a phone call from a dear friend who is 92. This woman who has had an extremely active life during her whole existence and who lived to serve (she also had a healing gift and once performed a "miracle" that stunned a professor of medicine who acknowledged its divine source) lives now in the most immense solitude, despite the fact that she has a large well-to-do family. There are millions in her case. Let us embrace them in our deep caring.

We bless the elderly who, often after lives of constant service, face the last years of their life in desperate solitude.

We bless them in their discovery or the strengthening of their relationship with You.

May they come to really *feel* that You are always by their side, that You constantly uphold, surround, care for, cherish, protect, support them every day in every way, especially those who fear passing on alone, unattended, in what feels to them the most desolate solitude.

We bless their neighbors, family, friends or just passing acquaintances in their awareness of the plight of such elderly, that they may be moved to offer a presence or practical assistance where needed and above all love.

We bless our politicians and administrators that they be inspired to seek innovative and exciting new solutions to what is becoming a major social issue with the ageing of populations worldwide.

Finally, may we always be aware that, because we are all one beyond any representation we could ever imagine of this oneness, my neighbor is myself.

Day 180
For the Incredible Beauty of Creation

The incredible beauty of nature defies the wildest imagination. From the perfection of a tiny alpine flower no one will ever even see to the splendor of a star-studded summer's night, through the intricate beauty of a seashell to the breathtaking harmony of a spider's web, all this grandiose symphony has been laid out for our pure enjoyment.

Mistress of the universe, we bless You for the incredible perfection and splendor of the spectacle You have created for our constant rejoicing.

For the sheer miracle of a substance as mysterious and omnipresent as water to the rugged beauty of a mountain range, for the amazing functioning of living creatures and systems of all sorts that challenge our deepest knowledge to the constantly renewed abundance of Your goodness expressed in the produce of the earth and seas, including the unbelievable variety and wisdom of the animal kingdom we have barely begun to grasp, we bless You.

In front of the utter perfection and symmetry of every single flower, seashell, plant, crystalline rock, we stand in awe and bless You. For the century-old sequoia or oak trees in their majesty which sprang from a tiny grain or acorn to the rolling of the galaxies, for the magic of microbes and all other microorganisms to the silent communication systems between plants and between animals and plants, we bless the incredible Intelligence that runs this phenomenal show called the universe and fall on our knees in utter awe.

Thank You, thank You, thank You for including us for our sheer enjoyment in this grandiose spectacle, the reason of which is beyond anything we could ever imagine.

And finally, may we be reminded that we are not spectators, but actors in this happening which is simply Your boundless Love expressing Itself out of sheer joy. Daily we are Your dance of delight, Your pure goodness in ecstatic motion, Your holy choir.

Day 181
A Blessing for Street Children

The existence of street children is one of the most unacceptable scandals on our planet. In the USA alone, a developed country, it has been estimated that in 2013 the number of homeless children approached 2.5 million. Of course, any exact statistic is by definition impossible, but that is not the real issue. One street child would be too much, especially if it were yours. In many countries, children as young as 5 or 6 are homeless. They often rove in gangs, clothed in rags, sniffing glue to find some acrid solace, eating on garbage dumps, sleeping on top of each other on cold nights to keep a semblance of warmth in their emaciated bodies. Let our hearts turn into oceans of love to embrace our cherished other selves.

I bless the street children of the world in their ability to face their incredibly challenging plight with courage, dignity and unbending grit. I bless them in their ability to turn away all those who would attempt to use their plight for some base material gain, and I bless those who would do so in their authentic goodness and divinity that they may abandon such dark plans.

I bless these children in their solidarity, that they may support one another in their daily fight for survival, and I bless them in their creativity that they may use the slightest opportunity to lighten their burdens.

I bless the social agencies dealing with them that they may have the will to really face the challenge head on, and find new means, however unorthodox, to handle the situation.

I bless the politicians and mayors of all concerned cities that they let their authentic compassion speak rather than political calculations.

And I bless myself in my profound caring that I may use any opportunity – financial, voluntary work or meditation – that we may rise as a race to eliminate this unacceptable evil once and for all.

Day 182
Blessing Reduces Prison Sentence (Testimony)

Emmanuel (name altered) was a gentle man who ended up in the Geneva jail on drug charges.

He was a modest businessman in his native Ghana. His mother was severely ill and serious medical care was extremely expensive. Friends told him he could make excellent business in his field if he went to China. So he invested all his savings on the trip. However, things did not turn out as planned and once in China he lost everything. He returned home completely broke – and desperate because he could not help his mother whose condition was rapidly deteriorating.

An acquaintance told him that he could make some quick, easy money if he agreed to deliver drugs in Geneva (there was a direct flight at the time). Very unwisely, he accepted and was caught at the customs on arrival. Off to prison – where we met.

We very rapidly came to talk about blessing. He just devoured the book The Gentle Art of Blessing and started to bless literally everyone: the prison guards and other personnel, the lawyers involved in his case, the district attorney and the judge with whom he met and who was to preside over his trial... anyone remotely close to his situation, not to mention his fellow inmates. Emmanuel just blessed and blessed and blessed.

The normal punishment for a case such as his would have been 7–8 years in prison. He received a year and a half. No one at the prison would believe him when he returned from court. As he had already served well over a year, he only had a few months more of the prison sentence to serve.

I have not seen Emmanuel since, but I believe he must still be blessing people.

(Pierre, Switzerland)

Day 183
Handling the Belief of Dualism

Dualism – the belief of separation in all areas – is possibly the greatest spiritual challenge of our age. Its healing will come as people realize that ALL is infinite Love manifesting itself in a thousand ways and that, behind all appearances, there is only Love calling to be acknowledged and cherished – starting with the street children of a precedent blessing.

I bless humanity in its ascending path from the rigors, suffering and feeling of separation born of dualistic beliefs to the deeper, joyful understanding that we are all one, nature, plants and animals included.

I bless myself in the revolutionary understanding that my neighbor – the drunkard on the street, the white-collar criminal, the unbearable fundamentalist on the same floor as mine – IS myself, whatever the material senses claim to the contrary.

I bless us in our openness to the cosmic energies pouring onto our planet to help us towards the next stage of planetary evolution as we slowly leave the dimension of materialism, conflict and separation to move to higher dimensions of harmony and growing oneness.

I bless myself as we all move from the most cherished dogma of dualism – the belief of lack – to the understanding of infinite abundance for all, which is the fundamental fact of non-dualism or oneness.

And may we as a race courageously face the huge challenges and planet-threatening dangers in front of us as the old energies of conservatism muster their last efforts in their vain attempt to delay the New World of oneness and harmony being born.

Halfway Through The Year

Here we are, halfway through the year. Many readers have certainly been faithfully blessing daily. And I do not doubt that many of you have occasionally asked yourself the question: but what impact are my blessings having on the world?

So before we continue, I would like to include a most inspiring text by a French spiritual teacher, Alyna Rouelle, who, when she was still young, received from divine grace an amazing revelation illustrating the impact of her meditation. I have had the privilege of taking a workshop and having a private session with this absolutely out-of-the-ordinary and very special illumined soul who lives solely from light (or prana).

After close to 30 years of blessing, this text gave me a new boost that continues daily. I trust it will inspire you too.

"I saw a child elude death in a dangerous city.

I saw an armed man on the verge of killing, stop what he was about to undertake.

I saw a desperate young woman about to commit suicide become suddenly enlightened and open her heart to life.

I saw a group of animals saved by a group of young men from being tortured and avoiding a death that seemed inevitable.

I saw a child give a sandwich to an old man dying of cold and hunger in the street.

I saw faces bathed with tears of joy, hands joining in brotherhood.

I saw people find the strength to heal, to get up again, to choose life.

I saw people manipulated to sow terror brought to repentance through compassion and change sides."

(Source: http://alynarouelle.wix.com/lumieredevie Blog for November 28, 2015. Her website is in French.)

It is my deeply held belief that every single sincere blessing, prayer, or meditation, if impelled by a clear intent and practiced with perseverance, has an impact, however modest. This is so encouraging, especially in the rather wild world we live in, because so many people don't believe they can have any significant impact on events.

So, my precious friend, just KNOW that your blessings, if enfolded in love and nurtured with deep compassion, can only heal. Like the seeds carried by the wind, you will maybe not know on what soil they fall, but they will carry fruit, they will illumine, they will uplift.

Day 184
For Children in Foster Care Worldwide

Children in foster care often come from very dysfunctional families. And too often, the foster parents are not up to the high standard of parenting which would be expected for such a role. So the children concerned show much higher rates of school failure, difficulties in social adaptation and delinquency than their peers.

I bless children in foster care, that the challenges of their past weigh not unduly on their future. I bless the hosting families that they may welcome their foster child with gentleness, deep compassion and caring and an understanding of their special needs.

I bless these children in their courage, openness and complete trust. And I send blessings to their classmates and neighbors of their age group in their friendliness and readiness to help them adapt, and to the social services concerned in their tolerance, patience, innovativeness and foresight.

I bless the school authorities and their teachers in their understanding of the challenges facing these children and their creativity in helping them adapt to their new surroundings.

And finally, I shower with blessings our societies in general that we the citizens and the authorities understand that the way we treat our weaker members is a measure of our own values and a yardstick enabling us to better walk our talk.

Day 185
A Blessing to Heal Racism

A dear friend of mine in St. Louis (USA) who has become a real brother invited me to attend a court proceeding which involved an African-American member of the church my friend attended. This member had been insulted and threatened by a white neighbor. I have never ever in my life encountered such distilled and hate-filled abuse as this neighbor's tirade in the courtroom. I composed this blessing while attending this session of the court.

We bless all those suffering from feelings of racism that their repressed fear of differences may be completely healed.

We bless them that the feelings of rejection, intolerance or hatred that haunt them may be replaced by wonder for the boundless physical and cultural variety of the human race and a deep appreciation of our human differences.

May they be freed from the mental jail in which they have unconsciously cloistered themselves, thus closing their hearts and minds to the divine beauty of every single human created by the Being of unconditional Love that runs the show called life or the universe.

We bless equally those who suffer from the impact of racism, be they in the social, economic or cultural fields, human relationships, employment and so many other areas, that they may muster the courage and wisdom to defend themselves nonviolently, with love, quiet strength and – why not – humor.

And we bless the whole human race in its march towards the growing understanding that we are one single family and that we have the incredible privilege of loving our neighbor as ourselves *because our neighbor IS ourself.*

Day 186
Native American Blessing

Originally a prayer, I have very slightly modified it to give it the form of a blessing. However, for the infinite Spirit which hears our calls, what counts is not the words they are wrapped up in but the deep sincerity of the heart that utters them.

O Great Spirit, whose voice I hear in the winds and whose breath gives life to all the world,

Hear me. I am small and weak, I need your strength and wisdom. May I walk in beauty and may my eyes ever behold the red and purple sunset.

May my hands respect the things you have made and may my ears be sharp to hear your voice. May I be wise so that I may understand the things you have taught my people.

May I learn the lessons that you have hidden in every leaf and rock.

May I seek strength, not to be greater than my brother but to fight my greatest enemy – myself. May I always be ready to come to you with clean hands and straight eyes, so when life fades, as the fading sunset, my Spirit may come to you without shame.

(From: *Native American Prayers*, published by the Episcopal Church)

Day 187
Blessing Concerning Child Labor

According to the ILO (International Labor Office), today, throughout the world, around 215 million children work, many full-time. They do not go to school and have little or no time to play. Many do not receive proper nutrition or care. They are denied the chance to be children. More than half of them are exposed to the worst forms of child labor such as work in hazardous environments, slavery, or other forms of forced labor, illicit activities including drug trafficking and prostitution, as *well as involvement in armed conflict e.g. as child soldiers. So as you bless please remember that the ONLY thing that gives healing power to a blessing is **feeling it in the heart**. Words per se have absolutely no power to heal.*

From the bottom of our hearts we bless the millions of children worldwide who are living in conditions often bordering on slavery – if they are not outright slaves.

We bless them in their courage, grit and determination, that they may be capable of simply imagining a better future, and never give up on these dreams.

We bless them in their health and strength, that they may survive their usually appalling working conditions and impossible work schedules.

We especially bless those small girls and boys who at the ages of eight or ten are employed in brothels for locals or rich tourists, that the unacceptable abuse to which they are submitted not distort their view of humankind or crush their self-esteem.

We bless all these children that divine Love may somehow find its miracle path to pull them and all the others out of the pit of extreme exploitation and open a path towards a more dignified life.

We bless the businesspeople who exploit these children, the civil servants and politicians who tolerate such exploitation that divine grace may lift them out of their pit of indifference or hardness of heart and lead them to take firm steps to definitively ban such conditions.

And finally, we bless the Western supermarket chains and we as consumers who often knowingly profit from such conditions that we may all awaken to our major responsibility in the creation of a world that works for all, starting with these children.

Day 188

Meeting Limited Circumstances with Unlimited Thoughts

Once more, I borrow a prayer from the beautiful book by Marianne Williamson, A Year of Miracles. *I have just added here and there a "may I..." to conform a little more to the blessing form (Day 49 in her book). It seems especially suited to follow the precedent blessing on child labor.*

While the world is changeable, the Truth is not. May I not be tempted by the drama of the world to forget the eternal peace of God. May I hold to the truth of who I really am and how the universe operates, despite whatever the world may say.

In a universe where only love is real, may I not be deterred by the appearances of fear. Where there is lack in the material world, may I proclaim the infinite abundance of the spiritual universe. Where there is discord or conflict on the material level, may I proclaim the love that unites us as one.

Today, may I meet limits with the thinking of unlimited possibility. Whatever occurs, may I remember that miracles are possible regardless of circumstances. May I proclaim the miracle, may I pray for the miracle, and may I rejoice in the miracle.

Day 189

Acknowledging My Divine Selfhood

With the understanding of the allness of Love, accepting and feeling one's divine essence or selfhood is one of the most important spiritual steps any individual can take. The lack of self-love is one of the most fundamental challenges I have encountered in my workshops for a quarter of a century, which is why its healing is so fundamental to meaningful living.

I bless myself from the heart as the utterly beautiful, totally divine being I AM.

I bless myself in my radiant goodness that constitutes the very marrow of my nature.

I bless the complete, untarnished integrity of my mind and heart.

I bless myself in the constantly renewed vitality and energy Life has bestowed upon me so as to serve with joy.

I bless myself in the unfettered vision that prepares me for all the miracles awaiting my openness and trust so as to manifest themselves in my existence.

I bless the perfect health already embedded in the essence of my being that it may be powerfully expressed despite matters' claims all shouting together for my attention.

I bless myself in my unconditional love and forgiveness which constitute the very foundation of my being.

I bless myself in the as yet unexpressed talents just waiting to blossom inside me.

I bless myself in my boundless resilience and grit that can carry me through any trial.

And finally, I bless myself in my ability to see all through the eyes of the love that *never* judges or condemns but tenderly embraces, encourages and uplifts.

Day 190
Blessing for an Illness

Views about disease have been changing very rapidly in recent years as we just begin to understand the complex nature of mind-body relations. Some MDs and health practitioners are beginning to describe an illness as a cherished friend of our growth: e.g. to heal cancer, first eliminate any deep-seated resentment; to heal stress dissolve your anger or your fear; to improve your declining eyesight, learn to see all with love instead of accepting the parrot-like mantra of inevitable ageing. Our future is in our hands (and still more our present!).

I bless this illness in its loving intention of supporting my inner growth toward a healthier state of being and improved lifestyle.

I bless and thank this disease in its aim of enabling me to face what could be an unhealthy lifestyle, eating habits, ways of thinking or any other claim I have ignored until now.

I bless this illness for challenging me to accept that through every single event in my life, the universe is conspiring towards my ultimate happiness.

I bless myself in my deep listening to what my body is attempting to tell me, that I may hear with gratitude and wisdom rather than react in fear.

I bless myself in my instant awareness of the negative thought patterns which may be dampening my energy levels, and my courage in facing long-repressed incidents of the past, that these be exposed to the healing balm of forgiveness, self-forgiveness and love.

And finally, I bless myself in my ability to unearth repressed negative emotions that harm the harmonious functioning of my immune system and replace them with the deep contentment that stimulates and nourishes my whole being.

Day 191
For Spending a Day in Gratitude

Such a great deal has been written in recent years about the power of gratitude it appears unnecessary to belabor this point. It is impossible – repeat, impossible – to hold at the same time the slightest negativity of any sort and authentic gratitude. Their coexistence is simply impossible, and the choice is always ours.

May this day be a constant canticle of gratitude from now on till I retire tonight.

May I welcome any negative event with gratitude for the growth it will produce in my life.

May I face every single encounter with gratitude for the

manifestation of divine love it represents.

May I face any disgruntled, depressed, angry or sad face with gratitude that my blessings can uplift and help dissolve such attitudes.

May I eat my meals with gratitude for all those who have participated in bringing them onto my table.

However tedious, unimportant or boring my work may appear, may I perform it with the understanding that the very act of giving thanks can profoundly transform it.

And above all, may I understand that the choice between complaint, indifference and gratitude is mine at every single moment of my life.

Day 192
To Overcome the Plague of Alcoholism

Alcoholism is one of the major scourges of the planet. According to the World Health Organization, its abuse kills well over three million people per year. Not to mention the tens of millions of marriages and families it destroys, the number of accidents and crimes it causes, the self-esteem it throttles in millions – this sad list could cover a whole page. Let us hold close to our hearts those plagued by one of the ultimate forms of self-destruction and misery – mental and material.

We bless those suffering under the heavy weight of alcoholism. We bless them in their authentic desire to shake off this condition once and for all.

We bless them in their ability to take a firm stand to end this self-destructive claim and to hold on to that stand, whatever the cost and however grueling the challenge.

When their body or their mind screams for a drink, may the invisible presence of grace nerve their endeavor to hold on at all costs and when "going through hell, to keep going."

May they find just the support they need in family, friends or an organization offering competent assistance.

And finally, may they arise above all self-condemnation and learn to behold themselves in their true divine status, untarnished by any claim of our material sojourn here on earth.

Day 193
To Heal the Challenge of Insomnia

The tempo and stress of modern life combined with many other factors have turned insomnia into a major health challenge, not to mention its serious impact on the quality of life. Let us embrace those who suffer from this claim in our tender, caring love. It is also important to know that there is absolutely no solid scientific proof that people need a fixed amount of sleep. There are people who lead perfectly normal lives sleeping one hour per night, and a good many well-known people sleep 4–5 hours per day. (Napoleon slept 3 hours per night.)

We bless those who night after night spend endless hours tossing and turning, often in anguish and desperation.

We bless them in their endeavor to seek what in their existence may be causing or aggravating this challenge and to adopt those simple practices that will help them heal it.

We bless them in their search for the professional or other support necessary or available.

We bless them also in their freedom from totally unscientific claims and cultural beliefs that everyone "needs" a given amount of sleep.

May they refuse the temptation of self-condemnation in any form and learn to trust that the infinitely loving Life-force that runs the universe from the smallest organism to the majesty of the heavens will lead them to exactly what they need to live an existence unfettered by this suffering.

Day 194
In Prison for Murder and Led to Use The Gentle Art of Blessing *(Testimony)*

At the local Geneva jail where I was a visitor for many years, I was asked to visit a young man who had read my book on Roger W. McGowen, Messages of Life from Death Row. *Roger speaks at length of the powerful impact blessing had on him during one of the most challenging periods of his 25 year stay on death row. He had read Roger's book three times and shed many tears.*

In November 2005, the young man wrote to me: "Pierre, your book is a marvel. [He is referring to the book on Roger, only available at Amazon.] It is opening my eyes on many things and brings me great joy and help in my daily life. Since reading your book, I bless all and everything nonstop. I have the impression it is bearing fruit and I am so happy about that.

I am going to find a way of having photocopies made of the (one page) text 'The Gentle Art of Blessing' which is at the beginning of the book and I will distribute it to the maximum number of inmates possible, because if everyone followed what the text states things would change rapidly."

(This young inmate corresponded for years with Roger on Texas death row.)

Day 195
A Blessing for Complete Transparency to the Divine

In many great spiritual traditions, the ultimate aim is to reach the complete elimination of the ego and its rather pompous and pathetic claims to self-importance. The following very brief blessing is one many find helpful in their striving for transparency. You can use it as a mantra and pray it many times a day.

Thank you for shining as me, infinite Love, and may I be so

Thee that all those I encounter may experience me as Thy radiant presence, Thy unconditional love and forgiveness.

May they no longer see me, but only, only, ONLY THEE.

Day 196
A Blessing for Inner Listening

Some great spiritual seers state that silence should be the very foundation of spiritual life and prayer, not talking nonstop to Divine Love, but listening to what Love has to say to us. So this will be our theme today.

I bless myself in my ability to go into the silence and listen to Spirit's words of unconditional Love and encouragement.

I bless myself in my ability to calm the constant, strident chatter of the human mind and rest by the deep pool of inner contentment that homes deep down inside me, awaiting my visit.

I bless myself in my ability to resist mind's suggestion that nothing is happening, or that I cannot hear what Spirit is whispering to me, as it is when nothing is happening that I can start listening.

I bless myself in my ability to simply sit still and just observe without resisting if any strong emotions or fears come welling up – just letting them be and observing instead of judging.

I bless myself in my ability to rearrange my daily schedule so as to make this precious practice of listening a daily gift to myself.

Day 197
To Heal the Belief of Incurable Diseases

To call a disease "incurable" is totally unscientific, yet it literally kills people, or at least drastically shortens the lives of numerous patients at whom their MD has in certain cases almost thrown this diagnosis (cf. the remarkable work of Norman Cousins in this area of medical practice). In such circumstances, the most one can say is that science has not yet found a cure for such and such an ailment.

We bless those whom limited, unscientific human beliefs have labeled as "incurable."

We bless them in their understanding that "to God all things are possible" despite what very narrow, material or lopsided views of reality claim to the contrary.

May they be inspired not to submit their lives to limited, short-term, material views of things but be inspired by the amazing healings of practically every known disease happening daily around the world, be it through alternative forms of medicine or health care or solidly grounded spiritual approaches which have amply proved their worth.

May they put aside once and for all old, tired theological beliefs of punishment or negative karma which may unknowingly influence them.

May they summon the courage to break out of the well-beaten tracks of conventional wisdom, "victimitis," or fears for their life, that they may dare try new approaches which are carriers of hope.

And may they take the ultimate authority for their own well-being into their own hands rather than surrendering it to some exterior authority or system, however well-intentioned it may be.

Day 198
On Miracles

What the human mind calls "miracles" is simply the normal functioning of reality at a higher level of manifestation, i.e. the realm of divine Love. I personally once had an instantaneous healing of symptoms of dysentery on a plane returning from Africa when I had a sudden, incredibly powerful vision of the omnipotence and unlimited action of infinite Love, and, above all, **felt** *this Love with my whole being.*

May we be open to accepting so-called miracles as the smile of God upon the earth.

May we gently set aside our analytical, rational minds that we may see with new eyes.

May we open our hearts to the unexpected and the miraculous functioning as the normal way of life beyond the very limited veil of material perceptions.

May we accept that the presence of grace supersedes the law of karma as we take off the blinders of a narrow material vision of things. May the tunnel vision of materialism dissolve in the joyful illumination of our soul suddenly attuned to the infinite abundance of the spiritual realm, the kingdom of heaven awaiting us now.

Day 199

A Blessing for My Setting Up Residence in the Inner Sanctuary of My Heart

I bless myself in my ability to discern the sacred sanctuary of Love already established in my heart.

May I grant myself the sheer grace of retiring there many times a day.

May I rejoice that at any moment I can rest in the holy Presence and emerge rested, rejuvenated and renewed.

Day 200

A Blessing for Moving into a New Home

I (we) bless this new space which divine Love has opened up for me (us) to live in.

I bless this home that it may become a sanctuary of love for all those who enter or live there.

May this space bring the deepest rest and quiet joy to all. May they feel the ineffable peace and quiet of Your Presence.

May they be abundantly blessed by the energy of this home and leave uplifted and enriched.

May it be for me a harbor from the stress, rushing and hectic consumption of a world desperately clinging to old models of living. May I find therein true refreshment for my soul and may it be an ever-welcoming wellspring of renewal that I may return to my daily activities with enthusiasm to serve, share and love more.

May those who are heavy laden or depressed find in my home a place of healing where their burdens may dissolve and vanish into their native nothingness.

And finally, may its gentle aura embrace the homes nearby as well as those who simply pass its gates.

Day 201
For Natural Catastrophes

Natural catastrophes – a good many man-induced – touch innumerable people each year, leaving them frequently homeless and with all their often modest belongings totally destroyed.

We bless those who have suffered the extreme disruption of a major catastrophe, be it water, wildfires, wind or quake-induced, or whatever its source may be.

We bless them in their resilience and strength in facing immediate losses and hardships.

We bless them in their courage in dealing with the often total disruption of their lives, and in their creativity and imagination in organizing new and innovative ways to rebuild their existences.

We bless the authorities of their region in summoning the means necessary to cover the emergency needs of the populations concerned, to organize mass-scale assistance and avoid any disorganization in the different forms of assistance offered.

We bless the regional and national authorities concerned

that they may act wisely and without loss of time, and the international community in its compassion and caring when its support is needed.

Finally, we bless consumers and businesspeople worldwide in their alertness to the fact that overconsumption has been and can be a contributing cause of major natural catastrophes that both may alter their modes of living or production to better meet the demands of our wonderfully generous planet which has ample resources to provide for all our real needs but not all of our unnecessary wants.

Day 202
To Find True Peace

I have made very minor modifications to this text by Native American chief Black Elk, an Oglala Sioux and Spiritual Leader (1863–1950), to give it the form of a blessing.

May I find the first peace, which is the most important, that which comes within the souls of people when they realize their relationship, their oneness with the universe and all its powers, and when they realize that at the center of the universe dwells Wakan-Taka (the Great Spirit), and that this center is really everywhere, it is within each of us.

This is the real peace and the others are but reflections of this.

And may I also find the second peace, that which is made between two individuals, and the third one which is made between two nations.

But above all may I understand that there can never be peace between nations until there is known that true peace, which, as I have often said, is within the souls of men.

(Source: www.sapphyr.net/natam/quotes-nativeamerican. htm)

Day 203
A Blessing for MDs

With the advent of modern medicine, especially in the postwar period, the public put MDs on a pedestal – a dangerous position many accepted willingly. But with the arrival of numerous forms of alternative medical care and the growing realization by many that no one else can carry the ultimate responsibility of a person's health than that person (barring special situations such as e.g. children born with abnormalities and some others), MDs are needing to rapidly adapt to change. At the same time, very encouraging developments have occurred in recent years in the curricula of medical schools which bode well for their ability to adjust to new trends.

We bless MDs in their ability to rediscover their practice first and foremost as a form of public service rather than a comfortable source of income.

We bless them in their ability to not only accept, but encourage the demand of a growing number of patients to accept the primary accountability for their own health.

May they learn to resist the constant attempt of the pharmaceutical interests to continually foist on MDs the latest miracle drug in the understanding that lifestyle, one's thinking and the environment, rather than drugs, are the primary source of health.

May they be led to take the time to truly listen to each patient with deep and genuine care and compassion, realizing that healing the root of a problem may require more than writing out a prescription.

And may all MDs come to discover with humility and gratitude what an increasing number of their colleagues have already realized, namely that in their healing work they are but an instrument of Life and a transparency to its amazing ability to heal all disharmony of any sort.

Day 204
Another Blessing on the Wise Use of Time

Hurrying, rushing has become a way of life for so many, despite the fact that it is very bad for our health and happiness! A university-educated woman holding a professional position in an environmental organization told her mother, a very dear friend of mine, "Mum, I just don't have the time to live!" How many in our societies could echo that statement. So here is a blessing on slowing down. I suggest you put it in the first person.

Today:

May you take time for worship and reflection.

May you take time for friends – they are a source of happiness.

May you take time to think, it helps make the right choices.

May you take time to laugh and sing – it makes life's loads lighter.

May you take time to dream and hitch your soul to the stars.

May you take time to play, it is the secret of youth.

May you take time to read, it is the foundation of wisdom.

May you take time to smile at a stranger, he or she IS YOU.

May you take time to love, unconditionally – it is who you are.

May you make a little time for silence – it refreshes and regenerates your soul.

And may you take time to be grateful and to count your blessings!

(Adapted from an anonymous poem in the book *The Treasure Chest*)

Day 205
The Native American Ten Commandments

I have transformed these beautiful Ten Commandments into blessings.

May I treat the Earth and all that dwell therein with respect.

May I remain close to the Great Spirit,
May I show great respect for my fellow beings,
May I work together for the benefit of all mankind,
May I give assistance and kindness wherever needed,
May I do what you know to be right.
May I look after the well-being of Mind and Body,
May I dedicate a share of my efforts to the greater Good,
May I be truthful and honest at all times,
May I take full responsibility for my actions.

Day 206
On Blessing People on Public Transport

When one has really delved into the depths of blessing, it becomes such a joy one ends up doing it everywhere! I love blessing e.g. in the public transport system (I have no car). Rather than my mind wandering aimlessly from one ad to another, it is such a delight to think one can freely help another person without them ever knowing from whence came the sunray that broke through the clouds of their sadness or fear.

May the heart of Love move me to realize the immense gift it is to bless people everywhere.

May I rejoice in the privilege of being an anonymous sower of light and joy knowing that, unbeknownst to me, people may receive comfort and strength through my silent blessings.

May I constantly be aware of the fact that so often a specific opportunity to bless the person in front of me may never repeat itself again and hence be moved to not miss the opportunity.

May my blessings always be joyful and light and never ever be made with a sense of obligation or duty which would automatically annul their healing power.

Finally, may I always be aware of the fact that, however shocking or sad the material appearance in front of me, in the realm of the unseen, right there is the resplendent manifestation of the divine Life in all its perfection and wholeness.

Day 207
Extreme Situation of Alienation Healed (Testimony)

Mahfoud and Idriss were brothers, living near the city of Mopti (Mali, West Africa). Mahfoud was the eldest brother – and in the African tradition, that means other brothers and sisters owe him special respect and obedience. On the occasion of his third marriage, he asked Idriss for two sacks of rice for the festivities. Idriss did not feel like complying, and from that day on a real feud started between the brothers. The situation got so bad the village elders asked Idriss to leave the village.

Idriss then settled in the nearby city of Mopti where his elder brother, still full of fury, hunted him out and shot at him while Idriss was eating his evening meal in the courtyard. He missed and was arrested. To appease his brother, Idriss gave his TV as a bond to the police so that Mahfoud could get out on bail. On leaving prison, he vowed not to miss his younger brother the next time.

My friend Mamadou met a rather desperate Idriss in the street who poured out the whole story. Mamadou told him to simply bless his brother unceasingly, which Idriss started doing. A few weeks later, a delegation of the village elders came to present the elder brother's apologies to Idriss, requesting him to reintegrate the village. Once settled again, Mahfoud would do everything he could to be of service to his brother. When Mamadou returned from a trip to Europe, Idriss came at 1am one morning, so eager was he to share the story with him.

Blessing heals – even in extreme situations.

Day 208
For a Released Prison Inmate with Nowhere to Go

It has always amazed me how inmates – like my friend Ibrahima from the Ivory Coast – are often released with no concern whatsoever as to whether they will have a place to stay, a potential job in view, a minimum of funds, or the slightest social contact (especially in a place like the Geneva jail where around 90% of inmates in December 2015 came from abroad).

We bless all these inmates worldwide who, after the trauma of jail, face the challenge of entering a world where often practically all doors are closed to them.

We bless them in their trust that, despite all material appearances to the contrary, they are cared for, yea, even cherished, by an infinitely compassionate Providence.

We hold them in that space where infinite Love is constantly conspiring for the good of every single one of its creatures and where "miracles" occur as the natural unfolding of divine law and its reservoir of unlimited possibilities in all areas.

We bless them in their health, their strength, their unlimited creativity, their positive vision, their perseverance and their ability to reject all attacks of discouragement or fear or any temptation to have recourse to illegal or criminal acts.

Finally, we bless them in the totally unexpected opportunities for a new life already awaiting them, whatever social statistics may scream to the contrary, and we open ourselves to any opportunity of assistance that might avail itself in this area we could contribute.

Day 209
On Finding Life's Purpose

It is rather amazing how some people can live their whole existence without asking themselves why they are here on earth. Others believe they are here to have fun – or to suffer! Yet the reality is rather different. This blessing can be given in the first person or the plural (i.e. I, we or "those seeking for their life purpose"). One can never repeat enough that a blessing you give in Brooklyn, Caracas or London can uplift someone in Timbuktu, Shanghai, Lima, Verkhoyansk or Yakutsk in Siberia – reputed to be the coldest cities on earth.

I bless all those searching for meaning in their life.

I bless them in their understanding that as every single person is unique in time and history, every single one of us has an absolutely unique purpose that cannot be duplicated by anyone else.

May they discern that they have a function to fill no one else can fulfill in the way they can, and may they grasp the fact that they have very special gifts which cannot be duplicated by others in the exact manner they use them.

May they understand that, however humble their talents or opportunities, because of their unique life history, they have a manner of offering them no one else can do in the same way.

May the very severely handicapped who are totally dependent on others realize their own unique role in encouraging their caregivers to express greater patience, goodness, calm, love and the many qualities these caregivers need to function.

And may we all understand that it is above all the pure love with which we perform our various tasks and activities which nourishes our lives with the deepest purpose and meaning of all.

Day 210
The Blessing of an Unending Love

On the blog by Edie Weinstein on beliefnet.com I found this beautiful text by Rabbi Rami Shapiro. The text is called "An Unending Love." I have added "May we..." to give it the form of a blessing.

May we be loved by an unending love.

May we be embraced by arms that find us
even when we are hidden from ourselves.

May we be touched by fingers that soothe us even when we
are too proud for soothing.

May we be counseled by voices that guide us even when we
are too embittered to hear.

May we be loved by an unending love.

May we be supported by hands that uplift us even in the
midst of a fall.

May we be urged on by eyes that meet us
even when we are too weak for meeting.

May we be loved by an unending love
embraced, touched, soothed, and counseled.

Ours are the arms, the fingers, the voices;
ours are the hands, the eyes, the smiles;
we are loved by an unending love.

Day 211
On Giving Up the Desire to Control

*The tendency to wish to control everything – hence the expression
"control freak" – is widespread in our societies. At a subconscious
level, it is the expression of some deep fear that things will get out
of hand and menace the stability of one's existence and upset one's
carefully designed plans or whatever. I truly believe that the question,
"Is the universe friendly?" is possibly the most fundamental question
each person needs to answer for themselves. Some spiritual paths teach
that the universe is an infinitely friendly place. If it is, then why not
"let go and let God"?*

May I make myself the precious gift of learning to let go of
these attempts to keep everything under control.

May I trust that the real control of *all* is in the hands of the
infinitely benevolent and loving Entity running this incredible
show called the universe (an Entity humankind calls by many
names and of which it has so many representations).

A great spiritual master once told us that even the hairs of
our head were counted and that not even a sparrow disappeared
by chance, so may I unreservedly trust that my path is outlined
down to the smallest detail.

And could infinite Love do less?

When I make plans, may they be as wishes I am ready to see

completely altered according to the foresight of the Higher Good governing my life.

And when my carefully laid plans run afoul of some obstacle or even human malice or hatred, may I learn to say "thank you" before I have even deciphered the lesson awaiting me. For it is always present, and always for my ultimate growth.

May "Thy will be done" be my constant prayer to the universal law of Love that ultimately runs the show – whatever powerful CEOs or dictators may believe to the contrary.

May I learn to so treasure this assurance of Love's control that trust becomes my fundamental attitude in life, a trust that all is well, that all is working out for my ultimate good – and of course the good of all mankind and of the whole planet.

I bless myself in my ability to express and rest upon this deep trust.

Day 212
Blessing the Infinite One

As has already been mentioned, blessing is also an expression of gratitude. When we bless the invisible One, we are thanking It for being What It Is.

Infinite Love, we bless You for Your infinitude which includes every speck, atom, molecule and living being of this fabulous universe.

We bless You for being unconditional in Your giving – not requesting a single condition or specific behavior before pouring Yourself out to us and expressing Yourself AS us.

We bless You because You are constantly and everywhere enfolding, embracing, caring for and cherishing us with such infinite tenderness, encouraging us at all times, whatever the circumstances and our mistakes, to nestle in Your ample bosom.

We bless You again and always because You are at every moment infinite, unconditional, total forgiveness. No crime, no sin, no withholding, no lack is ever too great for Your forgiveness which is ever available before even the act was committed! For You only can, and at all times, see the perfection of Your creation, as the Light You are cannot see the darkness only we in our fear believe is there.

We bless You for Your infinitely precious omnipresence. In the deepest dungeon, the darkest canyon, the devouring fire of treason or trial, the desolate vastness of human solitude, You are ever present. Were we alone drifting to nowhere on an iceberg in the Arctic sea, facing dangers unknown or total annihilation, even abiding in the valley of the shadow of death, You are with us and Your strong rod and tender staff are ever-present to comfort us.

Finally, we bless Your omnipotence. Whatever the screams of the material senses and the unending finger-pointing accusations of atheistic materialism, the ultimate triumph of infinite Love is assured, unavoidable and certain.

Such is our ultimate trust, o infinite One, and with the unseen hosts at all times surrounding us all, we bless You and we praise You.

And may we serve totally unconcerned by any need for gratitude or recognition, knowing that our reward is in the deep, quiet inner joy rising from a task well done rather than outside acknowledgment.

Day 213
Completing the Great Circle

Today's blessing comes from a group called The Terma. You will find quite a few websites on blessing apart from mine, which is at the address: www.gentleartofblessing.org.

May my feet rest firmly on the ground
May my head touch the sky
May I see clearly

May I have the capacity of listen
May I be free to touch
May my words be true
May my heart and mind be open
May my hands be empty to fill the need
May my arms be open to others
May my gifts be revealed to me
So that I may return that which has been given.
(http://blog.gaiam.com/quotes/authors/terma-collective)

Day 214
Another Blessing for Journalists

As one who was a journalist for a certain number of years, I am well aware journalists have one of the most important functions in our societies – that of, to a great extent, forming public opinion (although Internet and the social networks have started changing this). However, with the growing concentration of the media in the hands of a very few powerful groups or owners, it has also become a very challenging activity, and truly independent journalism has almost become a luxury. Hence the importance of our blessings for this profession.

We bless journalists in the demanding task that is theirs in a highly competitive field with new modes of communication surfacing constantly. We bless them above all in their deep integrity, that they may always put their highest sense of truth and loyalty to a strict deontology before professional pressures, however aggressive these may turn out to be, that would make them pliable to professional survival or advancement built on compromises, expediency and profit.

We bless them in their ability to denounce evil solely to correct it. We bless them in the total honesty of their being which enables them to avoid all seedy sensationalism or unhealthy curiosity with the private life of others.

We bless them in their ability to see themselves in the truly educational role that can be theirs, rather than purveyors of cheap entertainment. We bless them in their ability to resist a distortion of truth in favor of meeting deadlines and the temptation to pander to cheap or lewd information or presentations to meet a supposed public demand.

Above all, we bless them in their courage to become whistle-blowers if ever the need arises, whatever the professional cost, and so place their highest sense of duty before personal security or the esteem of their colleagues or superiors.

Day 215
A Blessing for Integrity

Being true to oneself as Shakespeare reminds us is something we all need to strive for above all else. A person who is true to their deepest essence is solid like a centuries-old oak tree, whereas someone who lacks this fundamental honesty is like a reed bending in all directions depending on the winds.

May I follow at all times my highest sense of what is right, whatever the cost and however lonely the path, or however loud the mockery of the Pharisees.

May I express the integrity that always speaks truth to power, as the old Quaker saying goes, when silence might better serve our interests, and which stays firm in the tempest when others disappear in the underground catacombs of their fears or timidity.

May I always express the authentic self-honesty that refuses to cheat with myself, lie to myself or reside in the shady light of half-truths. For one can lie to others and be forgiven, but when we deceive ourselves, who is there to forgive? Hence may I never be ignorant or foolish enough to let myself indulge in such self-defeating behavior.

May I stay always true to this integrity which is the very core of my being, the marrow of my identity. And when the winds of trials howl or when the tempter whispers, "Come on now, compromise is essential to your survival" and attempts to make me avoid the trials I need to grow, may I – whatever the cost – be true to this inner fount of my integrity, for therein resides true living.

Day 216
A Blessing for Perseverance

Few valuable aims in life can be reached without a good dose of perseverance, which explains this second blessing on this theme. Be it the musician aiming at perfection and practicing eight or ten hours a day or more, the mother never giving up on a child who constantly commits the same errors, the unemployed person filing their 66th application for a job, the person fighting chronic depression, the farmer attempting a very challenging graft for the nth time, the healer refusing to give up on a patient medicine has condemned as hopeless... in practically all areas of life, perseverance is a key ingredient of success.

I bless myself in my ability to just hang in there, whatever the challenge.

May I never, never give up, never, never give in however enormous the trial or the difficulties. When the odds against me seem overwhelming, when I feel at the end of my tether, maybe totally alone in my struggle, may I remember the legions of unsung heroes who went before me and ultimately won the day.

When the good intentions of friends, the sheer weariness of numerous hours of effort or simply the toll of endless, unsuccessful attempts suggest that I simply give up ("you'll try again another time," or "when circumstances are more favorable"), may I find the inner resources to just hold on a little longer, a little more, one day at a time.

And above all, may I never forget that – whatever the material appearances to the contrary, however lonely my trek appears through the desolate plain I may be crossing – I am in fact never,

ever alone. May I remember that Your tender Presence is ever available and the everlasting arms ever uphold me. Such is my trust.

Day 217
A Blessing by Barbara De Angelis

I offer my blessings to the planet Earth, my home while I am in this body.

May Grace now shower upon the world and restore it to Peace.

May all who suffer now be comforted and healed.

May all who are oppressed now be liberated and their dignity redeemed.

May all who are lost in forgetfulness now awaken from the Great Sleep and return to Remembrance.

May all beings now live together in perfect harmony.

May all souls now align with their Highest.

May all souls now find their way back to Love and may that Love be All that Is.

May the One Perfect Light now triumph over all darkness in all people and all places, seen and unseen,

And may that One Perfect Light prevail for all time.

May there be Peace. May there be Peace. May there be Peace.

Source: *Soul Shifts* ©2015 Barbara De Angelis Enterprises. All rights reserved: barbaradeangelis.com

Day 218
A Blessing When Faced with So-Called "Failure"

Every so-called failure is a gift of life which includes in its very existence a lesson we need to learn or an unlearning we need to grasp.

When faced with so-called defeat or a grave mistake of mine, may I be kind to myself and instead of rudely berating myself, may I gently open myself to Love's whispering and higher wisdom.

May I accept that in this phenomenal, incredible universe, everything happens on schedule, or for a reason. Every fall hides a coach waiting for my consent to grow, and if the very hairs of my head are counted, surely then every trial is a blessing waiting to be discovered. Hence what from my very limited view of things I might label "failure" could be the most incredible springboard to higher attainments and could reveal itself one day as a true victory.

May any incident help me transform myself into a simple observer of events I choose not to label as good or bad, rather than a harsh judge, be it with myself or any others involved.

And finally, may I understand that the courage involved in risking so-called failure or the very fact of simply moving on, whatever the consequences, is surely better than sleep-inducing immobility and the refusal to try or take risks.

Day 219
Stolen Bag Returned (Testimony)

On my way to visiting a friend who lived close to Lausanne (Switzerland), I boarded the train in Geneva on a Saturday, and left my small rucksack on the seat nearest the carriage exit while I went to the toilet a few feet away. I returned less than two minutes later – no bag! It had simply vanished.

Immediately, I started blessing the thief – in his integrity, his abundance (because if one steals, one is evidently suffering from a belief of lack), his goodness, his uprightness – all the qualities his behavior seemed to belie. I did that till I felt true peace of mind.

On Monday, I decided to purchase a new bag as I used it every day, and to replace the old, quasi paleolithic electric razor I should have replaced years before as even its grid was broken and it scratched my skin each time I shaved! Despite going to three different large stores,

I did not find the desired kind of bag but did purchase a new razor. Monday evening, a small businessman who had a shop near the station phoned me to tell me he had found my bag in a dumpster. He was even kind enough to bring it to my home – and I live quite far out of Geneva. The only missing thing was a toothbrush and toothpaste!

For months after the incident, I would bless the thief as I shaved with my wonderful new electric razor, so gentle it felt almost like my wife was caressing my cheeks!

(Pierre, Switzerland)

Day 220
For Our Sisters Working as Prostitutes

Tens of millions of women around the world (possibly more) earn their living through the trade of sexual favors (and now more and more men), most of them having been forced into it through poverty, sometimes from early childhood. Despite some rather pathetic efforts to "glamorize" this activity, it remains one of the darkest corners of our societies.

Our hearts go out in deep compassion to our sisters whom often tragic circumstances in their lives have pushed into this activity.

May the frequently degrading language, attitudes and behavior they are forced to submit to not eradicate their clear sense of self-worth.

We bless them that despite everything, they may miraculously access that consciousness of their divine identity and of their oneness with their divine Source and their total innocence as perfect reflections of the Godhead.

May they discover that space of pure forgiveness where they can forgive the circumstances that led them on this path (in some cases themselves), and those who exploit them, be they mafia networks, pimps or clients.

We bless them in their ability to truly love the beautiful child of God that will always reside in them, despite the extreme indecency they are often forced into and which would attempt to squeeze out of their hearts the last trace of self-worth and dignity.

May they feel that, whatever they have done or not done, they will always be unconditionally loved and deeply cherished, and if ever the circumstances arise, may we be the human expressions of that deep, deep caring of the universe for them.

Day 221

For Children Condemned to Spend Their Whole Life in Jail

Today we will bless one of the most terrible situations I can think of – children condemned to life imprisonment. The USA is the main country in the world to do this, and almost 3,000 of them are condemned to this fate (figure for 2015), some as young as 13. Until 2005, some of them were even put to death. Let us embrace them deep in our hearts and say this blessing with special feeling. (For further information, check www.eji.org/children-prison.)

I bless the numerous children condemned to spend their whole lives in jail. I bless them in their courage to never give up and in their hope that the impossible may happen to set them free. I bless their families that they may keep contact with them through thick or thin. May the prison guards grant them special favors and treat them as their own children.

I bless the legislators and politicians involved with the administration of justice, from local courts to the Supreme Court. May they take to heart to vote new laws making such "cruel and unusual punishment" illegal. And may the American public push for the reform of this intolerable situation.

And I bless myself in my ability to rise beyond necessary indignation to understanding that even behind this horror, there is a greater plan unfolding toward a world of universal brotherhood, compassion and authentic justice.

Day 222
For the Silent Servants of Good

All over the world, there are millions of people who serve in silence, who do good around them, who sow seeds of love and compassion, unheralded and infinitely modest about their achievements. However, they are the glue that holds our society together.

We bless all those the world over who carry out their silent missions of service, compassion and mercy, without any concern for recognition or applause.

We bless them in their awareness that, through them, divine Love is smiling upon the world and the Christ energy is silently percolating through the tissue of human affairs and regenerating it.

We bless them in their silent rejoicing, that what they have done for the least of their fellow sisters and brothers, they have done for the universal Christ which is beyond all labels (including "Christian"), denominations and theologies.

We bless them in their deep sensitivity to the suffering of the world and all its beings, animal and vegetable as well as human. May they never be dragged down by it, but on the contrary be stimulated to radiate ever more love and deep caring, including to themselves as Your humble and shining reflection.

Day 223
A Blessing by Chief Tecumseh (Crouching Tiger), Shawnee Nation (1768–1813)

I have turned this exhortation into a blessing and put it in the first person.

May I live my life that the fear of death can never enter my heart.

May I trouble no one about their religion; may I respect others in their view, and demand that they respect mine.

May I love my life, perfect my life, beautify all things in my life.

May I seek to make my life long and its purpose in the service of my people.

May I prepare a noble death song for the day when I go over the great divide.

May I always give a word or a sign of salute when meeting or passing a friend,

even a stranger, when in a lonely place.

May I show respect to all people and grovel to none.

When I arise in the morning, may I give thanks for the food and for the joy of living.

And if I see no reason for giving thanks, the fault lies only in myself.

May I abuse no one and no thing, for abuse turns the wise ones to fools and robs the spirit of its vision.

When it comes my time to die, may I not be like those whose hearts are filled with the fear of death, so that when their time comes they weep and pray for a little more time to live their lives over again in a different way.

May I sing my death song and die like a hero going home.

(Source: http://www.indigenouspeople.net/tecumseh.htm)

Day 224
For the Healing of Fear

Letting go of fear is a challenge that will probably occupy most of us till our last days. Learning to rest completely on Providence is anything but easy. However, it is possible.

Spirit of truth and love, I bless myself in my ability to pinpoint my fears and face them, rather than run away from them.

May I learn to observe them as the outside observer I really am in my true identity, rather than hug them close to me as if they belonged to me.

May I learn to stop describing them in terms that give them power (e.g. as "deep," "old," "persistent," "aggressive") and may I stop making myself afraid *in the present* of something that could eventually happen *in the future* (but probably will not).

May I remember there is no place where divine Love has not already preceded me and no time when Its strong and gentle arms do not enfold me.

May I remember with the Psalmist that "yea, though I walk through the Valley of the shadow of death, You are with me and Your rod and Your staff do comfort me."

May I rejoice in the assurance that "divine Love always has met, and always will meet, every human need" including my need for total trust, and that this unbounded Love cannot be deprived of its manifestation and triumph in my life, however dark the shadows.

And finally may I rest peacefully in the quiet assurance that the combined darkness of a thousand caverns cannot extinguish the simple candle of my life.

Day 225
For the Gift of Forgiveness

Forgiveness is first and foremost a gift we make to ourselves: that of walking in the glorious freedom of having so totally forgiven ourselves we cannot feel the slightest resentment towards anyone else. Try it, friend, and you will see if you don't start dancing for joy! For the reference to the Prodigal (son or daughter), see the Gospel of Luke, chapter 15.

I bless myself in my ability to see myself as divine Love sees me: totally innocent and free of the deadweight of any resentment.

I bless myself in my ability to totally and completely forgive myself – and hence all others – for any mistake, weakness, lack of caring or compassion, indifference or whatever I ever committed or manifested, knowing I was then at my highest level of consciousness – and hence that this is true of all my fellow humans, dictators and so-called human "monsters" included.

May I learn to forgive life for any injustice I feel I suffered, knowing that to really make such a judgment I would have to be able to grasp the *meaning* of every step I took since time immemorial (and maybe before) until I reached the Kingdom – and its *place or role* in my destiny. And who could ever claim such understanding?

May I learn to forgive anyone for any harm done to me, while also knowing that the harsh and cruel net of my resentment imprisons me still more than my neighbor, just as the gentle, caring mantle of forgiveness enfolds me as surely as it tenderly upholds all others.

And may we all bask in the deep understanding that divine Love never sees any of its creatures except as totally innocent because the Prodigal Son or Daughter who leave home only do so in their own dream of separation from their Source, just as the returning Prodigals who put on the robe of innocence and the ring of oneness recover the true state they never lost in their Father/Mother's eyes.

Day 226
A Blessing to Manifest Strength

Who does not need strength at one time or another? It is an indispensable quality of a life well lived and especially when crossing any period of trials such as we all face at one time or another. It mightily enhances our ability to claim complete responsibility for our lives, the most fundamental step to really becoming an adult.

I bless myself in my ability to express the needed strength at all times, especially in challenging situations of any sort.

When confronted with a threatening situation, may I stand as firm as the proverbial, centuries-old cedar that faces the wildest storm with unlabored, quiet stability.

When faced with jeers, hatred, anger or emotional floods of any kind may I exude the calm of one who rests in his true divine identity and bless the ones expressing such uncontrolled emotion as they can be but expressing their own inner turmoil or suffering.

When faced with challenging diseases or even death, mine or others', may I rest in the quiet understanding that the one and only true Life can never be touched by material discords of any sort.

When things fall apart outside me and maybe even inside me, may I remember that divine Love shepherds me every step along my way and that no trial will ever befall me that I am not able to overcome or could lack the courage and strength to face with quiet serenity and settled peace despite all.

Day 227
A New Day

This poem was inspired by a text by Swami Chidananda. I have adapted it and transformed it into a blessing.

This day is a new day.

It never existed before and will never return.

May we turn this day into a ladder

so as to access ever greater heights.

May we not allow the sunset to find us

the same as we were at sunrise.

May we make this day into something unique.

Enrich this day,

thereby enriching yourselves.

This day is a gift of God.

It is not something extraordinary or fortuitous,

something that could go without saying.

It is specially offered to us.

May we take it into our hands with a feeling of fervor,
And return it enhanced to its Maker.

Day 228
A Blessing for Home

Isn't home such a special place for most of us? So today, we will borrow a blessing on home from the book by William John Fitzgerald, Blessings for the Fast Paced and Cyberspaced.

God bless this house.

Make it a safe place, a place of warmth, a place of ease, a place of comfort, a place of rest, of pleasing colors, a place of stability, a place of memories, a place of dreaming, a place to talk, a place of table hospitality, a place of acceptance, a place of welcome, a place of laughter, a place of healing, a place of beauty, a place of romance and lovemaking, a place of pleasant aromas, a place of strength and security, a place of unconditional love, a place where we can most truly be ourselves, a place of refuge from hyperactivity.

In such a holy space, angels hover near.

Day 229
Our Blessings Compass the World

Let us be encouraged by the fact that a sincere blessing can reach to the furthest parts of the globe. (See Alyna's testimony at mid-year on page 159.)

May we be blessed by the understanding that our every felt, meaningful blessing is like a bird on wing, carrying its message of love far and wide, yea, to the end of the world.

May we understand that we are meshed with millions of silent spiritual seekers and carrying the world on our blessings and prayers.

May we trust in the impact of our blessings to heal worldwide, be it the immigrant family down my street or the native tribe in the Amazon fighting for its basic rights; the civil rights activist being tortured in the Middle East or the desperate mother abandoned by her husband in a Third World shanty town and struggling for her young children's survival; the multimillionaire ready to end his days because his life has no meaning or the teenager whose rigid fundamentalist family will expel her from home if they discover she is pregnant.

And may we have the clarity of vision to one day grasp that, beyond the needed healing brought about by our incessant blessings on the human plane, there is a realm of light and a space of Consciousness which cannot be invaded by any error, where no healing is even needed because all is always well.

Day 230
Karma and Grace

The universe is run by two sets of laws, the law of karma (we reap what we sow) and the law of divine grace which totally eradicates all karma and acts as divine Love's totally free gift. Our blessing today refers to both.

I bless my past that it may become wisdom and not karma. I bless my present that it may manifest the abundant life a great Master promised us over 2,000 years ago. I bless my future that it may be a totally new creation rather than the simple projection of my past.

I bless my body that it may be the strong, perfectly obedient and healthy partner I need to work, serve and play in life, free of the karma of medical or cultural beliefs of decrepitude, handicaps, beliefs about conditions which supposedly cannot be healed and other mental deadweights.

I bless my days that they may become unending tools of constant learning and spaces of joyful giving. I bless all those I met today that they may discover with wonder the divinity hidden in their hearts so that Divine Love may pour therein the unearned grace which is the totally free heritage of every single one of God's children.

Day 231
For the Happiness of Humankind

Authentic, deep happiness is certainly one of the most desirable aims of many if not most human beings. Yet how many find it? As most seek for it outside of themselves, few find it. This brief blessing suggests another approach.

I bless all those I meet in their deep happiness – the firm and unchanging happiness which comes from living in harmony with the divine law that runs the universe and reality.

I bless them in the happiness that comes from realizing that my neighbor *is* myself.

I bless them in the happiness that results from an unconditional forgiveness of themselves, which itself results in forgiving all others or all painful circumstances and sufferings ever endured.

I bless them in the happiness that flows from a life of unselfed love and joyful service.

I bless them in the happiness and peace produced by the understanding that their lives are governed and guided, down to the smallest detail, by divine Love. "I shall send an angel before you to guide you on your way and to take you to the place I have prepared." (Exodus 23:20)

What a blessing in that promise!

And I bless myself in the understanding of these same laws from which flow my serene contentment and unfailing happiness.

Day 232
Impossible Work Situation Resolved (Testimony)

The testimony that follows is particularly interesting. It shows very clearly the three fundamental qualities needed by anyone pursuing a spiritual goal: intention, sincerity, and perseverance.

"I had had a lot of problems at work. Each day I would go to work and sob and sob and sob. On the street, at home, all the time. My supervisors were cruel with me, retaliating against me because they had abused me, even assaulted me, and I had filed a legal complaint. The way they were treating me was horrible. They had been doing this to other employees and I felt strongly that I needed to stand up for it. But they were about 11 managers against me.

So, one day, at work, I was walking in the street in Washington at lunch time and sobbing once more. The suffering was too much. I had been praying, taken sessions with modern sages, meditating for hours. To no avail. My sorrow was too much. Each step I had taken to resolve the situation amicably had failed. The lawsuit would be taking a few years. I was so discouraged. And meanwhile, management wanted to push me to suicide or to resign. They knew they were managers and had the power. In another instance, they had even pushed an employee in my building to commit suicide.

So, that day in the middle of the street, out of the blue an idea came to me: 'God, I do not care if I win or lose. I just want to live in peace. I just want to bless them.' And from that day, I was so determined, I would put my timer for one hour and use my 105-bead mala (to help me be grounded and focused) and bless by name each manager at work that was hurting me.

Before long and even though my situation is still ongoing, a miracle ensued. I had been complaining for almost two years but nothing was moving. But all of a sudden after I started to bless all of them and my agency, the deputy of the head of my section who was orchestrating all this was put above him. He now reports to his deputy. This was a public humiliation for him. People were shocked and started to look at me differently. The biggest miracle is that since I started to bless them, I am able to handle whatever situation presents itself.

The matter is far from being resolved. They are still trying to retaliate against me and trying to hurt me, but I am handling every situation with peace, constantly blessing them while continuing legal action. I still have periods of insomnia and go through panic attacks, but I am able to weather it all – as long as I stay in a blessing mode.

I feel that discovering you through Lilou Mace has been an answer to a prayer. To find kindred spirits, a support system for the spiritual direction I want to give to my life. I pray that one day, this work becomes commonplace and that people discover the power of blessings. I feel that I have found my calling. I would like to dedicate my life to teaching people this. But of course, after I have mastered this myself."
(MF, USA)

(Lilou Macé is an independent interviewer who has her own program on the Internet where she interviews hundreds of people both in English and in French. She interviewed me on blessing. See http:// gentleartofblessing.org/interviews-with-pierre/316-video-interview-with-lilou-mace.)

Day 233
For Miracles

Fortunately, the universe does not function according to the Cartesian understanding of a material universe of material causes and effects, but according to the unlimited and gentle generosity of grace.

I bless myself in my understanding of the functioning of grace.

May I understand that where the materialistic mentality says, "Just impossible," my higher wisdom whispers to me, "What a glorious opening for a fresh vision of how the universe operates."

May I have the courage to shut out fear's chorus whispering the mantra: "Not enough, not enough, not enough," and replace it with Love's hymn, "You are always with me, and ALL that I have is yours too. *Infinite* abundance is my mode of operation."

May I see that where mortal mentality sees constant and growing division, the divine Mind sees present oneness and harmony between all its children.

Where rational cause-effect thinking claims limits as inherent to the human condition, may I see the omnipresence of unlimited possibility everywhere and at all times.

Day 234
Native American Blessings

Once more, here are two very brief Native American blessings with their special tone and gentleness.

May the stars carry your sadness away,
May the flowers fill your heart with beauty,
May hope forever wipe away your tears,
And above all, may silence make you strong.
(http://www.goodreads.com/quotes/72132-may-the-stars-carry-your-sadness-away-may-the-flowers)

Unspecified Origin
May you have the strength of eagle's wings,
The faith and courage to fly new heights,
And the wisdom of the universe
To carry you there.

Day 235
A Blessing on Following My Own Path

The stereotyped education of any culture or society tends inevitably to produce stereotyped forms of thinking and behaving. This is the very nature of the process called "socialization" which aims at making people conform to certain modes of behavior and customs including the path they should take in life. This blessing is for those who feel another calling.

I bless myself in my vision, ability and courage to truly follow my own path, however challenging this may be.

May I stay true to my deepest self, my divine self, which will always guide me in the right way. And may I do so without any aggressiveness, defensiveness or fear of losing some good if I step out of the secure highways of convention, custom, family or religious tradition.

May I truly understand that a path is formed by walking on it, however uneven its course and however far it takes me from the neon-lighted beaten track. And if doubt attempts to creep into my heart, may I choose the solitude and bracing winds of the unmapped plains over the crowded streets of social norms and security.

For divine Love has *already* mapped out my way to the amazing place that is awaiting me.

Day 236
A Blessing for Humility

Humility is a quality that is oft misunderstood. It does not mean groveling on the ground and trying to make oneself small or unimportant, nor battling with the ego or hiding it in the basement. It is more in line with a transparency to the divine acting through and especially as us. Rabindranath Tagore once wrote beautifully about becoming like a simple reed flute the divine could fill with its music.

I bless myself in the privilege of becoming clay in Your hands, O infinite Love, a song on Your lips, a windowpane so clear it fades away to let Your light shine through.

May I find my joy in the good deed done unnoticed and unheralded, the anonymous gift that brightens a heart captive of the fear of lack, the service performed with no thought of return of any sort.

May my heart sing as I labor in the dark, content to be Your tool.

And may I one day be so at one with You that even the sense of wanting to serve humbly disappears because I will have come to realize that You are I and I am You.

Day 237
An Ojibwa Blessing

May you walk in beauty, and may your eyes ever behold the red and purple sunsets.

May your hands respect the things the Great Spirit has made, and may your ears be sharp so you may hear the Great Spirit's voice.

May you be wise, so that you may understand what the Great Spirit has taught your people, and the lessons the Great Spirit has hidden in each leaf and each rock.

May you ask for wisdom and strength, not to be superior to your brothers and sisters, but to be able to fight your greatest enemy, yourself.

Day 238
Celtic and Irish Blessings

Ancient blessings incorporate the wisdom of centuries, which is why they still speak to us today.

Celtic
May the blessing of light be on you –
Light within and light without.
May the blessed sunlight shine on you
And warm your heart
till it glows like a great peat fire.

An Old Irish Blessing
May love and laughter light your days
and warm your heart and home.
May good and faithful friends be yours,
wherever you may roam.
May peace and plenty bless your world
with joy that long endures.
May all life's passing seasons
Bring the best to you and yours.
(Source: islandireland.com/Pages/folk/sets/bless.html)

Day 239
Love's Protection

There is no place we could go where divine Love has not been before us and no trial we can endure for which Love has not already planned both a lesson to learn, an opportunity to grow and a way out.

We bless ourselves in our understanding that Love's guarding presence can never be fooled nor sidetracked by error of any sort.

May we always trust that in the darkest cavern or the deepest abyss, Love's caring tenderness and unfailing strength will always uphold us.

Even if we appear to be on the road to nowhere, the ultimate dead-end street, the untrodden, most treacherous path, may we know and trust that Love's plan will always lead us to our divinely preordained destination.

When the heralds of materialism, all sirens wailing, scream: "There is no God, there is no hope, you are lost, all is falling through," may Love's quiet assurance shore up our hearts, return us to our green pastures and reduce our fears to their native nothingness.

When we "walk through the valley of the shadow of death," may we hold on to the serene understanding that Love's rod and Love's staff comfort and uphold us.

When faced with dark deception and the ultimate betrayal, may we quietly rejoice that Love's shield of truth will restore the innocence of the betrayer and the trust of the betrayed to their original wholeness.

Finally, should we feel at the very end of our tether, overwhelmed by life and feeling that just too many challenges are coming at the same time, may we find the ultimate rest in Love's assurance that we will never be tried beyond our ability to face the challenge.

Day 240
A Blessing for You My Friend

A friend sent me today's lovely blessing from Ralph Waldo Emerson which I have slightly adapted. It is a blessing just for you!

This is my blessing for you.

May you have comfort on difficult days and smiles when sadness intrudes. May rainbows follow your clouds and laughter kiss your lips. May sunsets warm your heart, and hugs abound when spirits sag.

May beauty open up for eyes to see, and may friendships brighten your being. May faith abound so that you can believe what is true and confidence appear when you doubt.

And may you have the courage to know yourself, patience to accept the truth and love to serenely complete your life.

Day 241
A Blessing to Simply Trust Divine Love

Jesus told us that unless we became as little children, we would not enter the "Kingdom" which of course is not a place, but a state of the consciousness of unconditional love and infinite contentment. Children are usually trustful by nature. Let us also learn from them to trust. The quotes are all from the Bible.

"Fear not, little flock, it is your Father's good pleasure to give you the Kingdom," the same Friend told us.

May we see that it does not have to be earned by virtuous living, good deeds or stringent discipline. May we rest deeply in the understanding that this gift is totally free. Just as the shepherd does not demand that his sheep produce good wool before leading them to the green pastures, may we relax totally in the understanding that the kingdom is ours by divine birthright – because it is already in us. Let go and let God.

May we trust in the promise of constant guidance because divine Love whispers to us, "I (infinite Love) will hold your hand and will keep you."

May we never fear for our daily bread but trust in the promise of infinite abundance provided by the Source of all good which tells us, "Prove me now herewith, if I will not open you the windows of heaven and pour you out a blessing that there shall not be room enough to receive it."

May we rest in the certainty of constant protection following the promise that "You, omnipotent Love, truly do protect me from behind, in front of me and You rest your hand upon me."

When we are (I am) hit with full force by tempest, trial or tsunami, may I know that I need not fear, because: "You sent from above, You took me, You brought me forth into a large place, You delivered me because You delighted in me."

And when the most grueling inner trial knocks me into the dungeon of despair and doubt, may I be reminded that all things (*every* single trial) will ultimately turn out to be a blessing.

May we trust the divine insight of the Master who told us that even the hairs of our head were counted, i.e. that an infinite Intelligence beyond all comprehension governs absolutely all, from the tiniest mental molecule to the rolling of the galaxies – which, somewhere in between, includes us too!

Day 242
A Blessing Affirming Divine Guidance of Our Lives

Retrospectively, so many people become aware of the fact that they were guided by an invisible hand, sometimes in the most treacherous situations, or that a decision which seemed very minor when it was taken changed the course of a lifetime. It is so comforting to really feel that we are not alone, that some incredibly loving Intelligence is really running the show, despite all appearances to the contrary.

May we rest in the calm assurance that a perfect plan is at all times running our lives, whatever we may feel.

When in some gigantic mess from which we see no way out, or hedged in by evil forces which seem to squash us, may we understand that the Gabriel of Love's presence has already mapped the way home.

When we feel we have made a mistake from which there is no return, the ultimate faux pas which does not forgive, may we be guided to see that the divine Mind is quietly rejoicing that only useful lessons are being learned.

Yes, we bless ourselves when faced with the most challenging decisions knowing that all things ultimately work for the good of them that follow their highest sense of truth.

We bless ourselves – when at a crossroads with no sign to guide us – in our ability to turn inside and find a signpost already awaiting us in our heart.

And finally, we bless You, infinite One, that You guide us in our passage from a material sense of existence to our ultimate spiritual destiny, from sense to Soul.

Day 243

For Children of Separated or Divorced Parents, or When a Parent Just Disappears

Divorces have become such a frequent phenomenon they go almost unnoticed – in my home city, Geneva, over 60 percent of marriages end in divorce. And in many cases, one of the two parents simply disappears (often with a lover), never to reappear. For the children involved, especially at younger ages, it can be deeply traumatic. Let us hold them so close to our hearts as we say this blessing.

Our hearts go out to the children whose families have been torn or deeply challenged by divorce or unexpected separation.

May they find in themselves the courage to face the situation with fortitude, strength and serenity.

May they gain the wisdom that enables them not to make either parent feel guilty nor to make any accusations. And especially may they never be tempted to feel that they are in any way to blame.

May they on the contrary become agents of healing for their parents and siblings as they receive their own inner healing through the workings of grace.

When tempted to be torn between loyalties, to feel discouraged or even abandoned, may they understand that they, and their parents as well, are always embraced by an unconditional, all-encompassing divine loving Presence which will guide and protect them always.

And may the inner growth they will attain during this challenge enable them to develop the compassion to help friends going through similar trials.

Day 244
God Be Me

This blessing is by the Rev. Jim Cotter from his book Prayer at Night. *It is also used in the foreword of Caroline Myss' book,* Anatomy of the Spirit.

God Be

God be in my head and in my understanding
God be in my eyes and in my looking
God be in my mouth and in my speaking
God be in my tongue and in my tasting
God be in my lips and in my greeting
God be in my nose and in my smelling/inhaling
God be in my ears and in my hearing
God be in my neck and in my humbling
God be in my shoulders and in my bearing
God be in my back and in my standing
God be in my arms and in my reaching/receiving
God be in my hands and in my working
God be in my legs and in my walking
God be in my feet and in my grounding
God be in my joints and in my relating
God be in my gut and in my feeling
God be in my bowels and in my forgiving
God be in my loins and in my swiving
God be in my lungs and in my breathing
God be in my heart and in my loving
God be in my skin and in my touching
God be in my flesh and in my paining/pining
God be in my blood and in my living
God be in my bones and in my dying
God be at my end and at my reviving

Day 245

Harmony Restored Before Concert (Testimony)

With a Cameroonian friend, I was organizing a benefit concert in favor
of peasant-farmer groups in Senegal. The concert had been publicized
on the radio and in the local press, and was to be held in the large

auditorium of a college which was lending it to us free of charge.

However, the technician cum caretaker of the college would have nothing to do with our concert, and the college director informed us that he could not force the technician to work after office hours! So we had to call upon the services of another technician from another college.

Two hours before the concert, my Cameroonian friend and I arrived to see if everything was in order. Upon arriving on stage, we were distressed to discover there were only two mikes left. We went to see the caretaker who was extremely hostile towards us.

At first, I felt anger, but a little voice inside me said, "Pierre, you are not going to resolve this situation with anger. Just bless him." And while he was talking aggressively to my friend, I just started pouring blessings on him.

Suddenly, between two sentences, his whole face lit up with a big smile, he went to his laboratory, came back with a whole pile of mikes and wished us a splendid evening. This is how it turned out to be – thanks to the art of blessing!

(Pierre, Switzerland)

Day 246
A Blessing by Laurel Burch

Laurel Burch, a self-taught artist-painter in California, left home at 14 with a paper bag in which were a few clothes, and a serious bone disease, osteoporosis. Still a teenager, she started making such original necklaces people would stop her in the street to enquire about them. That was the beginning of the career of a remarkable woman who once said, "I refuse to have anything in my life I can't turn into something magical and beautiful." We can do the same and blessing is a wonderful tool for magically turning all into beauty, whatever the initial appearance.

May we live life like a sacred dance
and from our hearts speak our truth
and from our souls find our courage.

May we stand strong,
May we soar high
Believing in ourselves and one another.

Day 247
Seeing the Day with Fresh Eyes

The Irish people have produced such a rich lore of blessings adapted to all situations. Here is another one.

May you see the world each day with fresh eyes.

May you always know day from night, true from false, wisdom from convenience.

May your every step be on firm earth.

May you see through illusion to reality.

May you bring splendor and joy to all you touch.

May you always know what it is to live in freedom.

May you be a support to those who have fallen, a guide to those who wander to return to their true path.

May your needs be fulfilled.

May you draw strength from your community.

May you be part of the splendor that crowns Israel.

May you remember in whose image you are created.

May you remember the joy of freedom even in times of bondage.

On life's path, may you never know weariness of body, mind or spirit.

(Source: http://islandireland.com/Pages/folk/sets/bless.html)

Day 248
Lakota Instructions for Living

I have slightly adapted the first four paragraphs of these beautiful Lakota instructions which show how far in advance of us these original inhabitants of the United States were centuries ago in the

understanding of the links of all things.
Friend, may you do it this way – that is,
whatever you do in life,
may you do the very best you can
with both your heart and mind.
And if you do it that way,
the Power Of The Universe
will come to your assistance,
if your heart and mind are in Unity.
When one sits in the Hoop Of The People,
one must be responsible because
All of Creation is related.
And the hurt of one is the hurt of all.
And the honor of one is the honor of all.
And whatever we do affects everything in the universe.
If you do it that way – that is,
if you truly join your heart and mind
as One – whatever you ask for,
that's the Way It's Going To Be.
(Passed down from White Buffalo Calf Woman)
(Source: www.sapphyr.net/natam/quotes-nativeamerican.
htm)

Day 249
Blessing for Earth-Healers

Traditional cultures have almost always been deeply respectful of the earth and its resources. However, now, even in the West, a new race of Earth-healers is spreading, hopefully in time to save Mother Earth from major wounds of which we would be the first victims. Let us support them by our blessings.

We give thanks for all those who are moved,
in their lives, to heal and protect the earth,
in small ways and in large.

Blessings on the composters, the gardeners,
the breeders of worms and mushrooms, the soil-builders,
those who cleanse the waters and purify the air,
all those who clean up the messes others have made.
Blessings on those who defend trees and who plant trees,
who guard the forests and who renew the forests.
Blessings on those who learn to heal the grasslands
and renew the streams, on those who prevent erosion,
who restore the salmon and the fisheries,
who guard the healing herbs and who know the lore of the
wild plants.
Blessings on those who heal the cities and bring them alive
again with excitement and creativity and love.
Gratitude and blessings to all who stand against greed,
who risk themselves, to those who have bled and been
wounded, and to those who have given their lives in service of
the earth.

(Source: excerpt from The Earth Path: Grounding Your
Spirit in the Rhythms of Nature by Starhawk, quoted in: www.
blessingfiles.wordpress.com)

Day 250
A Franciscan Blessing

*Henri Nouwen has said that "to give someone a blessing... is more
than a word of praise or appreciation; it is more than pointing to one's
talents or good deed; it is more than putting someone in the light. To
give a blessing is to say 'yes' to a person's belovedness." Here is a
blessing from that rich lore of Franciscan spirituality.*

May God bless you with discomfort
at easy answers, half-truths and superficial relationships
so that you may live deep within your heart.
May God bless you with anger
at injustice, oppression and exploitation of people

so that you may work for justice, freedom and peace.
May God bless you with tears
to shed for those who suffer pain, rejection, hunger and war
so that you may reach out your hand to comfort them and
to turn their pain into joy.
May God bless you with foolishness
to believe that you can make a difference in the world
so that you can do what others claim cannot be done
to bring justice and kindness to all our children and the poor.
(Source: http://blessingfiles.wordpress.com)

Day 251
A Blessing to be a Tool of Love's Healing Touch

Dr. Joe Dispenza is one of the key players in the emergence of the New Medicine that is helping to profoundly transform the inhabitants of this planet. In one of his collective e-mails received early January 2016, there is a stunning brief video of Elsa Saks, an Estonian-born adventurer of life and the spirit, who decided to cycle through seven Central American countries using gratitude as her only currency. It is an incredible tribute to the power of love, which Elsa says met her every need. It inspired the following blessing.

We bless ourselves in our ability to see the love that undergirds all reality, whatever the material appearances to the contrary.

We bless ourselves in our ability to see all with the eyes of love, saint or sinner, angel or villain.

We bless ourselves in the understanding that sees absolutely every single encounter, challenge, fear, appearance of lack… as an opportunity to grow in love.

May we meet every hurting soul with the oil of compassion which lifts up, consoles, and pours the healing balm of love on every wound or resentment, every hatred or hurt.

May we meet every broken or solitary heart with the gentle companionship of love so that those concerned may feel the deep caring born of such solicitude.

May love be our constant inspiration and energy – and mold every thought, word, deed or feeling which we express, that those we encounter may experience us as the very presence of the Divine in its radiant splendor.

Day 252
For Those Consumed by Anger, Hatred or Resentment

Few attitudes are more harmful to those who harbor them than the three above-mentioned ones – not to speak of their environment. One cannot help feeling the deepest compassion for people who are eaten up, especially by resentment, which is a bit like a rat gnawing at your entrails (which is what is does to your immune system!). Let our hearts be literally inhabited by this compassion as we carry them in our blessings.

My heart goes out to all those who are consumed by all dark emotions such as resentment or hate.

I bless them in their consciousness of the harm they are doing to themselves by harboring such dubious companions in their hearts, not to mention their human environment.

May they abandon all attempts to justify their attitude by any injustice, loss or harm of which they might have been victim by understanding that such persistence in error just mires them deeper into the pit they have dug for themselves.

May the divine essence hidden in their soul awaken in them the deep yearning to be free of these heavy chains and their constant clutter as they drag them through life.

And finally, may they harken the whispers of love gently prodding them to awaken from their zombie-like state of mind and yearn for the glorious liberty and green pastures of forgiveness.

Day 253

A Blessing for Every Day

I would like to rename this beautiful blessing (which its author Debbie Ford entitled "Drenched in Holiness: Prayer for a New Year") simply: A Blessing for Every Day, as it expresses what so many people would like to live by.

Dear God,

On this day I ask You to grant this request.

May I know who I am and what I am, every moment of every day.

May I be a catalyst for light and love, and bring inspiration to those whose eyes I meet.

May I have the strength to stand tall in the face of conflict, and the courage to speak my voice, even when I'm scared.

May I have the humility to follow my heart, and the passion to live my soul's desires.

May I seek to know the highest truth and dismiss the gravitational pull of my lower self.

May I embrace and love the totality of myself, my darkness as well as my light.

May I be brave enough to hear my heart,

To let it soften so that I may gracefully choose faith over fear.

Today is my day to surrender anything that stands

Between the sacredness of my humanity and my divinity.

May I be drenched in my Holiness

And engulfed by Your love.

May all else melt away.

And so it is.

Day 254

For Children Who Have Temper Tantrums

A moment ago I was on the bus and a child entered with her mother.

There and then, the child threw a real tantrum. I had my notebook ready as I was preparing to write a blessing or two, and here was the golden opportunity to live it first. The child calmed down in a few moments and I proceeded to write this blessing.

I bless this precious mother and her sisters in motherhood everywhere in their unlimited patience.

I bless her in seeing that right where there appears to be a rebellious, screaming child, right there, just beyond the veil, is the very presence of God, Life, Love smiling at her and teaching her to uplift her vision to the true spiritual reality.

I bless her child that she may feel the boundless kindness of Soul moving in her heart and prompting her to gentler responses and greater dominion.

I bless all parents raising their offspring in the tremendously provocative environment of a totally connected world and the enormous challenges it poses for all those working with children. I bless them in their understanding that, for some, to simply grow up normal can be a feat.

And I again bless all parents faced with frequent tantrums and similar situations in their unfailing self-control and settled serenity.

Day 255
A Blessing for Awareness of the Divine Presence

For numerous mystics and spiritual seekers, feeling the presence of the divine has been a major spiritual practice. However, to paraphrase Rumi on love, we may well try to describe the divine Presence, but when we truly experience it, we are utterly speechless. So we again return to this theme which for many has been the foundation of spiritual practice.

May the warmth of Love's Presence be felt all through this day. May we rejoice that no circumstance of any sort can sever us from this ever comforting companionship with the Divine.

Behind the eyes of every person I meet, may I become aware of Your constant Presence. And may the wonders of nature remind those who have a heart to see of the beauty of Your resplendent face everywhere.

From the incessant or strident clamor of the city or workplace to the anxious waiting of some feared outcome or decision, may I take refuge in Your gentle, ever-available Presence and therein find my peace.

When in the parched plains of deep doubt, the clamor of battle, or when I shout out to You and hear no response, when my friends abandon me and life itself appears to close down on all sides, may I descend into the hidden cloister of my heart and discover You had never left me.

May I above all learn to savour and truly cherish the gentle sweetness and quiet strength of this Presence surrounding me on all sides, hovering above me, constituting the very ground on which I walk – for truly it is a paradise that none can steal, that years cannot corrupt, that suffering or injustice cannot tarnish. *This* is my eternal home.

Day 256
A Blessing for Friends

We borrow this written as a prayer for friendship from Marianne Williamson's book Illuminata: A Return to Prayer *(section on friendship).*

May angels fill their nights and bless their days.
May they find peace and joy and harmony.
May I be a source of happiness in their lives.
May our bonds be strong and based on truth.
May they always know that in me, they have support.
May I live a life that supports this prayer.

Between Friends

We surrender this relationship to You.
May it serve Your purposes and be blessed by You always.
Fill our minds with Your thoughts.
May we always be led to the highest vision of each other.
Remove any obstructions to our highest love.
May we find joy, and peace, and harmony.

Day 257

A Blessing for Joy

A spiritual life without joy is missing an essential ingredient. One of the great spiritual leaders and avatars to walk this planet, Jesus, when sharing his vision with his followers, implied that this vision, understood, would bring with it perfect joy. However, one does not strive for joy for joy's sake – it is often the result of giving one's self to a higher purpose.

I bless You, infinite One, for having created JOY!

For what is life without joy but honey without sweetness or a bird without wings!

I bless myself in letting that joy well up from deep inside me where it always was and always shall be.

I bless myself in my opening to that unexpected joy which suddenly fills our heart like the sun breaking through the clouds invades all with its warm rays – a pure gift of grace.

May my life be a canticle of joy that uplifts the brokenhearted and the desolate and those in prisons of their own making.

In the quiet sanctuary of true listening, may I still all inner noise and mind's interminable ramblings until I hear that deep inner silence from which all spiritual joy is born.

And may my life become that special space where the geyser of Your joy springs forth into eternity.

Day 258
Blessing Brings Deep Peace After a Theft (Testimony)

Recently, I was on the train, entering phone numbers into my iPhone, with my laptop in a closed black cover in a black bag touching my thigh. Sometime later, I happened to look for my laptop... and no laptop. Someone had managed to steal it without either me or the many people on neighboring seats realizing what was happening.

The very second (not the very minute) I became aware of the theft, I started blessing the person concerned in their integrity and abundance (because if you steal you necessarily suffer from some deep feeling of lack of some kind), in their goodness and peace, for quite a while. Immediately I was overwhelmed by that "peace that passes all understanding," a peace I had not felt for a very long time. This was followed by a deep sense of the most sincere compassion for the person concerned. My heart really went out to them. Can you imagine what it must mean to spend your life stealing from others? Your brothers and sisters? What state of mind that person must be in. Even now, as I type this message, my heart is filled with a deep desire that this person change their ways, first of all for their OWN good (not to mention all the other people concerned), if they have not already done so.

Blessing is the ultimate healing balm, and the ultimate protection from so many forms of evil. Dressed in the armor of love, human hatred cannot touch us (and blessing is one of the highest, purest forms of love).

(Pierre, Switzerland)

Day 259
A Blessing to See God Everywhere

Hafiz was one of the very greatest Sufi poets. In the beautiful translation of his poems by Daniel Ladinsky (The Gift), there is this poem entitled simply "Everywhere" in which the poet describes a series of completely crazy acts like tying everything he owns to a stick and setting it on fire

and he concludes:
What else can Hafiz do tonight
To celebrate the madness
The Joy,
Of seeing God
Everywhere.
His poem inspired this blessing.

I bless myself in my ability to see God everywhere, from a small tuft of moss on a piece of bark to the endless forests of Siberia and the Amazon,

From the tiny mountain stream to the huge expanses of the world's oceans, from the mental molecule to the rolling of the galaxies in the heavens.

May I see You in the eyes of sinners as well as of saints, be it the murderer I visit in jail or the mystic in ecstasy on a mountaintop.

God, God, only God everywhere.

In the acid taste of a freshly pressed lemon and the sweetest wild honey I discover in the hollow of a tree,

From the trial that knocks me flat at the bottom of the canyon of soaring granite cliffs where I travel in deep pain to the lush green pastures where Your Grace awaits me,

In the awesome silence under the star-spread heaven in yonder valley to the roaring rush of the busy city street,

In the joy-filled pilgrims flocking to the holy shrine and the terror-filled refugees fleeing a pitiless foe,

God, God, only God, everywhere, all the time.

What else?

Day 260
For Learning to Love Well

Jack Kornfield is someone one could call one of the true American sages of the day. We have simply given this prayer of his the form

of a blessing.

May I in all things learn to love well.

May I learn to touch the ever-changing seasons of life with a great heart of compassion.

May I live with the peace and justice I wish for the earth

May I learn to care fully and let go gracefully

May I enjoy the abundance of the earth

May I, through my own life, thought, word, and deed, bring benefit to all that lives,

That my heart and the hearts of all beings learn to be free.

(http://www.onespiritinterfaith.org/2013/09/september-2-2013-jack-kornfield/)

Day 261

A Blessing to See Everyone's Innocence

Many years ago I had an incredibly powerful mystical experience. I was in the streetcar in my home town of Geneva, Switzerland, going to a meeting, and I suddenly not only saw but felt the absolute, radical innocence of every single person in the vehicle. When I got off, it continued in the street, and I felt like raising my arms and shouting at the top of my voice, "You are innocent, you are innocent..." However, as that might have led me to the local lunatic asylum, I held my peace!

I bless myself in seeing the radical innocence of every single one of Your children.

From high level generals to mafia leaders, from heartless speculators or pimps to greedy businesspeople or pedophile priests, through all the categories of those whom society castigates and rejects as unmoral, criminal or worse, may I hold on to seeing what You do see: the utterly guiltless nature of every single one of Your creations.

However loudly society may scream and condemn the guilt of fellow humans, may I insist and persist in seeing what You so clearly see and only see: guiltless being.

May I also discern that this vision has nothing to do with what the material eyes behold or the society or media describe, but with the vision that Soul instills in my heart.

May my compassion be so deep that I prefer companying with grace so as to visualize people's innocence than joining the loud bandwagon of society's jeers and outrage.

And may I steadfastly hold them in Love's sight, thereby hastening the day of awakening which shall one day come to them as surely as the sun rises each morning.

Day 262
A Blessing for Child Soldiers

The website www.dosomething.org states that: "Child soldiers are any children under the age of 18 who are recruited by a state or non-state armed group and used as fighters, cooks, suicide bombers, human shields, messengers, spies, or for sexual purposes. In the last 15 years, the use of child soldiers has spread to almost every region of the world and every armed conflict. Though an exact number is impossible to define, thousands of child soldiers are illegally serving in armed conflicts around the world. Some children are under the age of 10 when they are forced to serve." There are also many very young girls among them. They urgently need our blessings.

From our heart of hearts, we bless children who are abducted and forced to serve in armed conflicts.

We bless them in their innocence, that despite the trying and sometimes dramatic situations they are in, deep down inside them the consciousness of this innocence stays awake.

We bless them in their fundamental integrity, that the horrendous things they are forced to witness and often to accomplish may not erase their desire to escape from the human hell they have been forced into, or their belief in another more humane and normal life and the possibility of one day achieving it.

We bless them in their consciousness of their oneness with

You and of their essentially perfect divine identity.

When they walk through death canyon, may Your hand keep them safe from all evil – both from performing it or being its victim.

When solitude, hunger, sheer despair or the desire to give up on life cruelly grips them, may the comforting presence of Grace support them and lift them up.

And finally, we bless the adults who so uncaringly force children who could be their own into such situations that Your Spirit may awaken them to their true nature as children of God.

Day 263
A Simple Blessing

In the following blessing by Susan Larson, I have simply replaced the word "tomorrow" by "today" in the last line.

May God give you perspective on the things that frustrate you.

May your heart of compassion grow for those who suffer in unimaginable ways.

May you pray as passionately for them as you do for yourself.

May God protect you from a small, selfish mindset.

May He fill you up with thanksgiving and joy for the freedoms you enjoy!

May He renew your resolve to be a grateful, humble soul.

And may He use you today in ways that surprise and bless you!

(Source: www.afriendofjesus2013.com)

Day 264
A Blessing for My Positive Impact on Life

We are collectively realizing more and more clearly that our every thought, word or deed has an impact somewhere in the world. And it is my deeply held belief that every single sincere blessing, prayer, or meditation, if impelled by love and a clear intent and practiced with perseverance, has an impact, however modest. This is so encouraging, especially in the rather wild world we live in, because so many people don't believe they can have any significant impact on events. If ever you believe they are too small to make any significant impact on the world, remember the statement attributed to the Dalai Lama, "If you think you are too small to make a difference, try sleeping with a mosquito." It weighs less than 25 million times your weight (2.5 milligrams) but its impact on you...

I bless myself in my surrendering of every thought, word and deed to the divine Love that runs this universe.

May my every thought go out like a gentle spring breeze, blessing all Your children worldwide, wherever they may be, from my neighbors through a Johannesburg shanty town to a Wall Street trader's room.

May my every word inspire, uplift and heal, from the stressed salesgirl who fears for her job to the street mendicant who pulls at my shirtsleeve, from the self-important university professor who looks down upon me to the fresh-eyed young volunteer distributing leaflets in the street.

May my eyes, wherever they rest, be like a soothing balm, a ray of sunshine, a messenger of gratitude and love to all they rest upon, beggar, bird, beast or bush.

May my every deed be a conduit for Your Love, lived in mindfulness and total attention, with no aim but to bless my neighbor and further Your Kingdom on earth.

And may my every feeling touch all those around me like the invisible but so present odor of the lavender bush wafting through the atmosphere in the spring.

Day 265

A Blessing by Buddhist Teacher Thich Nhat Hanh

Today we will be inspired by his blessing: "May I be peaceful, happy, and light in body and mind."

May I be safe and free from accidents.

May I be free from anger, unwholesome states of mind, fear, and worries.

May I know how to look at myself with the eyes of understanding and love.

May I be able to recognize and touch the seeds of joy and happiness in myself.

May I learn how to nourish myself with joy each day.

May I be able to live fresh, solid and free.

May I not fall into the state of indifference or be caught in extremes and aversion.

Day 266

For the Happiness of All People

There are probably few aspirations on which more people in the world could agree upon than the desire for happiness. Which explains the presence of a second blessing on this theme. Our consumer culture, with the active collaboration of so many of us, has created and continues to feed the myth (or huge lie) that accumulating possessions or money can increase happiness, when often the exact contrary is true. I have encountered in some of the poorest areas of the world where I have lived people owning almost nothing who radiated happiness.

I bless all the inhabitants of this magical planet in their deep, deep happiness.

May they discover that it is first and foremost a state of profound inner contentment and not of outer signs of wealth.

May they discover that it flows much more from what we

give than what we receive, from saying YES – THANK YOU to life in *all* circumstances.

I bless us all in our clear understanding that the "Kingdom of Heaven" – that space of deep inner peace, quiet, radiant joy, unshakable trust, which is the hallmark of true happiness – *IS* within us, as a great teacher once told us, and that we don't need to run after something that is already ours, albeit hidden in the most secret chamber of our heart.

Finally, may I above all become conscious that happiness is not a delicate plant to be fearfully protected from the frost or hail in a greenhouse, but a gift to be shared with all, a garden where all are invited to rest and pick the flowers of their choice.

Day 267
A Blessing for Security

Some theorists of human behavior have postulated that the search for security is the basic striving of humankind: security in food resources, in relations, in health, in income, protection from dangers of all sorts… the list is endless (and for some would include salvation!). At the same time, spiritual seers of all climes and times have reminded us again and again that true security is first and foremost to be found in the Divine. The spiritual literature is interspersed with so many instances of just amazing protection in apparently totally helpless situations, stressing that insurances, vaccines or sophisticated locks are perhaps not the last word in terms of security.

I bless myself (my family, my community, my country…) in my (our) understanding that true security is first and foremost to be found in divine Love's government of all things.

May I accept a divine Master's promise that "I give you power to tread on serpents and scorpions and over all the power of the enemy: and *nothing* shall by any means hurt you" – and that the "serpents and scorpions" of modern life no longer hold sway over me.

I bless myself in my grasp that, however somber a material or human situation may appear, there is a divine law that supersedes all human means and efforts, however valorous they may be.

May I understand that however hopeless a medical diagnosis may sound, there is the higher diagnosis of divine Love that can overturn any limited human prediction, whatever its claims to scientific validity which are always terribly limited and hypothetical.

When the media depict some imminent catastrophe – financial or other – and despite every material appearance to the contrary, may I hear the silent yet insistent whisper of Soul inside me saying "all is well, all is well, all is very, very well" for "divine Love *is* my Shepherd and I shall not want" – ever.

Day 268
A Blessing for a Husband/Wife/Companion Who Has Left Home

The following is just one of the numerous testimonies of the impact of blessing I have been receiving over the years, taken from the blessing website (gentleartofblessing.org):

"My husband S. fell in love with another woman and then left a couple of months ago to live with her. Although my initial reactions were shock, anger and resentment while I came from a place of fear (mainly of being on my own without him), I quickly started to bless them both (and myself of course!) and the transformation was almost immediate... I felt guided to write two letters of forgiveness, thanks and blessings just a couple of days ago after he left: one was to both of them if he chose to stay with her and the other was to her if he chose to return to me and our children. I still have those letters and I am not sure whether I will ever send either one of them but they have helped me now to arrive where I know there is nothing to forgive as I myself called this forth! For what purpose I am not entirely sure, though I

have during the last few months started to be able to love myself after all these years."

(Karen)

I bless myself in my ability to forgive...... (his or her name) for their departure from our home, and to see that they were at their highest level of consciousness and still are now.

I forgive myself totally for any eventual shortcoming on my part which may have contributed to or caused their departure.

Despite my pain, may I learn to bless them and their new partner in the integrity of their relationship and their happiness together.

I bless myself in my understanding that behind the pain of this experience there is an infinitely precious and important lesson awaiting us both.

(If any children): I bless the children that they may receive the strength and understanding to weather this immense challenge with serenity and trust in their capacity to cope with it.

And finally, I bless myself in my ability to face this trial with wisdom and courage and to learn, every step of the way, to trust in the infinite plan for good Providence *has* already outlined for me and mine.

Day 269
A Blessing for Increased Trust

It is extremely difficult to function adequately in life when one lives in constant worry or fear that something might go wrong. Some try to manage this by being control freaks, which just represses the fear without healing it. But the picture changes completely if one believes in a loving Providence which guides all.

I bless myself in my ability to just let go and let God.

When faced with an apparently insurmountable challenge, may I remember that miracles are Love's normal way of functioning.

When feeling deeply unsettled or fearful because of the state of the world, the environment or some other major planetary or international issue, may I remember that the oriental carpet, which seen from below is just a medley of woolen strands, viewed from above is a picture of perfect harmony, beauty and color.

When faced with raving anger or outright hatred, may I trust in the serene power of love to nonviolently heal the situation.

If misled, cheated, deceived, or wronged in any way, may I trust in the power of forgiveness to set right or repair all wrongs and may I make myself this supreme gift of forgiving all and everything.

May I trust that, however confused the path or direction, Your guarding angel walks beside me and Your comforting Presence always surrounds me, that however somber the night, the light of truth pierces the darkest shadows.

Finally, may I trust that whatever mistakes I make, Your infinite goodness ultimately settles all things right.

Day 270
Welcoming a Child into the World

What will tomorrow's world be like? Some believe it could be a mighty, mighty strange place with robots taking over human activities in all areas, even running the place according to some no longer science fiction scenarios, with an environment which could be causing tens of millions to emigrate from coastal zones… Or maybe the Bright New World some predict? At least now, uncertainty is the dominant key.

We bless…… (name of child) who is joining us in this amazing and challenging adventure called humankind advancing.

We bless them in their ability to face the immense challenges that their generation will certainly have to meet. We bless them in their constant adaptability, creativity and inventiveness as they face unsettling or strange conditions.

We bless them in their resiliency to potential pressures of all sorts, their courage and openness when faced with dangers and possibly strange beings from other planets.

We bless them in their keeping a firm grip on their vision, in their "hitching their chariot to a star."

We bless them in their firm rootedness in the practice of love as the ultimate power enabling them to say "YES" to any and every situation they will encounter in their life, to those persons or situations which would attempt to frighten, humiliate or tempt them, or discourage them from following their highest calling.

And we also bless them in their green pastures that they may therein rest and dance, be joyful and creative without ever dropping their vigilance and alertness.

And we bless them in their unshakeable trust in Providence that watches over their every step, that furnishes them with the wisdom and insight to follow their own path, the resilience, determination and grit to never, ever give up, the clear intention that can never be swayed and the vision that ignites a flame in their eyes and draws a smile on their lips.

Day 271

Blessing Heals Resentment and Solves a Problem (Testimony)

"Some time ago I gave a very precious garden bench to a local carpenter for repairs. The bill for the job hit the ceiling, but I decided to pay without comments because this bench (which could comfortably seat four people) was so precious to me.

However, immediately after paying the bill just after the work was delivered, I noticed two large, deep cracks in the woodwork. I immediately flared up inside. How dare this man deliver the bench with such a glaring imperfection? I jumped on the phone and immediately called him, but was told he was in a meeting. As he lived in a nearby township, I decided to drive to his shop. Such a bill for such shoddy finishing! I would tell him what I thought of this, me, such a good client.

As I drove to his place, a little voice in me said: what about trying blessing? So I immediately started blessing him – in his diligence, his craftsmanship, his integrity, etc. Of course, this produced an instant change of heart, and when I reached his shop my tone was warm and friendly and he immediately apologized profusely and came to fetch the bench which he finished to perfection."

(Marie Louise, Switzerland)

Day 272
To Express Our Greatness

The Sufi poet and thinker Rumi is for many people one of the greatest poets ever and, with Hafiz, probably the greatest Sufi poet. In one of his wonderful non-dual aphorisms, he makes this startling statement: "Stop acting so small. You are the universe in ecstatic motion." So...

I bless myself in my infinite grandeur

... as God expressing Itself,

... as God smiling at you and all those I meet,

... as God quietly rejoicing in seeing Its reflection everywhere and Its perfection in all.

I bless myself in my wide-open heart ready to welcome the downtrodden and the sick, the fearful and faint-hearted, the sinner and the saint, the most inglorious scoundrel and those who humbly serve... and all those ready to sit at my table that I may serve them the food that truly restores.

I bless myself in my understanding that my only greatness is being Your greatness expressed, that I can only love authentically if I am a total transparency of Your Love, that I can only act wisely as I allow the divine Mind to be my mind.

Oh! I truly rejoice in and bless myself as the universe, You, infinite Love, in ecstatic motion.

Day 273
Another Blessing for Prisoners in Solitary Confinement

As one who has visited a prisoner in solitary confinement on death row in the US for 12 years, I can confirm the horror of this practice in cells 45–60 square feet, with no human contact of any sort, sometimes even with no windows. It is only in 2016 that President Obama stopped the practice of this "cruel and unusual punishment" (supposedly banned by the Eighth Amendment of the US constitution) for juveniles – but in federal prisons only. Long-term inmates of solitary spend an average of over eight years in total isolation, the record being 43 years (Albert Woodfox, released February 2016). It is more and more considered an abuse of human rights and a form of torture (which of course it is).

We bless our brothers and sisters in solitary confinement all around the world.

We bless them in their resilience, their indomitable courage, their fearlessness and especially their trust in a Providence which, despite all appearances to the contrary, never, never abandons them.

We bless them in their ability to maintain their mental balance in an environment with often not the slightest mental stimulation of any sort.

We bless their families and friends that they keep up contacts with them despite the drag of time as year upon year piles up. We bless the officers who supervise them in their authentic compassion that they may always remember that they are their brother's keeper, not only physically, but especially spiritually.

We bless their lawyers that they never tire of taking any legal steps that could lighten their plight. We bless the victims that they may realize that resentment and vengeance harms them more than anyone else, and we bless the inmates in their ability to forgive themselves.

Finally, we bless the politicians that they be led to "do as you would be done by" and the citizens of all countries that they work in all ways possible to end this affront to human dignity and compassion.

Day 274
Blessing to Heal World Belief of Lack

It is my conviction that the belief of lack is the world's number one problem: lack of time, of compassion, of work, of money, of health, of creative ideas, of solutions, of tolerance, of housing, of safety, of customers, of opportunities, of self-confidence, of a future... you name it, it is everywhere. Even billionaires who own 20, 30 billion or more want still more! Yet we have already quoted the biblical promise that if we trusted we would receive blessings that there shall not be room enough to receive all the abundance available.

I bless myself in my ability to see abundance where the human mind sees lack.

Where a homeless person is quietly sobbing in the street, may I be aware of the abundance of love and possibly practical help I have to give.

Where a parched earth cries out to a brazen sky, may I see in my mind the clouds heavy with rain ready to pour forth their treasures.

Where there appears to be a desperate lack of fresh, new ideas, may I rejoice in omnipresent Mind, available to all.

When I seem to be pressed by a lack of time, may I be reminded that my every minute belongs to divine Love which supports me in my endeavor to express it in the present moment, the only time that will ever exist.

When I appear to be lacking in funds or some pressing need shouts for attention, may I become alert to the fact that the "Kingdom of God," the one and only source of all true abundance, is within me.

Oh, I bless myself in my ability to discover the Niagara of Your grace just awaiting to pour onto me and all.

Day 275
A Blessing to Raise World Consciousness

The number one priority for the planet today is not eliminating poverty and extreme hunger or peace between nations, cleaning up the environment or reducing growing income disparities, although all these issues and many others are vitally important. It is raising individual – and hence collective – consciousness. And there, we are all the Number One player. And before reading this blessing, if so moved, please reread the text by Alyna Rouelle in the middle of this book on the power of meditation to heal (page 159).

I bless myself in my grasp of the infinite beauty of a world where ALL IS CONSCIOUSNESS.

May I see that every single one of my thoughts contributes to the barometer of our collective consciousness, pushing it up or pulling it down.

I bless myself in understanding that, because we are all linked by One infinite Mind every time I take special care of my environment, I am helping all humans do the same, wherever they may be.

May I rejoice that every positive, loving, awakened thought I have is a building block in the new win-win world we are all building together.

May I find deep meaning and joy in mentally reversing all negativity I am alerted to, and become aware that the divine understanding is the only true understanding, is literally *all*, and that at a higher plane, there *is* no other consciousness.

May I include every single being, animal, plant or so-called material object that comes my way in my consciousness that I may bless it, respect it and treat it with love.

And may my blessings be so part of my consciousness that

they no longer need words but become simply a deep and unceasing yearning for the good and happiness of all creation, myself included.

Day 276
Bat Mitzvah Blessing

It would be unconceivable to publish such a book and not include a traditional Jewish blessing, so important is this practice in the Jewish faith.

May you live to see your world fulfilled,
May you be our link to future worlds,
and may your hope encompass all the generations to be.
May your heart conceive with understanding,
may your mouth speak wisdom
and your tongue be stirred with sounds of joy.
May your gaze be straight and sure,
your eyes be lit with Torah's lamp,
your face aglow with heaven's radiance,
your lips expressing words of knowledge,
and your inner self alive with righteousness.
And may you always rush in eagerness to hear
the words of One more ancient than all time.
– *Talmud Berachot 17a*
(Source: https://blessingfiles.wordpress.com/2011/)

Day 277
A Blessing for Oppressed Native Peoples

All round the world, native groups have been oppressed and often purely and simply eradicated (Brazil and other Latin American countries, USA during the colonization of North America by the Europeans, many parts of Asia, Africa and Australia). Apart from a few occasional observers, only very recently have we been discovering the incredible wealth of wisdom and knowledge these people have cultivated over the centuries... and which large pharmaceutical multinationals are now exploiting for their own benefit.

We bless our sisters and brothers whom we have so long considered "uncivilized" as stewards of immense wisdom which might one day be of great value for our own survival.

We bless them in their consciousness of their value for the contemporary world, and of the unique worth of the storehouse of knowledge of nature and its plants they represent.

We bless them in their ability to resist the innumerable physical, chemical, cultural, religious and other aggressions, including the outright occupation of their lands, which have over the years decimated or destroyed so many of them.

We bless them in their capacity to combine with sensitivity and wisdom the best of their own traditions and the good that modern civilization can nevertheless bring to them.

We bless ourselves in our ability to treat these peoples with the deepest respect we are capable of, and to repair to the utmost the harm already done so that together we may move, each in our own unique way, towards a world that works for all.

Day 278

A Blessing for a Clearer Understanding of God's Allness

Mystics of many spiritual backgrounds, ages and countries have claimed that there is another totally harmonious reality behind the veil of material appearances. And when we bless following the approach explained in the brief text "The Gentle Art of Blessing" we are referring to and appealing to this other "real" reality. Hence the importance of grasping its nature.

I bless myself in my understanding of the true reality of being behind the distorted veil of the material appearances. I bless myself in my ability to still the stridency of the material senses and the rational mind which really believe they understand something of true reality.

I bless myself in my desire to still my emotions that I may simply feel the divine happening within.

May I truly grasp that the reality of Your Presence admits of no contests, that whatever the rattling and ranting of the human senses, to infinite, ever-present Love, ALL IS LOVE, and there is no disharmony of any kind, no sin, disease nor death.

May I truly *feel* that divine Love is the only substance, Presence, power, cause and effect, true consciousness, intention and being in and of the universe, and that to an elevated consciousness, there is no other power or presence.

Day 279

For Immigrants, Refugees and Others Arriving in a Foreign Country

In recent years, millions have had to flee their own country for a variety of political, economic, social and other reasons, such as civil war. The challenge of adapting to a new country, culture, language, climate, customs… is daunting, as anyone who has worked with or befriended such people knows. Just to survive you sometimes need to be a hero, especially if you are a mother with small children. Let us open our hearts wide to these brothers and sisters and really put ourselves in their shoes: how would we respond to such a situation?

We bless all those who have had to flee their homes and are attempting to adapt to a completely new setting.

We bless them in their unwavering courage, sheer grit, perseverance and stamina in face of the huge obstacles facing them daily.

We bless them in their innate intelligence and adaptability when facing complex rules and regulations, customs that seem to them really strange if not utterly bizarre.

We bless them in their equanimity and strength when facing

outright hostility from nationals resenting their presence out of fear or ignorance.

We bless the host nations in their spirit of compassion and sharing so that their citizens may be awakened to the immense human, intellectual and cultural wealth these newcomers represent for them.

And finally, we bless all concerned in their consciousness that my sister or brother *is* myself and that the challenge of integrating these immigrants is truly an amazing gift of the universe in helping all work toward a world built on collaboration and cooperation in all areas that will alone guarantee the survival of the human race.

Day 280
A Blessing for a Forthcoming Trip

This blessing can either be used in the first person singular or plural, depending on whether the trip is individual or collective (which starts with two!).

I bless this trip I am about to undertake to...... (name of place or country).

I bless myself in my understanding that You truly do guard me on my way and that Your protecting Love is my shield. I bless myself in my constant *feeling* of Your Presence and the assurance that no harm can befall me in the inner shelter built on peace and trust.

I bless myself in my openness to all the encounters Your tender caring has already prepared for me, new customs and new foods, to all that takes me totally by surprise, so as to learn new lessons and deepen my love.

I bless myself in my welcoming and eager anticipation of the Unknown, of unheard vistas of the heart, mind or soul, that I may be ready to take them all in so as to broaden my own inner and outer horizons.

I bless myself in my constant sense of humor when faced with the strange or bizarre or simply the little quirks of existence, my equanimity when unexpected encounters or an upsetting of my plans would attempt to put me off balance, my deep tolerance for all that does not fit into my little mental cubbyholes.

And above all I bless myself in the love, joy and generosity of the heart I may bring to every single encounter on my way.

Day 281
Native American Blessings

These blessings have such a deep and trusting relationship with Mother Nature and the living Earth – an attitude we have much to learn from amongst many other qualities. I have very slightly adapted this very moving prayer to give it the form of a blessing.

Earth, May You Teach Me
Earth, may you teach me quiet ~ as the grasses are still with new light.

Earth, may you teach me suffering ~ as old stones suffer with memory.

Earth, may you teach me humility ~ as blossoms are humble with beginning.

Earth, may you teach me caring ~ as mothers nurture their young.

Earth, may you teach me courage ~ as the tree that stands alone.

Earth, may you teach me limitation ~ as the ant that crawls on the ground.

Earth, may you teach me freedom ~ as the eagle that soars in the sky.

Earth, may you teach me acceptance ~ as the leaves that die each fall.

Earth, may you teach me renewal ~ as the seed that rises in

the spring.

Earth, may you teach me to forget myself ~ as melted snow forgets its life.

Earth, may you teach me to remember kindness ~ as dry fields weep with rain.

(Source: www.sapphyr.net/natam/quotes-nativeamerican.htm)

Navajo Blessing
Before me peaceful,
behind me peaceful,
under me peaceful,
over me peaceful,
all around me peaceful.

Day 282
For a Person Suffering from a Serious Disease

In recent years there has been a growing consciousness of the amazing ability of the human mind to alter the body (even elements like DNA, which was thought of earlier on as unalterable, can be modified). This is opening up vast new areas of unconventional (and sometimes supremely efficient) healing. There are carefully well-documented cases of chronic or terminal diseases healed solely by spiritual means. These and many other developments make it realistic to envision completely new approaches to health and healing.

We (I) bless...... (name of patient) in the great trial she(he) is facing with this major challenge to their well-being and even life. May they find the courage and determination needed to face any situation that could present itself.

May they feel deep down inside that however tough the going and dark the valley, Providence's constant and tender caring always surrounds them.

May they understand that if a human body can be temporarily derailed or even terminated, the divine Life in them knows no death, for there is none in Its omnipresence.

May they acquire such a clear grasp of their own divinity and oneness with their Source that all fears for their health just melt away, whatever the medical predictions and concerns.

May they delve deep down into the most secret chamber of their heart so as to contact their perfect being hidden behind the veil of material beliefs and appearances.

We (I) bless all the doctors involved that they may be guided to the most appropriate treatments, the nursing personnel in their deep humanity, and the family in its constant trust and encouragements of their beloved one.

Day 283
For Someone Considering Suicide

Each one in life is at their highest level of consciousness at every single moment. Truly understanding this makes judging our neighbor impossible. This is particularly true of people considering taking their own lives. Our hearts can only go out to them with the most immense compassion and tenderness. Which is what we will do now.

We extend our love and burning compassion to the thousands all around the planet who are considering at this very moment taking their own lives.

We bless them from the depths of our soul that they may by some miracle (i.e. the normal functioning of Grace) be touched by some event, experience, feeling which puts an end to their somber plans or halts their unpremeditated self-destructive impulse.

May the magic of Grace break through all the darkness in their heart, that they somehow feel the unconditional caring of the Source for their good and their wholeness, yea, even their deep happiness. Despite all the self-loathing and self-condemnation or simply their utter and total despair, may they feel that infinite Love has already forgiven in advance any – and everything –

they could ever do.

We bless them that they may understand that the lessons they might be avoiding here on earth will have to be learned in another realm or another incarnation – and that these lessons are solely for their good, however tough they seem to be (and some are admittedly horrendously challenging).

We bless those that surround them that they may find just the right words to turn them around and evoke in them that glimmer of hope that makes all the difference.

And if they have made a failed attempt at taking their own life, may they be received not with condemnation or a frown, but with open arms and hearts and loving faces and words that evoke in them the desire to live a full and useful life.

Day 284
Blessing Heals Hatred and Contempt (Testimony)

"These days I am spending a great deal of time reading and meditating on (the book) The Gentle Art of Blessing. *I cannot tell you how much good it does to me. It's strange. I read it quite a few years ago, underlining the passages that seemed important but it seems that the seed did not grow. This time, I have the impression literally of a change of level. I will be sure to stand strong in this inner reality when I am confronted with the aggressions of the world.*

I took a few days' retreat as certain circumstances of my life have represented a real challenge for me in the past years. I am the first to acknowledge that I had come to harbor a great deal of negativity in the form of despising people, hatred and violence which I did not know how to counteract and that often knocked me out with this ego that seemed stronger than me.

That is why reading your book, and especially applying it, constitutes such a balm for the wounded soul! And I realize how the simple act of blessing connects me immediately to the spiritual dimension from which I so wish to live. Because I am aware that, as I read somewhere,

'We are not human beings in the quest of a spiritual experience – rather, we are spiritual beings undergoing a human experience.' So blessing and living in a state of gratitude for the present moment seems to me the best way of manifesting our spiritual essence in our psychic and material world."

(Philippe, Belgium)

Day 285
Bodhisattva Prayer for Humanity

The following beautiful prayer/blessing is performed each morning by His Holiness the Dalai Lama. It was written by Shantideva, the Indian Buddhist sage of 700AD.

May I be a guard for those who need protection,
A guide for those on the path,
A boat, a raft, a bridge for those who wish to cross the flood.
May I be a lamp in the darkness,
A resting place for the weary,
A healing medicine for all who are sick,
A vase of plenty, a tree of miracles.
And for the boundless multitudes of living beings
May I bring sustenance and awakening,
Enduring like the earth and sky
Until all beings are freed from sorrow
And all are awakened.

Day 286
For Those on Death Row

I have been corresponding for 20 years with an inmate from Texas who was for 25 years on what is probably the worst death row in the US. Wherever they are, such places are among the toughest on the planet, and usually amount to the "cruel and unusual punishment" forbidden by the US Constitution. In the US, their cells are often 6–10 feet (or even less), sometimes with no window or then just a bare slit in the wall, and inmates can stay there year after year, sometimes decade after decade, without the slightest human contact, in total isolation. Many go mad. It is estimated that 4% are innocent. Such a percentage represents a huge failure rate for any legal system, still more so in matters of life and death.

We bless inmates on death row in their courage as year after year *really* drags by.

We bless those who are guilty that they may come to peace with what they did, and beyond their very real human guilt, discover their divine innocence.

We bless those who are innocent that they may find inside themselves the strength to fight for their release despite the challenges of little or no funds or legal help, and often very little or no support from family or society.

We bless the prison administrators and guards that, despite often heartless regulations, they may show inmates authentic compassion and understanding and attempt to lighten their terrible plight.

And we bless the public, wherever they may be in the world, that their level of consciousness may rise enough so as to press for immediate change and the end of the death penalty itself.

Day 287
A Blessing for Us All

May your endings be embraced with fervor equal to what you gave your beginnings.

May the stopping places in your life create a space for what is yet to be known.

Instead of sorrow, may you find joy.

Instead of hopelessness, may you find possibility.

Instead of terror, may you find peace.

When you face an ending,

may you know it is a beginning
tinged with the potential of a small seed in dark soil.
In the blackness of grief may life push through
And soften your sadness.
May the blessing of light be on you – light without and light within.

(Source: www.explorefaith.org/faith/explore_christianity/ holy_days/lent/lenten_blessings.php)

Day 288
Another Blessing for Deeper Compassion

There is a great difference between sympathy (from the Greek sym-, with – and pathein-, to suffer, i.e. to suffer with) and compassion. With compassion, one's heart goes out to the other to uplift and console them, strengthen them and express the deepest caring for their plight, but never taking their suffering onto oneself. The contemporary world is in immense need of compassion, possibly the most fundamental virtue in Buddhism.

I bless myself in my ability and desire to express the most authentic, unselfed compassion towards all, person, plant or beast.

May I have this deep, burning desire to be that gentle flame of loving compassion that embraces all, everywhere, at all times.

May my compassion tenderly embrace and uplift the most heinous criminal as well as the most dedicated servant of humanity, the most criminal and perverted dictator or the greatest saint, the cruelest sadist or my friendly neighbor, the illiterate street sweeper and the most learned erudite, the most distorted cripple or the beauty queen – all, all, all – without distinction of any sort.

May my compassion embrace Your wondrous creation, from the miniscule insect to the huge blue whale, from the modest shrub to the towering sequoias or the 3,000-year-old cedars of the Sahara, from the tiny stream to the infinite ocean, for You have created them for our enjoyment and pleasure.

And as I enter the inner silence, may it embrace my neighbors near and far of whatever kind or hue, religion or absence thereof, social status, political conviction, level of education, opinion or belief.

And finally, may my compassion embrace my past and my nation's past, my future and that of our race and cleanse any old shadows from the past or fears of what is to come in the most authentic embrace that deeply cares for, heals, appeases and uplifts.

Day 289
How Blessing Trials Heals

Buddha is said to have stated that, "Every experience, no matter how bad it seems, holds within it a blessing of some kind. The goal is to find it." When I look back upon my own life, I can see how the most terrible trials which appeared without any redeeming aspects turned into incredible blessings. So...

We bless our trials as precious gifts in disguise, as proofs of Love's care for us. We bless ourselves in our desire to listen for the hidden lesson rather than burst into complaint. We bless ourselves in our ability to trust that every cloud truly does have a silver lining, and that it will become apparent to us as we continue our path with our head high rather than take refuge under the blanket of self-pity.

May we have the discernment and patience to learn the exact lesson awaiting us in every situation in life, especially our trials.

May we persevere whatever the cost, however deep and dark the valley and especially however long the waiting before the first glimmer of hope appears on the horizon.

When the storm clouds of despair and total discouragement seem to engulf us, may we trust that, despite all appearances, our guardian angels never leave us nor would Love ever cause us unneeded suffering or abandon us.

Day 290
For Openness and Receptivity to Grace

Grace is the completely unexpected goodness of divine Love manifesting itself in our lives, often at the most unexpected moment. Some people call it "miracle" which is a word we use when we do not understand the perfect laws governing the nonmaterial sphere of being.

May I be open to the extraordinary fact that, at every moment and for all creation, grace is hovering in the wings of space-time, waiting to manifest itself.

May I see that what appears as a totally unplanned blessing is very much the expression of a higher Plan for our good.

May I at all times, and whatever the circumstances, be open to the presence of grace ready to assist, heal, encourage and uplift the willing heart.

When I see total despair in the eyes of my neighbor, may I rejoice that, even now, grace is working to heal the wound, dispel the sorrow and erase the damning belief of lack.

Finally, may I rejoice that the gentle workings of grace can undo the arrogance of human or material power in any form to heal, repair and transform.

Day 291
For Commitment to a Win-Win World That Works for All

It is becoming clearer every day that either we create a world that works for ALL, animals and nature included, or it will soon work for no one, starting with us humans. As citizens of the world – and we are all, whether we know it or not, such citizens – this should be one of our very top commitments.

We bless ourselves in clarifying our vision of a world that works for all and in our deep commitment to making it come to pass.

We bless ourselves in our willingness to give up those forms of consumption that do not enhance our ability to serve and work for this unified world – be it water use, transportation, keeping up with fads and fashions in all areas, or anything that oversteps the limits of having enough but not more.

We bless ourselves in our ability to share this vision with great simplicity and sincerity and without a trace of "preachiness" or self-righteousness.

We bless ourselves in our ability to see that such a vision is implicit in the very structure of the universe we live in, where absolutely everything is linked to everything else, that we may *feel* it and not only believe it.

And may we have that unshakeable trust that, at this very moment, our wonderful home, the universe, is conspiring to make this true for our beautiful blue planet and all its inhabitants.

Day 292
Blessing for My Ability to Adapt to Change

Never in history has the pace of change approached what we experience today. Nearly all of us are challenged by this deluge, which, however, has some great hidden benefits (otherwise it would not be happening).

I bless myself in my ability to crawl out of the timorous shells of the ego's fears so as to face the bracing winds of change with humor and courage.

I bless myself in my readiness to challenge the psychological mechanisms that cause me to resist change rather than welcome the possibility of growth and renewal it often brings.

I bless myself in my understanding that in a universe completely governed by the law of Love, down to the smallest detail, no humanly engendered changes or events can foil Love's plan of universal salvation, i.e. complete fulfillment for all and the final triumph of good.

May I also have the courage to refuse changes dictated by fashion or group pressure and hold my ground – if coming from my highest sense of right rather than timorous refusal of what is new.

And may I always peacefully continue on my path in the quiet trust that divine Love guards my every step and will allow no circumstance to foil its plan of total blessedness for my existence.

Day 293
For Life's Abundance

As my basic text on blessing states, blessing and gratitude are in a sense the two sides of the same coin. When you bless a situation or a person, you are also saying thank you to the universe for a given quality they express. And gratitude for a situation or a person implies necessarily that they constitute some kind of blessing.

Infinite Love, we bless You for the unbounded blessings that descend on us from all sides. Truly You are constantly opening the sluice gates of heaven and pouring on us such blessings that there often seems no room to receive them all – or even to number them. We bless you for the incredible beauty and abundance of nature that is pouring its gifts on us season after season, year after year.

We bless You for the innumerable people who cross our paths and enter our lives and enrich our existence by their different vision of things and the challenges they force us to face.

We thank you for that quite incredible support machine You have given us called the human body. Its intricate workings simply defy any attempt to describe it and the greatest scientists can only bow their heads in front of its perfection that defies our wildest imagination.

We bless you for our daily bread which takes such varied

forms, and for homes that offer support, warmth and peace.

We bless you for the innumerable difficulties that are as many opportunities to grow, expand our horizons and love more.

(Please continue this blessing with your own themes of gratitude.)

Day 294
To Eliminate Mass Rape as a Tool of War

Rape and genital mutilation used as an instrument of war has been going on for 15–20 years in the Kivu region of the Democratic Republic of Congo, where an estimated 500,000 women and even babies and men have been raped. Dr. Denis Mukwege, a modern saint, who can only leave his hospital in Panzi under police protection, has over the years operated on tens of thousands of women who have been not only raped but whose sexual organs have been destroyed out of pure sadism. Let our deepest compassion tenderly surround all concerned.

We open wide the doors of our hearts to all the participants in this drama in Kivu.

We bless the women who have been raped that they recover their sense of wholeness, holiness and health.

We bless the female children and even babies, victims of this barbarity, that their physical, mental and psychic integrity may be healed and restored.

We bless the families concerned that they have the courage to overcome social barriers to the loving and full reintegration of the victims and the national and local political authorities, usually run by men, that they take decisive action to stop this massive violence.

We also bless from the bottom of our hearts the perpetrators of this horror "who know not what they do," that they may awaken to the sheer insanity and cruelty of their actions and to the fact that they are piling hot coals on their own heads as they will have to reap what they sow.

And finally, we bless the international community that it may go beyond the all too easy moral denunciations of these events written in the restful comfort of plush meeting rooms to taking decisive action to stop this silent war which is an affront to the dignity of us all.

Day 295
To Express Kindness, Part I

Kindness is one of the most civilized expressions of the human being. The well-known US writer George Saunders has written a book on this theme, Congratulations by the Way: Some Thoughts on Kindness, *where he stresses that "expansive awareness of the greatest gift one human being can give another – those sacred exchanges that take place in a moment of time, often mundane and fleeting, but echo across a lifetime with inextinguishable luminosity." He says that what he regrets most in life are failures of kindness. Anonymous blessing is a unique manner of expressing kindness. (Quote from: https://www.brainpickings.org/2014/04/28/george-saunders-on-kindness-)*

I bless myself in my ability to stay open to the innumerable opportunities in my life to express loving-kindness: giving up my seat or carrying the bag of an elderly citizen, saying a kind word of appreciation to the supermarket cashier for her smile, exchanging a few words with a homeless beggar rather than just anonymously giving some change and hurrying on – and the thousand other opportunities with which my life is graced.

I bless myself in my ability to see that every act of kindness is also a gift to myself, broadening my heart's outreach, often softening the use of my time, awakening my awareness, filling me with quiet joy and above all teaching me to see myself in my sister or brother. For truly we shall love our neighbors only as we recognize them to be the reflected image of who we are.

I bless myself in my ability to express my innate loving-kindness to all nature: to avoid walking on the ant or the fly on the ground, to spare swatting the mosquito whose strident buzz drives me crazy, to gently raise the bended daffodil and to take the time to support it with a small stick, to dig a grave for the fallen sparrow because for me it is meaningful, to donate generously to a specific activity aimed at supporting some urgent or important environmental issue, to talk to a caged dog that seems so desperate for a kind word.

To just let the innate kindness of my heart arise and shine.

Day 296
Expressing the Gentle Fragrance of Kindness, Part II

I remember a friend sharing with me the infinitely sad story of this young man from San Francisco who was on the verge of committing suicide and decided he would give life a last chance: he would cross the whole city on foot and if one single person smiled at him, he would not commit suicide.

He committed suicide.

I ardently pray that I never be the person who passes him without smiling!

I bless myself in my deep yearning to sow everywhere the spiritual fragrance of anonymous blessings.

When I see or feel the slightest hint of suffering in my sister or brother, beast or bird, may I help allay it by claiming the opposite of what the material senses scream.

When I become aware of any situation of distress or lack on this gentle blue planet that supports us all, may the kindness woven into the texture of my soul rise to alleviate it in any manner available to me.

May I never later in life ever regret a missed opportunity to express kindness.

May I never pretend or claim I am too rushed by time to perform a random act of kindness, or that my act of kindness is really unimportant, or that in any case it is too insignificant to be of any meaning, for the tiniest act of kindness is of more value to the progress of humankind than the donation of a huge fortune for a wealthy man's self-aggrandizement.

And may I, through every single act of kindness of mine, planned or spontaneous, challenging or easy, be seen as Your smile upon the earth and Your comforting Presence upholding all. May people no longer see me, but only, only, only YOU.

Day 297
Blessing Restores Peace and Results in a Cleaner Living Environment (Testimony)

"At the time I was living in Yverdon, Switzerland, on the ground floor of a small four-storied building and I had access to a little lawn with some flowers. One day, I noticed several cigarette butts on the lawn; irritated, I picked them up. From then on, every day, new butts were tossed in front of my window, and the location suggested that they were thrown from one of the windows of the apartments above my own. Angered I tried to catch the offending smoker, without any success.

Suddenly, I remembered that Pierre had introduced me to the art of blessing, and I decided to put it to a test.

So I thought about this person and felt compassion for them. Indeed, one often lights a cigarette because of hassles, worries, wounds that trouble our lives. Moreover, this person was very likely addicted to cigarette smoking.

So I began blessing this individual in their life, to claim peace and new hope on their behalf as well as freedom from the smoking dependency. Each butt became a motivation and a reminder to bless. To my surprise, within a few weeks, the cigarette butts disappeared, although nobody in the building had moved out.

The practice of blessing first brought me peace of mind by eliminating my irritation, and then specifically, my lawn remained clean."

(CG, Switzerland)

Day 298
For the Healing of Racism and Ethnic Rejection

Racism and the rejection of people because of their ethnic origin are still very widespread in our societies. In a world where communications and the sense of oneness are growing by leaps and bounds, such outdated and parochial attitudes have to disappear if we wish to set up the win-win world of the future.

I bless all those who are tempted to reject their neighbors because of their color or ethnic background.

I bless them in discovering that part of themselves they unconsciously reject which in turn nourishes their rejection of others.

Because we are all one, may they understand that in rejecting their brother or sister, they are also unwittingly rejecting themselves.

Rather than squatting in the comfortable, closed mental seclusion of their racial or ethnic identity, may they open wide their arms and hearts to our polychrome humanity and its wonderful diversity of forms, shapes, colors, odors and sizes.

And may all who are victims of rejection or persecution due to their ethnic background or color feel deep down that their true value has nothing to do with appearance but solely with their true identity as children of the light and of the Creator of all life who says to them, "I am so happy to express Myself as you."

Day 299
To Be Aflame with Divine Love

In a variety of teachings, unconditional love is the heart and soul of the spiritual life and the ultimate aim of the spiritual path – and by love is meant love in action of course (be it meditation or feeding the hungry), not discourses about love.

We bless ourselves in our desire to have a heart consumed with love.

We bless ourselves in our ability to extend this love to every living thing and even inanimate ones.

We bless ourselves in our ability to embrace so-called enemies in the warm embrace of this forgiving love.

May this love be our first cry of joy when we awake in the morning and our last thought of gratitude when we fall asleep at night.

May this love so permeate our thinking, dreaming, hoping, speaking, and acting that we ultimately cannot exist outside of its radiant splendor and constant warm presence.

May we radiate such love that all those who cross our path feel caressed by its gentle aura, and may we look at all with the eyes of love; where human vision sees poor sick humanity may divine Love so fill our soul that we no longer see but Your beauty and splendor.

Finally, may we understand and feel that, clad in the panoply of Love's transcendent power, human envy or hatred cannot come nigh our mental dwelling place.

Day 300
A Finnish "Pagan" Blessing

How strange words can be! In the very traditional Christian family in which I was raised, "pagan" described something dark, ominous, foreboding and quasi sinful. Today, I can see that this attitude simply reflected the fear of the unknown that inhabited the church I belonged to. So as this book on blessing is also about extending our understanding, our hearts' compass and our love, I am so happy to include this beautiful blessing of the sower of Nordic origin.

Blessing to the seed I scatter,
Where it falls upon the meadow,
By the grace of Ukko* mighty,

Through the open finger spaces
Of the hand that all things fashioned.
Queen of meadow-land and pasture!
Bid the earth unlock her treasures.
Bid the soil the young seed nourish,
Never shall their teeming forces
Never shall their strength prolific
Fail to nourish and sustain us,
If the Daughters of Creation,
They, the free and bounteous givers
Still extend their gracious favor,
Offer still their strong protection.
Rise, O Earth! from out thy slumbers
Bid the soil unlock her treasures!

*Ukko in Finnish mythology is the god of the sky, weather and harvest.

(Source: https://blessingfiles.wordpress.com/2011/01/12/blessing-of-the-sower/)

Day 301
Seeing Through Appearances

More and more people are becoming aware that we live in a world of illusion – the material world – and that behind the veil of appearances there is a reality of such awesome beauty, harmony and depth that once one has tasted it, no human experience can even remotely compare with this true world.

I bless myself as Love's gentle smile on every living being.

May I have the deep spiritual insight that sees through all material appearances.

May I have the spiritual strength and clarity to discern the divine behind even the most horrendous human form.

May I understand that absolutely all that enters my life is infinite Love and its infinite manifestation for the Godhead truly is All-in-all.

And as I rise every morning may I rejoice that I am Your radiant goodness and beauty in ecstatic expression for all those I meet.

Day 302
For a Couple Learning to Live Together

The challenges of daily living can rapidly dampen the romantic enthusiasm of the early beginnings. To approach each new day with a sense of freshness rather than déjà vu, a sense of adventure rather than of habit, of "more of the same," a firm inner decision and a clear vision are needed. As the psalm says, "My age is clearer than the noonday, I do shine forth, I am as the morning."

We bless ourselves in our understanding that the enduring freshness of our relationship is a daily creation.

We bless ourselves in our ability to silence the indignation, protests or silent moans of our little egos by being better transparencies to divine light.

We bless ourselves in our ability to challenge the soporific, downward pull of humdrum daily living and its tendency to fall into the ruts of routine and habit which are sure killers of freshness, newness and our adventure *à deux*.

May we understand the magic of forgiveness in maintaining harmonious communication between us, including first and foremost the ability to forgive ourselves for our shortcomings and missed goals.

May we constantly renew our sacred commitment to loving ourselves and being true to ourselves without which authentic acceptance of the partner becomes a real challenge.

May we embrace wholeheartedly the bracing goal of living totally without judgment, knowing our partner is constantly at their highest level of consciousness.

And finally, may we take time in the rush of modern life to

keep open spaces of togetherness just to be with each other, without demands or expectations – just present to the beauty of our partner as the child of the Divine they are and always will be.

Day 303
For Deep Contentment of Our Fellow Humans

There are few more universal aspirations among humankind than the desire for authentic contentment. Who has not at one time or another felt a deep yearning for such contentment?

We bless every single one of Your children in their deep, lasting, unselfish contentment, a contentment that needs not be merited because it is the free gift of Your unconditional Love to all Your children.

We bless those who understand that it is only in sharing it that they can keep it, and also those who don't, that they may come to this realization.

We bless those who have reached the understanding that no lasting contentment can ever be found in things or possessions, prestige and power, and that it is solely to be found in the treasures of the heart.

We bless ourselves in our comprehension that as long as a single being on earth is dissatisfied, our work is not finished.

And may our deep yearning for the authentic contentment of every single being keep us socially and spiritually active till we move to our next destination.

Day 304
In the Aftermath of a Terrorist Attack

We live in a world where it appears that in most countries, almost anywhere, anyone can be blown up anytime. Yet many know that spiritual power, if intelligently harnessed, could be a major tool in offsetting this insanity so often due to desperation or hate. (Written the day after a terrorist attack in Ankara in October 2015 with a toll of close to 100 killed.)

From the deepest wellspring of my heart I bless all the victims of this terrorist attack, their families and friends. I bless those who were killed in their new understanding of why their destiny put them there, just at that moment.

I bless those who were wounded and their families that they may be given the courage and strength to overcome their natural human response of shock, extreme anger or hatred, despair and confusion, and regain their poise and peace. May they learn the lesson that awaits us all in every single challenge we all face at times.

May all those who were involved, either as victims or simple bystanders, summon the clarity enabling them to grant themselves the gift of unconditional, radical forgiveness. May the governments concerned receive the wisdom leading them to attack the root causes of this evil rather than turning to useless revenge or the temptation to counter violence with violence.

And finally, I bless the perpetrators of the attack, whether alive or dead, that they may sincerely repent of their extreme fanaticism and violence and discover that, despite all material appearances, they too are children of the light – and our brothers.

Day 305

I Am the Space of Love

One day, when we wake up to our true identity, we might be in for some major surprises. We will realize that this material body has absolutely nothing to do with our permanent identity, which appears to be completely spiritual. So here is a brief blessing to help us open up to this (for some, challenging) perspective.

I bless myself as that space of Love which constitutes my true permanent essence.

I bless myself in my resting in this new vision where people, events, things are just passing through a totally Love-imbued space which constitutes my true being.

I bless myself in the unshakeable assurance that nothing can disturb or harm such a purely spiritual reality.

May I just observe what goes on in that space without ever reacting, just blessing all those who pass, all that which happens but is never my essential divine being, totally and for always at home in Love's gentle embrace.

Day 306
For Someone Trying to Kick Substance Abuse

The drug trade is one of the main forms of business in the world today. In terms of income, the drug trade would represent the 19th economy in the world! Because of the hold that not only the drug but the whole lifestyle has on its victims, kicking the addiction to certain drugs like heroin represents a heroic achievement. Let us tenderly hold these brothers and sisters in the innermost chamber of our heart.

We bless all those who are valiantly attempting to get rid of their enslavement to drugs.

We bless them first and foremost in their sincere intention that it may carry them through moments of doubt in their ability to achieve the liberation from this slow suicide, and moments when their mind and body scream for their daily dose or the wish to quit everything and leave the human scene.

We bless them in their intelligence to seek the right form of support and the strength to break the old group attachments that kept them so long in the rut of dependency.

We bless them in their desire and opportunities to embark on new forms of training, to find a stable job, to create new, healthy relationships that support them.

We bless them in their understanding that the victory is already in sight the day they truly set their mind on this sacred aim, and that even though they walk through the darkest canyon, they are not alone, for Your rod and Your staff support them all the way to the lush meadows of deep contentment and peace.

So be it.

Day 307

For Those Earning Their Living Deceiving Others (Testimony)

Recently, I was a victim of computer pirates who managed to extort money from me by telephone claiming to repair my system, which my webmaster had to reinstall urgently. I also had to cancel my bank card. The total cost amounted to close to $500. The second I became aware of the deception, I instantaneously started blessing the people concerned. How incredibly sad to spend one's days deceiving one's neighbor, not to mention the bad karma one is amassing on one's own life.

We bless all those around the globe who earn their living by tricking and swindling their neighbor in their becoming conscious at the deepest level of their soul of the harm they are perpetrating and negative energies they are unleashing.

May they become intensely aware not only of the suffering and maybe personal catastrophes they are causing others, but the deep harm they are causing to themselves.

May they awaken to the law of right returns – i.e. that we always and without exception reap what we sow until divine grace intervenes – and may they truly repent of the harm they have caused.

And may those who were fooled discover the overwhelming beauty and healing power of true forgiveness, that they may be led to forgive not only those who deceived them but themselves for having been tricked.

And finally, we bless ourselves in our ability to discover in our neighbor's face, even behind the sometimes ugly mask of human, material appearances, the very face of God.

Day 308
For True Listening

Listening is a true art, be it listening to one's neighbor or anyone who is suffering, to one's partner or children, not to mention the most important of all, listening to the Godhead. For this, I believe, is the true value of prayer: not telling an omniscient Deity what It already knows, but listening to what It is telling us of the infinite abundance that is already ours at another level of reality.

I bless myself, first in my *desire* to truly deeply listen, and then in my *ability* to master this art.

Despite the constant background noise of a culture on the run, may I learn to make regular spaces of inner listening to tune in to You, divine Love, and to Your message of deep trust and constant encouragement.

May I learn to listen to the suffering of the world and my neighbor and decipher the meaning beyond the words.

When I open the morning newspaper or put on the TV news, may I listen to the message You are giving me behind or despite the pictures and words that appear on a page or a screen.

When I turn to You, may I grasp that the highest and most profound petition is not asking You to listen to my needs which You already know of, but hear Your millennial promise: my child, you are always with me and *all* that I have is – and will ever be – yours; and all that I AM, you are – and always will be.

Day 309
A Hindu Blessing

This blessing is from the Taittiriya Upanishad. The Upanishads refer to a series of sacred Hindu texts considered to be of revealed origin and dating approximately between 700 and 300BC. Their aim was to free believers from the cycle of reincarnation.

May the Lord protect us together!

May He nourish us together!
May we work together uniting our strength
for the good of humanity!
May our learning be luminous and purposeful!
May we never hate one another!
May there be peace, peace, and perfect peace!
(Source: https://blessingfiles.wordpress.com/2011/01/29/a-hindu-blessing/)

Day 310
I Refused to Judge (Testimony)

"I'd like to share a story which left me flabbergasted. Recently I read the book, The Gentle Art of Blessing. *It filled me with love. I already believed lots of the ideas but I never found how to stop someone from doing something wrong in any book I have read... I am referring to the affirmation, 'he is the perfect son of God.'*

Obviously I wanted to try it out. And I did on some occasions especially when I heard someone gossiping. There were a few times when it worked, but I was not sure. And other times when it did not work.

Then last Friday I had the confirmation that it really works. A woman spoke to me threateningly. As soon as she did, silently I stopped myself from judging her and said, 'She is the perfect daughter of God.' And I forgave her immediately. Then with a calmness I never thought I possessed (because in such situations I am frightened), I explained why I acted the way I did (which must have infuriated her). And wonder of wonders it really worked! We talked calmly until everything was settled between us.

I kept thinking about this incident, why it worked so quickly. And I came to the conclusion that it worked because I did not judge and forgave her immediately."

(Claudine – originally shared in:
https://www.facebook.com/groups/316404038484282/)

Comment by Pierre: It worked for you, dear Claudine, because there exist spiritual laws that are as rigorous and certain as those of physics if one knows how to activate them. However, they have to be felt on the level of the heart (and not on the mental level, which is the level on which most Westerners function 90% of the time). In such cases the result is often instantaneous.

Day 311
A Blessing for Equilibrium

Like the joy of the sea coming home to shore,
May the music of laughter break through your soul.
As the wind wants to make everything dance,
May your gravity be lightened by grace.
Like the freedom of the monastery bell,
May clarity of mind make your eyes smile.
As water takes whatever shape it is in,
So free may you be about who you become.
As silence smiles on the other side of what's said,
May a sense of irony give you perspective.
As time remains free of all that it frames,
May fear or worry never put you in chains.
May your prayer of listening deepen enough
To hear in the distance the laughter of God.
– *John O'Donohue, from* Benedictus: A Book of Blessings

Day 312
A Blessing for Silence

I weave a silence onto my lips.
I weave a silence into my mind.
I weave a silence within my heart.
I close my ears to distractions.
I close my eyes to attractions.

I close my eyes to temptations.
Calm me, O Lord, as you stilled the storm.
Still me, O Lord, keep me from harm.
Let all tumult within me cease.
Enfold me, Lord, in your peace.
(Source: *Carmina Gadelica: Ortha nan Gaid heal*, Alexander Carmichael, 1900, quoted in Blessing Files, op.cit.)

Day 313
All We Do Has a Planetary Impact

I receive daily inspirational messages from a variety of sources, including from The Universe (http://www.tut.com/inspiration/nftu; email: theuniverse@tut.com), which combine depth and humor. A recent one stated: "Did you realize that whenever you gave anything, to anyone, you gave to the entire world? And did you realize that for every path you've walked, for every stone you've turned over, and for every door you've knocked on, you did so for everyone? And finally, did you realize that whenever you felt love, for any reason whatsoever, you irrevocably lifted the entire planet higher into the light?"

It is an amazing realization.

We bless ourselves in our understanding that we are all linked in a planetary web of incredible intricacy beyond anything we can even start to imagine.

May we realize that with every single thought, we can help raise planetary consciousness by one notch, however tiny it may be and that a sincere and deeply felt blessing can change a life the other side of the globe.

May we realize that with every single glance we transmit a message of rejection, indifference or love.

May we have the awareness that the words we say can carry messages that communicate hope and healing rather than disinterest or negativity.

May I become conscious of the fact that every feeling I express sends out positive or negative energy to the whole planet.

May we be alive to the fact that every act of consumption sends out a powerful message on the kind of society we wish to build. And that at every moment, by our thoughts and deeds, we are all choosing the world of tomorrow in which we wish to live.

And finally, may we rejoice in the fact that every door of new possibility we open broadens the horizon of fresh opportunities for all humanity.

Day 314

Moving Out of Our Comfort Zones or Paid Parking Lots

We probably all have our mental comfort zones where we have given up attempting to progress. (I call them "paid parking" as the cost in terms of personal and spiritual development can be very high.) May this blessing help us ease out of them.

I bless myself in my ability to discern those areas of my life which I have chosen to neglect, or put between brackets because they disturb me, or which I simply prefer to ignore.

I bless myself in my ability to confront them and see what active steps I could take to start healing the issue, in whatever area of my life it may be: eating habits, finances, health, "TV-itis," various forms of sloppiness or physical or mental disorder, deeply ingrained attitudes or fears and so on.

I bless myself in my ability to shine the spotlight of alertness on my mechanisms of avoidance to facing a specific paid parking and in my courage to really confront this issue, *realizing that I am at the same time helping all those worldwide facing similar challenges.*

Above all I bless myself in my understanding of my true divine identity which enables me on the human level to muster the strength and wisdom to heal them in the most appropriate manner, and on the divine level to see that, as Love's reflection, they were never ever part of my true identity.

Day 315
Native American Blessings

I have given these brief texts the form of a blessing.
When you were born, you cried
and the world rejoiced.
May you live your life
so that when you die,
the world cries and you rejoice.
White Elk

Lakota Prayer
Wakan Tanka, Great Mystery,
May you teach me how to trust
my heart,
my mind,
my intuition,
my inner knowing,
the senses of my body,
the blessings of my spirit.
May you teach me to trust these things
so that I may enter my Sacred Space
and love beyond my fear,
and thus Walk in Balance
with the passing of each glorious Sun.
According to the Native People, the Sacred Space is the space between exhalation and inhalation. To Walk in Balance is to have Heaven (spirituality) and Earth (physicality) in Harmony.
(Source: www.sapphyr.net/natam/quotes-nativeamerican.htm)

Day 316
For Developing Infinite Kindness Towards Myself

We do not normally overflow with kindness towards ourselves, any more than we normally love ourselves unconditionally. Yet a psalm says, "I praise You that I am such a wonderful creature." Is that being not worthy of your ultimate kindness?

I bless myself in my ability to express infinite kindness to the child of the Universe I am.

May I unhesitatingly express to myself the kindness I am so willing to extend to others.

When I stumble or fall, may I grant myself a tender word of kindness rather than a harsh reprimand.

When I procrastinate, play tricks with myself or knowingly avoid a needed challenge, may I allow myself to become aware of the harm I am doing myself rather than knocking myself around with angry words.

When I am struggle-weary and feel like giving up the fight, may I allow myself a rest in Your green pastures rather than hitting myself on the head or whipping myself along.

And finally, may I always be aware of the barrier between the deceitful hammock of self-indulgence and the true wisdom of authentic kindness towards myself, remembering Your words spoken through a great spiritual seer, "This is my beloved child, in whom I am well pleased" – a statement that applies to every single one of us on the planet (and other planets, too).

Day 317
Blessing for a Heart of Fire

May your presence always deepen
May your exploration never cease
May not a speck of God's creation elude your heart's embrace

May you live as you die – awake, ablaze.

May you live as you dream – garbed in miracles.

May you explode with loving light, in the mirror of your beloveds,

And may the sparks rain down forever toward an undivided world.

(Source: *Setting Your Heart on Fire: Seven Invitations to Liberate Your Life* by Raphael Cushnir, quoted in Blessing Files, op.cit.)

Day 318
A Blessing for a Vision of Our Future World

A dear friend who made many helpful suggestions for this book sent me this blessing she had composed which I am grateful to include, as vision is one of the two or three most needed ingredients to create a new world that works for all.

May we cultivate a vision of a world where love and compassion are stronger than hatred, fear, and self-interest.

May we envision a world where justice is administered impartially and not influenced by politics, race, social and economic status.

May we all work for a world where individuals and nations choose cooperation and sharing over competition and hoarding.

May we learn, individually and collectively, that we are stewards of our planet and its riches, not its abusers.

May we create a world where we all understand that we are one another's keeper, and that what happens to one individual affects everyone.

May we all learn to listen to, understand, support, and nurture one another.

And in the words of Paramahansa Yogananda, may we know that "the happiness of one's own heart alone cannot satisfy the soul; one must try to include, as necessary to one's own happiness, the happiness of others."

Day 319

For Children and Adolescents Forced into Prostitution

Child prostitution is as great a scandal as street children. It is estimated that between 2 and 3 million children are victims of sexual exploitation, mostly girls. As time progresses, the victims are younger and younger, often barely 10 years old. There is a transnational traffic run by well-organized mafias, e.g. from Nepal to India. The West is in no way protected from this huge money-making machinery, and it has been estimated that in Northern Italy 40% of the prostitution concerned adolescents. (See e.g. www.equalitynow.org and many other sources.)

Spirit of Truth and Love which infinitely cherishes all your children, I bless all the children worldwide forced into prostitution.

I bless them in their hope, trust, courage and vision that they may never lose sight of their goal of becoming free. I bless them in their protection from excessive violence and HIV/AIDS.

I bless them in their spirit that the divinity that is always in them may carry them through this trial and give them the courage and strength to bear it as long as it lasts.

I bless the leaders of the mafia rings which organize this traffic that they may one day have the integrity and courage to see what they are doing and the still greater courage to change their ways.

I bless the clients of these children that they not rationalize away their misdeeds by claiming they are helping their clients and their families survive and that they dare come face to face with the great harm they are committing.

And I bless the governments of the numerous countries concerned that they too have the courage to face their apathy and inaction in this field and take vigorous steps to restore the children's dignity – and their own.

Day 320
A Brief Blessing by Eileen Caddy

Today we are once more borrowing a blessing from Eileen Caddy. May I add that Findhorn Community runs workshops in many languages and is certainly one of the main centers in the world of what one might call a form of eco-spirituality. I have personally been blessed many times by my stays in that community.

May we make a habit of dwelling on all the glorious things of life,
Of seeing the very best in everyone and everything.
May we refuse to dwell on the depressing things
But raise our thinking.
May we let it soar higher and higher like the tiny lark
And sing your songs of praise and thanksgiving.

Day 321
For a Rapid Awakening of World Consciousness

Our world is in dire straits, to say the least. A visionary like Andrew Harvey, the founder of the sacred activism movement, even speaks of the apocalyptic times we are living. Yes, there are occasional outbursts on the environmental side but at the same time in the same newspaper or news bulletin, the governments of the countries concerned rejoice that the rate of economic growth is expanding, i.e. that we are consuming always more. Time to wake up, friends!

We bless our fellow citizens on this planet that they may awaken to the fact that the house is on fire and that, as a race, we are facing unprecedented challenges to our survival.

May we become really conscious of the accumulation of dangers in key areas of existence: the environment, huge and still growing gaps between the rich and the poor, the risk of tens of millions of citizens in threatened areas migrating to Europe or elsewhere, the survival of numerous species, and so many other threats that require our concerned attention and involvement.

May we have the courage to challenge the powers that be that, faced with the huge difficulties of today's world, they take more than purely symbolic or dilatory measures and that our mainline media dare face the hard facts rather than continue serving us soporific doses of entertainment and juicy scandals – not exactly the urgent call to action we are in so dire need of.

May we have the deep desire to seek guidance as to what each of us can do as a person co-responsible for the survival of the planet.

And we bless ourselves in our integrity and vision that our concrete commitment to action may be daily more aligned with our words and beliefs.

Day 322
A Blessing for Politicians

Being a politician in our society is not the easiest of jobs.

Between being lauded one moment for their achievements and maligned the next for their failures, the difficult adjustment of personal ambition on one side and authentic, unselfish public service on the other, resisting the temptation of the many subtle forms of corruption while at the same time keeping one's political punch... the challenges are numerous. Some manage brilliantly, others less. This blessing can be personalized as well as kept in its collective form as here.

I bless the politicians of...... (a given city, party, country, region, i.e. European Parliament) in the demanding task of keeping their moral integrity while attempting to meet the challenges of their office.

May they muster the courage to resist all undue pressures, whatever the origin, all attempts at corruption, all temptations to pander to public approval or media popularity at the cost of the quality of their achievements.

May they have the moral grit to resist courses of action that bow to public fears rather than true wisdom and intelligent foresight.

May they always live true to their deep convictions and highest sense of integrity rather than toe the party line, whatever the cost of such consistency.

Finally, may they manage the delicate balance between honorably filling the public demands on their time with the demands of their family life and/or personal relationships.

Day 323
Healing of Psychiatric Problems (Testimony)

"After a burnout, I had to give up my job as the head of a store belonging to a supermarket chain. With medication, a stay in a clinic and psychotherapy, I tried to put my life together again, and in the past year I have again been working in a store of the same company.

Constant mood changes brought me very close to a relapse. Depression and negative thoughts again started to control my days. In mid-December 2014 I had an appointment with my psychiatrist, Dr. J. Do you know what he prescribed me? Not medication which I have stopped taking for quite a time. No, he prescribed two books! The Gentle Art of Blessing *and* The Power of Now *by Eckhart Tolle.*

I recently finished both books and could see in them the solution to all my problems... These books show me a path that I can tread and they give me a new zest for life.

I started blessing everything – even my burnout. Maybe the illness was a sign to me that I should change my life, that I should live more consciously and follow another path. It is an opportunity to reconnect with and experience again happiness and love and above all to share them.

Since I started blessing – and believe me, in my job there are many, many opportunities to bless – the negative thoughts have decreased, the past is no longer so present and I feel better from day to day."

(Urban V., German-speaking Switzerland)

Day 324
A Hindu Prayer

We have transformed this brief text adapted from the Upanishads by Satish Kumar to give it the form of a blessing.

May I be led from death to life, from falsehood to truth.

May I be led from despair to hope, from fear to trust.

May I be led from hate to love, from war to peace.

And may peace fill our heart, our world, our universe.

Peace, peace, peace.

Day 325
For the Complete Fulfillment of All Beings

One who has left all judgment behind ends up being just filled with the deepest desire for the total fulfillment of all beings – not only humans, but all the inhabitants of the planet – i.e. all forms of life – from the "queer" creatures that exist at 15,000 feet below sea level to the "worst" gangster or greatest saint. It is just a deep, deep yearning beyond all explanation or justification.

I bless all my fellow beings on this planet in their deepest, most radiant fulfillment, whichever expression it may take for the form of life they manifest.

I bless my fellow humans in their radiant freedom, as they fully enjoy the weightless walking on this planet of one who has let go of all attachments.

I bless them in their unconditional love and forgiveness as they experience the complete serenity of one who accepts all beings just as they are, with no expectations or demands that they be otherwise.

I bless them in the deeply settled contentment and lasting peace of one who has realized that (s)he who has enough is rich – a wealth that no bank crash, social crisis or belief of lack can disturb, because it is rooted in the Kingdom within.

I bless my neighbors – and all humans are my neighbors – in their fundamental equanimity and poise that no outward circumstance or encounter can ruffle or upset. And I bless them also in their luminescent joy that it may illumine all those they encounter.

I bless all my neighbors of the animal and plant kingdoms that the huge challenges the planet is undergoing which often seriously endanger their habitats may not upset their role on this planet.

"May all beings be happy, well, and content."

Day 326
The Real Internet

Because we are all one, my every thought, word or deed has an impact on the whole planet. To become aware of this is so exciting, because it transforms us automatically into world healers the minute we understand this.

We bless ourselves in our complete interlinked body as one glorious whole and in our understanding that our every thought links us through Mind to the being and the thoughts of others.

That when we overcome an old weakness or some temptation, we are lifting up all those on the planet struggling with the same issues.

That when we fend off an aggressive advertisement for something we don't really need, we are strengthening those struggling to replace the strident "me, me, me" of wants with a peaceful assessment of their real needs.

That when we counter a collective wave of hatred or rejection aimed at a specific racial, ethnic, gender, social, religious or other group with feelings of deep love, we are uplifting the race and preparing the way for the coming win-win world, for such a world alone will ultimately enable us to survive on this planet.

And when I give the slightest message of caring and love to

our animal or plant brethren, I am sending to Mother Nature the message that more and more of us see our mutual survival as the condition of our continued existence on this planet.

Day 327
For Listening to – and Hearing – Divine Love's Messages

Infinite Love is speaking to us the whole time and in a thousand ways. Those who say that they can't hear the messages of the divine maybe simply need to learn to listen or translate Love's messages that are all around us.

I bless myself in learning to hear Your constant, gentle whisper to me everywhere and at all times.

When I see a mother bird taking such incredible care of her young, may I hear Your gentle murmur saying, "Can't you see, Janet, that if I take such loving care of a baby thrush, I will surely do the same for you?"

When I think of the manner in which the 37 trillion cells of my body function 24/7 without a day's vacation for umpteen years, may I hear You saying, "If I have put in place such a superb support system for one single human being, do you really believe I am not capable of running this small blue planet and keeping it on course, despite all humanity's mistakes, arrogance or fears?"

When after weeks of desperate or ardent prayer you see nothing happening, rather than complaining that I am not replying, may you learn to understand that I answered before you even asked and that to hear the reply needs your sharper listening and hearing, not my louder talking.

When a ton of ballast in the form of a challenging trial hits you on the head, may you hear my insistent murmur, "Jim, remember that trials are often just what is necessary for you to learn a much-needed lesson. So now yours is the choice between Yes and No."

And if perchance you complain that you do not have the time in your busy daily schedule to really pause and listen to me, might I suggest that you choose between the daily TV news and me, or, better still, learn to hear me *through* the news?

Day 328
The Wings of Defeat

The British writer Neil Millar once wrote a powerful text with this title which has helped many people who had gone through extremely challenging situations they termed "defeat." It was the source of my inspiration for this blessing.

I bless myself in my ability to learn and grow through this apparent "defeat" I have just experienced.

May I understand that the only possible way of being defeated is by labeling "defeat" a precious lesson life has crafted for me that I may learn exactly what I needed to learn just at the moment.

May I listen to what life is teaching me rather than waste my energy accusing others, circumstances, or, worse still, myself.

May I understand that in a universe completely governed by Love, despite all material and visual appearances to the contrary, all things work together for the good of those who invest themselves sincerely in the creation of a better, saner world – and ultimately of all beings.

Where forgiveness is needed, especially of myself, may that forgiveness be total and unconditional.

May so-called "defeat" nourish my resiliency and my determination to succeed next time rather than feed my discouragement and apathy.

And when I meet one utterly crushed, or in the shambles of shame, due to what they consider an unredeemable defeat, may my deepest tenderness surround them with the cloak of a new vision and hope, that they may rise and walk, eyes bright and head high.

Day 329
A Blessing for Global Oneness Day (October 24)

The wonderful organization Humanity's Team, an international spiritual movement whose purpose is to communicate and demonstrate the timeless truth that We Are All One, asked me to write a blessing for Global Oneness Day 2016. Here it is. I would like to preface it with a few lines from that great Sufi master and poet Hafiz:

Look, one gets wings and gifts to the world
Music each morning;
One turns into such extraordinary light
He actually becomes a sustainer of a whole planet

We bless ourselves in our ability to express the light we truly are at the heart of our being, and thus to become willing tools to uphold, heal and sustain our beautiful planet.

We bless ourselves in our deeper understanding that we are all one, and that my neighbor truly is myself, and vice versa – but also that all living beings are equally my neighbors.

We bless ourselves in our profound yearning to build a win-win world that works for all, animals and plants included, and to never, never give up until that glorious day is here.

We bless ourselves in our inspired understanding that all life on earth, all beings, are meshed in the most intricate and miraculous manner, and that our every thought, word, and deed impacts the whole planet far beyond anything we ever imagined possible.

We bless ourselves in our desire to become caring stewards and consumers of the planet, with the added intelligence to take the needed steps to do so without a trace of guilt or self-condemnation when we have not met the standards we set up for ourselves.

We bless those who out of greed, envy, or an unconscious fear of lack suffer this insatiable lust for "more, more" that they be brought to an understanding that a wise stewardship of the planet will provide true and unending abundance for all. And we bless ourselves that we may replace any anger or condemnation we might have felt for them with the overflowing, caring love that sees them as Divine Love's children and cherishes their peace as we cherish ours.

Finally, may we reach that unshakeable trust that "He's got the whole wide world in His hands" and that the Supreme Intelligence which so lovingly crafted this incredible marvel, this precious little planet – our home – will not allow ignorance, fear or greed to destroy it, but will guide us through "the valley of the shadow of death" to the Fertile Valleys awaiting us all.

Day 330
For Fresh Inspiration

Few things are as soul-killing as routine, drabness, repetitive, mechanical activity. Let us open ourselves to the possibility of ever-renewed freshness in our everyday lives, activities, relationships, spiritual life. That which is performed with love can never be drab. Do you imagine a thrush or nightingale singing its glorious melody thinking, "I'm so tired of this same old song," or the alpine edelweiss perched on an unreachable ledge at 10,000 feet lamenting, "Oh gosh! No one ever sees me – why preen myself every morning to make myself beautiful," for it knows itself to be God's smile to the planet and the passing eagle.

I open myself to ever renewed freshness and, like Brother Lawrence in his modest kitchen, may I feel that no action, however humble, can be boring if performed in the consciousness of Your magical Presence.

Whether I be a writer, surgeon, counselor or secretary, teacher, mother, street sweeper, may I know that Niagaras of ever-fresh divine inspiration are just awaiting my openness and gleeful expectation to pour in.

May my innate and maybe dormant enthusiasm be awakened by the understanding that, as Mind's ever-renewed expression, I never ever need give in to cynicism, mental fatigue, boredom, humdrum habit, etc. For as divine Life expressing Itself as me, true inspiration and ever-renewed wonder are my essence and not the result of some arduous spiritual labor, of adding on some additional knowledge or zest, but of peeling off the layers of false belief concealing my present divine nature.

A great Master told us we would never enter the Kingdom – that space of constant wonder and joyful praise – unless we became as little children. Not bankers, rabbis or preachers. Little children.

Are you ready?

Day 331
A Grand and Glorious Adventure

Every morning on awakening, one of my very first thoughts is: "What grand and glorious adventure is awaiting me today?" Then I stand up next to my bed with outstretched arms and pronounce 7–8 times the most powerful word in human language (Dr. David R. Hawkins, MD dixit): YES, followed by: thank you! (to whatever is to happen).

I bless myself in my complete openness to all that You have planned for me today.

May I learn to put aside all my human planning for what I believe *should* happen to be open to anything that *could* or *will* happen.

May I learn to welcome, rather than fear, the Unknown for its amazing potential for unexpected inner growth.

May I be ready to be totally surprised at every moment, and remember that every single situation, opportunity or encounter is a precious gift from You, whatever the packaging.

I bless myself in my readiness to discover the incredible power of a YES that comes from the heart and said with total trust in the ultimate perfection of the plan You have already lovingly laid out for my life.

YES, YES, YES.

Thank you.

Day 332
Mass Slaughter of Animals

In recent years, a growing number of people have become aware of the number of animals (including fish) slaughtered in the world yearly – 80 billion just for the egg, food and dairy industries (for fish multiply by ten) – sometimes in the most horrendous manner, as for instance the terrible videos shown on YouTube in the spring of 2016 by the French collective L214 illustrated. Somehow, the dark energies set in motion by this massacre influence us all. There has to be a better way of feeding ourselves healthily.

We bless all humankind in our understanding that our neighbors include the animal kingdom.

We bless You for the millions of animal species that inhabit our planet and enrich our lives and enable to a great extent the very functioning of our environment, from the humble earthworms to the industrious bees, not to mention the innumerable insects, each one with its perfect function and role.

We bless those who run slaughterhouses in their awakening to the horrendous crimes thus committed on our helpless animal neighbors, part of Your wondrous creation, in the name of profit. May they become aware of the destructive energies thus unleashed on the planet and be led to an authentic change of heart. We bless them in their innate goodness and compassion and their awakening to the divine essence which constitutes their true being.

And we bless ourselves and all humanity in the understanding that one can lead healthier lives without meat, and that nature has provided us all we need to live perfectly balanced lives without resorting to killing totally innocent beings unable to defend themselves.

And may those attempting to abandon their meat-eating habits avoid all self-condemnation however slow and uneven their progress and however frequent their relapses. And may those still producing meat be led to treating their animals with respect and gratitude rather than as anonymous pieces of meat waiting to be slaughtered.

And finally, we bless ourselves as a race in our ability to open ourselves to our divine nature and its urge towards living our divine destiny ever more coherently in all areas of existence.

Day 333
My Neighbor Is Myself

To really grasp that my neighbor is myself – i.e. that we are all one – is one of the most important spiritual insights we can reach on earth and one that the world community urgently needs as we face the huge challenges confronting us. Which explains a second blessing on this theme.

We bless ourselves in the deep spiritual understanding that all is infinite Spirit, Love, and its infinite manifestation, hence that we are all expressions of the same divine Life that upholds all, that I am infinite Life living itself just as my neighbor is.

May we really comprehend with the most intimate fiber of our being that the radiant joy my neighbor expresses is also my joy, and that the deep suffering she or he is undergoing is also my suffering – hence also my responsibility and privilege to lighten or relieve.

May we really realize that there are no more private paradises in this world, and that to a material sense we will either make it together or sink together. At the same time, may we understand that in a universe governed by an unerring, loving Principle or infinite Intelligence, the more intense and widespread this consciousness of being all One is grasped by us all, the more trustingly we will be able to face the challenges already present and the greater ones ahead.

And may each one of us realize that she or he is the key actor in the game!

Day 334
A Blessing for Inner Silence

Silence is a rare presence in the constant noise of our hustling and bustling world. Yet a great American mystic like Joel Goldsmith could say that the essence and very heart of true prayer was silence, not talking and expressing needs and wants, wishes and desires. We can't even encounter ourselves if we live in constant inner and outer noise and agitation.

So shhhhhhhhh...

May I learn to tone down the strident clamor of our strange world which, like a police car all sirens screaming, rushes nonstop to its unknown destination.

May I return many times a day to that clear pool deep down inside where I will always find food for my soul and the freshest waters for my heart when parched or tired.

May I learn to listen to the gentle murmur of divine Love which, like a stream running under the moss-covered carpet of a forest, whispers messages of peace and hope and gentle promptings to all receptive hearts.

And may the loudest noise of all, that of a constantly parading ego for whom passing unnoticed is a quasi-death sentence, quietly disappear in the presence of Love whose firm insistence ultimately dissolves the tallest monuments of man's pride.

Day 335
A Blessing for Clear Thinking

A precious friend shared this brief blessing with me. It is so deep in its simplicity. May I suggest that you learn it by heart and use it as a spiritual tool to keep your thoughts centered throughout your days?

Bless my thoughts so they will reject discord and dwell in Your peace,

Bless my eyes so I may see everyone and everything through the eyes of Love,

Bless my ears so that I may hear the still small voice through the chatter,

Bless my mouth so my words may speak truth and love,

Bless my hands so they can do the work I am meant to do,

And bless my feet so they may take me where I need to go.

Day 336
Family Conflict Resolved (Testimony)

"I am using my vacation time to read your books. Thank you is the simplest word that comes to mind for your spreading of the practice of blessing. It is such an essential key which opens up the invisible and which enables us to detach ourselves from the widespread and morbid idea of returning evil for evil.

Blessing on the other hand is so clear and right and it opens the heart.

My mother, who is 86, had been very badly treated by my brother. I invited her to bless him and I helped her do it that same evening and the next day at noon. In the evening of the next day, my brother phoned to apologize. My mother really thanked me as my brother's apologies were truly miraculous. And that the 'miracle' happened because of her change of attitude was a great discovery for her. I really rejoiced because I know that now my mother will feel less alone and less helpless to face what is painful for her in life.

I no longer have any news of my son-in-law, but my daughter has

decided to return with her son to his father, who had threatened me. I continue sending out blessings and to support all and it continues to change me. The judgment I was making about my daughter's decision to return to her husband is little by little replaced by trust.

Each one is at his highest level of consciousness...

May the practice of blessing enable many, many, many people to feel less lonely and less helpless as they discover the power of the intention of the heart."

(Pilar, Switzerland)

Day 337
For a Drunkard Causing Disturbance in Public

A drunkard shouting obscenities on public transport isn't usually the immediate object of a wave of tenderness, caring and compassion from the onlookers. What a wonderful opportunity for us to step in and silently bless.

We bless this brother that he may awaken to his true divine identity – and we claim our ability to see him exclusively in this light.

We bless all those who are aware of his presence that they may be filled with compassion rather than judgment.

We bless him in his openness to grace that he may thirst for You rather than for a drink, that he may find his deep contentment in Your Presence – and why not today? – rather than in a substance that slowly destroys him.

And we bless him and all those facing the same challenge in the miracle encounter that could turn their lives around – even in an instant.

Day 338
Native American Blessings

Native American blessings are an endless treasure chest of deep, pure thinking and flowing inspiration. Here are three more.

Apache Blessing
May the sun bring you new energy by day,
may the moon softly restore you by night,
may the rain wash away your worries,
may the breeze blow new strength into your being,
may you walk gently through the world and
know its beauty all the days of your life.
(Source: http://www.worldhealingprayers.com/2.html)

Quero Prayer
May I look behind and be filled with gratitude,
May I look forward and be filled with vision,
May I look upwards and be filled with strength,
May I look within and discover peace.

In one short line, the following blessing summarizes one of the greatest insights anyone can have.

Bless those who challenge us for they remind us of doors we have closed and doors we have yet to open.

Day 339
For Someone Looking for Employment

As one who was at a time 30 months unemployed without any compensation payments (this is what most European countries pay to the unemployed) I have tasted this situation firsthand. But if the ultimate source of wealth is within us, all true supply comes from within, not without. I discovered this by creating my own job!

I bless this predicament for the important lessons I am going to learn, knowing divine Love would never have allowed it were it not in some way to bless me.

I bless myself in my courage, that I never be disheartened by the refusals or negative replies to my job applications I might receive, and I bless all those in the same situation.

I bless myself in the deep trust that unknown blessings are already on their way, however stark the external material picture may appear.

I bless myself in my imagination that I might discover original ways of hunting and applying for jobs, and also in the high energy I express when I present myself for job interviews.

Finally, I bless myself in my unlimited creativity and my openness to the exciting possibility that I might need to create my own source of income rather than depend on a regular job.

(*You can of course also change the tense and say:* "We bless the unemployed" *– or* "my friend or neighbor who is unemployed," *etc.*)

Day 340
To Express Our Full Divine Potential

For centuries sages and saints of all hues have been telling us that in our most authentic selves we truly are divine. And this is true of absolutely all human beings, from the jihadist kamikaze terrorist to the spiritual seeker who lives solely off light and the prana in the atmosphere.

We bless ourselves (family, neighbors, enemies…) in our innate divine essence.

As we rise in the morning, may we affirm first thing on awakening: I claim my beautiful and wholly perfect divine identity.

It is my divine right to uphold this identity for me and all in the face of the denials and screams of the material world, of psychological theories, guilt-obsessed theologies or the human and social sciences and so many other forms of human wisdom which claim to know what is.

We bless ourselves in our vision of this incredible truth and in our deep desire to reach out for it and make it the measuring rod of all our endeavors.

May our intent to hold on to this vision be so firm, so unshakeable, that no event of any sort, no drama or tragedy, individual or collective, may ever turn us from our path. And may our conviction be so strong and our vision so radiant and clear that others too may hold to this understanding, for truly it is the path of life.

Day 341
For Another Day of Blessing

"A blessing is a 'yes' to goodness, to grace, to an ultimately friendly universe. Blessings connect us to the wellspring of our very being," writes William John Fitzgerald, a retired pastor and author of eight previous books including One Hundred Cranes. *This wonder-filled book helps us see what the Celts used to call "the long hand of God at work in the midst of our busy lives..." Not only can we give thanks for the blessings of the day, as the author of the blessing below suggests, but we can give thanks for another day of blessing, of having uplifted our own thoughts through the practice of blessing.*

At the end of your day
Kneel down in gratitude
And give thanks for the blessings of the day.
Release all sense of accomplishment for now.
Let go of any entitlement.
It was all a gift.
Find a picture of one who represents the divine to you,
Or pictures of all those who do.
Give thanks for each and every thing.
(Source: Arjuna Ardagh)

Day 342
A Blessing for Simplicity

We live in a world of growing complexity in all fields. It is also a world where the consumer choices have gone far beyond any definition of what a reasonable choice would be – Amazon offers a possibility of over 200 million items on its site (New York Times International Edition, *October 24–25, 2015). This represents a massive loss of time and energy for consumers and the world. Yet, kneeling in adoration in the company of our Beloved One offers a wealth greater than all the kingdoms of the world. Don't take my word for it. Try it for yourself.*

In the whirl and swirl of our modern world, I bless myself in my ability to step aside, stop, and enjoy the greatest gift of all: the infinite simplicity and riches of Your Presence.

May I learn to prune my life of all its useless trappings and activities and simplify it down to its essentials, that I may have the time, energy and desire to hold on to what really matters: listening to You and serving my neighbor who also happens to be myself in disguise.

May I drop the hectic and impossible challenge of keeping up with the Joneses, the latest news, the latest book "I just must read," and the latest fashion of this or that. May they just fall by their own weight, and may I stand in the simple elegance of one who has discovered the fundamental truth that the "Kingdom of God" is simply that place of sublime beauty inside us where there never entered a single unessential presence or thought, where reigns but the feeling of God happening within.

I bless my fellow humans that they may discover the healing peace of uncluttered lives, the healing simplicity of an existence guided by one single and only desire: to love more, to serve more faithfully and hence to rejoice more constantly.

Day 343
For the Elderly

The ageing of the world population is a "first" in world history. The over-60-year-olds will more than double between now and 2050. This raises major challenges but also opportunities for the human community. The famous Tarahumara tribe of Mexico were for centuries the only known people in the world to believe one got more vigorous with age and demonstrated it by living usually well beyond 100 years, not to mention being the greatest known marathon runners ever discovered. Which goes to show that decrepitude is planned in the mind as much as the body.

We bless our countries in their ability to find new and creative ways of dealing with ageing populations, be it in the areas of minimum income and retirement plans, rapidly accelerating health costs, communal living arrangements and others.

We bless our communities in their ability to avoid labeling the elderly, and those advancing in years in their refusal of the stultifying or demeaning impact of such labels.

We vigorously refuse, both for ourselves and the elderly, the degrading and harmful concept of inevitable decrepitude which false beliefs have injected into our cultural background.

We bless the elderly in their ability to keep making plans for the future – which is such a powerful source of vitality and zest for life – rather than settle into a humdrum soul-killing daily routine. We bless them in their continued alertness and interest in the new developments going on all around them and in staying Internet literate.

We bless them in their consciousness of the unique treasure trove of wisdom and experience they have to pass on to the younger generations and in the ability of our communities to find ways to organize this exchange.

And especially, we bless them in their firm spiritual conviction that life is eternal and that passing on is but a springboard to a more expansive existence and the continued learning experience which is inscribed in our divine destiny.

Day 344
Tao Blessing

If there is to be peace in the world,
There must be peace in the nations.

If there is to be peace in the nations,
There must be peace in the cities.
If there is to be peace in the cities,
There must be peace between neighbors.
If there is to be peace between neighbors,
There must be peace in the home.
If there is to be peace in the home,
There must be peace in the heart.
May you have peace in your heart.
– *Adapted from a Taoist prayer by Lao-Tse*

Day 345
On Openness to Grace

The last five lines of this blessing are borrowed from the wonderful Daily Wisdom Messages of Paul Ferrini to which you can subscribe for free at: orders@heartwayspress.com.

I bless myself in my constant openness to grace – to grace happening in totally unexpected and often startling ways in my life.

I open myself to grace speaking to me in a thousand magical manners:

- the ecstatic song of praise of a lark soaring into the sky,

- the "chance" encounter with an old friend of many years' standing or meeting a total stranger who opens up an undreamed of and totally unexpected door to solving a challenging problem,

- the beauty of sunset or the melody of a stream which appeases my deeply troubled heart,

- the sudden and unheralded healing of a human relationship or of a seemingly hopeless, menacing disease,

- the right text that "just" brings the needed enlightenment or wisdom,

- a silent moment when I suddenly feel the presence of an angel by my side.

"Grace happens when you accept,
Struggle happens when you reject or resist.
Grace is effortless. Struggle takes great effort.
Struggle means that you get in the way.
Grace means that you stand out of the way."

Day 346
A Blessing for Those Who Feel They are Lost

Our aim is to bring about a world that works for all and blesses all (not just humankind but everything on the planet: plant, mineral and animal kingdom, environment). What Andrew Harvey calls "Sacred Activism" is needed from all of us.

The following blessing is a statement from the Vision Alignment Project which I adapted as a blessing.

We bless ourselves in our capacity to create a world where...

all those who feel lost have found their way home;

all who are cold have found shelter from the winds and a fire to keep them warm;

all who are hungry have found food in abundance;

all who are in pain are comforted and cared for;

all who are confused or struggling with their emotions have found peace in their hearts;

all who are lonely have found someone to hold them and love them;

and where all who yearn to wake up from the dream of separation and be One with their divine Source find that they never left home.

(Source: http://www.visionalignmentproject.com/)

Day 347

For Those Going Through Major Upheavals in Their Lives

Does this theme need an introduction? I doubt it – and those who have never had any such upheaval can skip it – or bless others going through such turmoil! "Smile" as my incredible death row inmate friend Roger would say, he who transformed his cell in the sheer hell of Texas death row into a place of peace and happiness. (After 25 years there, he is now off death row but still in prison.)

My heart goes out to all those who, through circumstances in their life (death of one close to them, a dramatic accident, major betrayal or bankruptcy, psychotherapy... the list is endless), are going through intense trauma, self-doubt or anger, or myriad other forms of inner turmoil.

I bless them in their deep trust that no experience befalls us without a reason, and that the greatest tragedy may just be hiding the greatest blessing.

I bless them in their trust that we live in a friendly universe which wants the good of every one of its creatures beyond anything we can even imagine.

I bless them in their understanding that this same loving universe is literally conspiring at every instant to bring into their lives exactly the right contact they need, just the right inspiration or new idea, the needed break in their inner turmoil and above all the activity of divine grace which, in the twinkling of an eye, can change absolutely everything for good.

I bless them that when life seems to them a canyon with sheer granite walls reaching to the sky, constant dark storm clouds and no way out, no rescue team of any sort, a little voice in their soul whispers the ultimate remedy, "You can always love. However desolate the path, be you totally broke or crippled for life in an armchair, you can always share love."

Day 348
When Struggling with Substance Abuse

May the God of mercy, who ministers to all who come to him, give strength to you, a servant of God.

May God enfold you in his love,
and restore you to the freedom of a child of God.
May God look with compassion on you
and all who have lost their health and freedom.
May God restore to you the assurance of divine, unfailing mercy,
strengthen you in the work of recovery, and help you to resist all
temptation.
To those who care for you,
may God grant patient understanding and a love that perseveres.

– adapted from "Blessing of a Person Suffering from Addiction or from Substance Abuse" on CatholicCulture.org. quoted in Blessing Files, op.cit.

Day 349
Resentment and Nightmares Healed Through Blessing (Testimony)

The testimony which follows is a short excerpt from a wonderful article, "Feel Free To Shower Blessings On Yourself," by Marguerite Theophil, PhD, of Mumbai, India, published March 14, 2015.

"The act of blessing – whether for others or oneself – interrupts the habitual way we see, feel and think about things, the shift allowing us to experience things differently than we normally would.

One example that I find inspiring is about a woman who told me that she had to undergo surgery of her leg at a very young age. Many years later she began to have nightmares about not knowing what had been done to the limb that had been removed during surgery.

When I spoke of blessing oneself, she wondered if she could bless that part of her that was no longer there, and began to do so. As she did this not only was she able to first get in touch with her buried deep anger about not being told much about it by either parents or doctors, but she was able to work through her emotions. The nightmares stopped. And now she blesses her prosthesis each time she uses it."

Please click on the link below to read the entire article!

(http://www.speakingtree.in/public/spiritual-articles/new-age/ feel-free-to-shower-blessings-on-yourself)

Day 350
For Wholeness in Our Being

In a commencement address I listened to by distinguished US writer and speaker Parker J. Palmer, I was struck by the following moving statement, "Wholeness means embracing the broken parts of you with love and gentleness." It inspired the following blessing.

I bless myself and all humans in our radiant wholeness.

I bless myself in my willingness to tenderly embrace those broken, repressed or unhealed parts of myself crying for attention and love.

May they know I acknowledge their presence and hear their cry.

Rather than delving into those subconscious areas of my being in the questionable pursuit of causes, may I offer them up to You that they may be completely dissolved in the warm radiance and penetrating gentleness of Your unlimited Love.

And may I realize that in Your eyes, no part of me was ever broken, hurt, bruised, distorted or depleted by life, but that I stand for eternity in my radiant wholeness as Your perfect child.

And may I see this for all fellow inhabitants of our little blue planet, animals and nature included, for ALL IS ONE.

Day 351
A Muslim Sufi Blessing

I have transformed what was originally a prayer into a blessing.

Inspirer of my mind, consoler of my heart, healer of my spirit,
May Thy presence lift me from earth to heaven.
May Thy words flow as the sacred river,
May thy thought rise as a divine spring,
May Thy tender feelings waken sympathy in my heart.
Beloved Teacher, Thy very being is forgiveness.
May the clouds of doubt and fear be scattered by Thy piercing glance.
May all ignorance vanish in Thy illuminating presence.
May a new hope be born in my heart by breathing Thy peaceful atmosphere.
O inspiring Guide through life's puzzling ways, in Thee I feel abundance of blessing.
(http://www.soitoronto.org/prayers-sufi-order/more)

Day 352
Blessing for a Sick Child

Who has not at one time or another had a sick child? Or known the child of a friend or family member who was very sick, maybe in danger of their life? Here is a blessing for such a situation written for a dear friend who had a seriously ill child.

I bless (name of the child) in their divine completeness hidden behind the veil of appearances. I bless them in their innate perfection which, as a child of God, only awaits to be revealed. I bless them in the perfect functioning of all their organs which always tend towards operating harmoniously.

I bless the doctors who take care of the child so that their heart and their thoughts be constantly open to the inspiration that comes to them from their Source and that they may always be led to use the most appropriate treatments for this child.

I bless the parents in their serene assurance that their child's GPS (God Positioning System) can never be derailed or err and that infinite Love's plan for their child cannot encounter any obstacles, no matter what might appear to the material senses. I bless them in their profound peace "which passes all understanding", so that no outside circumstances can cause them to lose their courage and clear vision.

And finally, I bless all the children on this planet who are facing the same challenges in the assurance that the infinite Life which is in all of us forever envelops them with Its active and unceasing tenderness.

So be it.

Day 353
A Prayer by Martin Luther King

I have adapted this brief prayer by Martin Luther King to give it the form of a blessing.

May we love you with all our hearts, souls and minds.

May we love our neighbors as we love ourselves, even our enemy neighbors.

In these days of emotional tension when the problems of the world are gigantic in extent and chaotic in detail,

May you be with us in our going out and our coming in, in our rising up and our lying down, in our moments of joy and in our moments of sorrow,

until the day comes when there shall be no sunset and no dawn.

Day 354
A Blessing for Serenity and Inner Strength

The following blessing by Evelyne Sinimale is translated from the French.

May you find serenity and tranquility in a world you can't always understand.

May the pain you have experienced and the conflicts you have survived give you the strength to pass through each new situation with optimism and courage.

May you be aware that there are always people who love you and understand you even when you feel very lonely.

And may you discover sufficient goodness in others to believe in a world of peace.

May a kind word, a reassuring touch and a warm smile be with you every day of your life – and may you make these gifts to others and receive the same.

Remember the sun even when the storm seems to never end.

Teach love to those who are full of hate and let that love envelop you when you go out into the world.

May you not be overly concerned with material issues but instead give immeasurable value to goodness flowing from the heart.

Take time each day to see beauty and love in the world around you.

Be aware that each person has unlimited competences but that each one is different in their own manner. What you believe is a weakness in you can become one of your strengths in the future.

May you find enough inner strength to appreciate your own value of your own self and not be dependent on the judgments of others for your accomplishments.

And may you always feel loved.

(http://evelynesinimale.over-blog.com/article-puissiez-vous-trouver-la-serenite-et-la-tranquillite-dans-un-monde-que-vous-ne-pouvez-pas-toujours-comprendre-57064681.html)

Day 355

The Courage to Follow My Own Path

We return once more to this theme, because being true to oneself is possibly the very first demand of authentic self-development and a meaningful spiritual path. Denying this absolute necessity once cost me the toughest – and hence most needed – lesson of my existence. However, once the lesson is really learned, it is highly improbable the lesson will need to be repeated!

I bless myself in my ability to stay true to my highest sense of right,

However far it takes me from the beaten track,

However loud the mockery of the Pharisees,

However sharp or hurtful the biting judgments of the self-righteous,

However nagging the pressures to conform to the accepted path, to custom, family, national or social tradition, professional pressure or time-honored mores,

However hurtful the emotional blackmail of those dear to me or a group to which I belong.

I bless myself in my ability to hang in there, again, and again, and again, however dark the night, however searing the solitude and however challenging the path.

May I stay anchored in my vision, not out of stubborn self-righteousness or pride, but out of simple faithfulness to what I feel to be true and right for me.

And may I trust that divine Love will always pull me through and that my guardian angel accompanies me step by step all along the rugged way – for a deep sincerity, unflagging perseverance and right intention are sure of success.

That is life's promise for all.

Day 356
The Ripple Effect of My Blessings

This blessing was inspired by the beautiful little video on YouTube, The Ripple Effect *(https://www.youtube.com/watch?v=TLMj6T0VNtY)3 57).*

I bless myself in my trust that my blessings ripple to the end of the world.

I bless myself in my deep faith that my loving, heart-impelled blessings can heal those in need the other side of the planet, even without me knowing about them.

May I trust that my little ripple, added to millions and millions of similar intentions, blessings, prayers all round the world, will create tidal waves of healing that will ultimately move history and bring down the frozen walls of selfishness, greed, bigotry, prejudice, hatred and fear that for too long have divided mankind.

May I rejoice daily in the gentle tool divine Love bestows upon me via this practice, that I may become every day more alert to the needs of those near and far and respond to them with my highest sense of what is right, be it in thought, word or deed.

And may I rest in the peaceful assurance that all is well, yes, all is very, very well, that the script of the show is not in our hands, and that because we live in a friendly universe, if each one does her or his part, the results will be in alignment with the harmony of the blueprint.

Day 357
A Blessing for Those Unjustly Incarcerated

All round the world, people continue to be incarcerated, often very unjustly, either for crimes they have never committed, or for political or other reasons. Many stay incarcerated for decades, some for life. Their existence is almost that of zombies buried alive. Only their moral strength enables them to survive. Let our hearts go out to them and embrace them in our deepest sisterly/brotherly love.

We bless all those around the world who have been unjustly imprisoned, due to harsh laws, defective justice, grave dysfunctions in the police work on their case if not outright concealment of testimonies in their favor, political manipulation, social, racial, religious and other forms of intolerance.

We bless them in their ability to rise above all resentment or desire for vengeance.

We bless them in their unwavering courage, so as to face day-to-day harassment, inhumane living conditions, deprivation of most or all human rights, often the total lack of hope and the absence of human contacts and support.

We bless them in their discovery of, or holding on to, their divine identity and their closeness to You, despite the sheer hell of their cruel fate.

May they experience the inner breakthrough that will enable them to see the clouds lifting and the blue sky of hope manifesting itself on the horizon.

May they trust then even in the valley of the shadow of death and quasi entombment, omnipresent grace can perform miracles.

And above all, may they reach that saving truth that even in the desolate spaces of their no man's land they can love, yes, love the hateful guards, the sinister judge and administrators, their fellow inmates and above all – themselves.

Day 358
A Blessing for Illegal Immigrants

With the chaotic state of the world, the number of illegal immigrants is bound to increase. 12 million in the USA (spring 2016), countless millions in Europe (no exact figure available). I have personally been befriending one of African origin for years. He lives like a kind of ghost or zombie with almost no contacts, incredible gaps in the most basic understanding of the culture where he exists (rather than lives), no one to employ him even illegally, hardly an envious situation.

We bless all those who because of the challenging situation in their country or their personal predicament seek asylum under what they hope will be friendlier skies.

We bless them in their ability to adapt to totally foreign customs and a new language.

May they learn to face hostility with serenity, outright rejection with strength, and discrimination with wisdom and even humor.

We bless them in their unfailing courage in their search for work, lodgings, contacts and all the other essentials of settling down in a new culture and country.

We bless them in their unbending determination to succeed.

We bless all those who meet them and have contacts of some sort with them in their ability to empathize deeply with the situation of these immigrants and to extend the hand of neighborly kindness and benevolence to them and their families.

We bless the population and politicians of the host countries in their realization that, at some point in our long history, we have all been immigrants from one area of the planet to another, not to mention when our countries invaded or colonized others; that we ultimately all migrated to our common planet in some form or another, and that in a world of growing oneness, we urgently need to learn to live together if we do not wish to die apart.

Day 359
Blessing for a Pregnant Mother

If we choose to bless others, we will inevitably end up feeling more blessed. This is of course not a reason to bless, but it is good to know. So today our blessing will be for one of the most precious groups on earth, pregnant mothers. Why not post it in your local maternity ward?

I bless the little life in me in all its perfection.

I bless it in its harmonious development, perfect health and the spiritual food it will receive from me during the whole pregnancy.

I bless myself in my constant peace, knowing that this little life immediately captures all my moods and emotions.

I bless it in the divine light that already surrounds it and the guardian angels that already protect it.

I bless myself in my deep serenity, knowing that the divine Love that is also the essence of my being protects me from all harm, all fear, all trauma.

I bless these pregnant months of joyful learning and blessing.

I bless myself sincerely and joyfully in the beauty of the divine being I am now.

And I bless us both in our perfect Oneness with the divine Life which maintains every single cell and atom of our beings in their total perfection.

Day 360
For Assuming the Full Responsibility of One's Life

"Victimitis" – feeling a victim of some situation or person or any other claim – is one of the most widespread syndromes of our societies. Many people live their whole lives feeling victims of one thing or another – hence never become truly adult, as the first characteristic of an adult is that of assuming full responsibility for everything that enters one's life. That does not mean one caused it, but that one accepts the full responsibility for one's response to the situation.

I bless myself in my ability to say YES THANK YOU to every person or situation that enters my life, knowing full well that it contains a treasure for me to discover, a hidden gift of divine Love to make me grow – that ultimately everything is grist for the mill to help me access the true reality behind material appearances.

May I absolutely shun complaint in any form and under any guise, for it is the bed companion of feeling a victim; and may I discover the amazing power of gratitude as the absolute antidote and perfect vaccine to feeling sorry for myself or a victim of circumstances or others.

May I understand that at every moment I have the choice of my attitude, and that infinite Love has endowed me with the ability to respond with intelligence, creativity and love to any circumstance, rather than wax faint in the arms of timidity, doubt or fear.

May I see that at another level of reality, there is a perfect plan for my life, and that at every moment, the universe is conspiring for my total happiness and profound contentment, hence that "trials are proofs of Love's care" and that ultimately all things *will* work out for my good.

Day 361
Living Each Day to the Fullest

I have transformed the text by SH Payer, "Live Each Day to the Fullest," into a blessing.

May you live each day to the fullest.

May you get the most from each hour, each day and each age of your life.

May you look forward with confidence and back without regrets.

May you be yourself – but your best self.

May you dare to be different and follow your own star.

May you never be afraid to be happy and enjoy what is beautiful.

May you love with all your heart and soul and believe that those you love also love you.

When you are faced with a decision, may you make it as

wisely as possible and then forget it, for the moment of absolute certainty never arrives.

Above all, may you remember that God helps those who help themselves, then act as if everything depended on you and pray as if everything depended on God.

(Source: http://www.anxietyslayer.com/help-with-anxiety-podcasts/2010/6/30/poem-live-each-day-to-the-fullest.html)

Day 362
Saved from Tuareg Rebels by Blessing (Testimony)

"It is truly a joy for me to give this testimony of an adventure that might well have ended very badly had it not been for the power of blessing.

I am an anesthetist physician, and in 2007 I got a call from a surgeon colleague in Toulouse on behalf of an association, 'The Children of the Aïr region,' which was urgently looking for an anesthetist for a mission to Niger. I jumped at the opportunity and got ready, albeit with a strange feeling that I might lose my life. I can't explain why, but this prompted me to send to a few friends your text The Gentle Art of Blessing. *They received it warmly.*

Upon arriving in Niamey, we immediately left for the small town of Tanout, in the north, where a curfew had been imposed because of the presence of Tuareg rebels. We reached the camp where we were to be lodged, fairly close to the hospital. The very next day we were put to work. Surgical operations began at an intense rate, since the hospital had been without an anesthetist for months and the waiting list was very long.

As we finished the last operation, we noticed that the phone lines had been cut. Black smoke rose from the nearby camp, and shelling started – not exactly a reassuring situation. Still, we decided to go back to the camp. We left the town in a 4X4 when suddenly we were stopped by rebels who had barricaded the road and were aiming their

Kalashnikov guns at us. Here I was, a lone woman among these rebels, held in detention deep in the boondocks, a French hostage likely to provide them with ransom money – a rather worrisome prospect!

Soon after, we arrived at a base camp teeming with masked Tuareg rebels. At one point, one of the rebels in the Jeep tried to recover a cartridge that had fallen to the ground. He turned towards me – he couldn't be older than 15 years old. Inexperienced and doubtless trigger-happy! It is at this moment that I started blessing him, because what else could I do in such a dramatic situation? It truly was my only weapon.

Moments later the Tuareg rebels' top chief appeared, leaned across the door of the vehicle and said to us in French: 'You may go.' Stunned silence! Everything stopped within us and around us. Then slowly, hardly daring to believe our good fortune, one of us took the wheel and we left the rebel camp slowly, thinking they might strafe us from behind. But nothing happened and we joined our mission colleagues who related to us how they were able to evade shots while several barracks near ours were pierced with bullets.

And the following morning we resumed work, 'business as usual.' In spite of urgent warnings by the French Embassy, we decided to complete the mission. Later, we learned that we had been freed because one of the best friends of the rebel chief was the companion of Annie Claire, a midwife member of our mission.

Upon my return, Patrick, one of the friends with whom I had shared the text on The Gentle Art of Blessing, told me that one evening he felt impelled to bless us all, myself and my team. And that evening was January 21, 2008, the evening we had been arrested by the Tuareg rebels.

And to think that some people still believe in chance and 'coincidences'!"

(Florence, Toulouse, France)

Day 363
A Blessing for the Weather

Such blessings need to include the wild hurricane and tsunami as well as the gentle spring rain or sweet softly-scented evening breeze, for if really everything is part of a wider plan for our good, this has to also include such dramatic events. As the great old spiritual goes, "He's got the whole world in His hand... He's got the wind and the waters in His hand..." – and all the rest too!

We bless You, Infinite One, for the incredible intricacy of nature in its thousand and one manifestations.

We bless you for the marvel of the gentle rain feeding my neighbor's freshly sown corn field, yams or cocoa plantation and the sun which makes all things grow.

And we bless You also for the catastrophic floods, the wild tsunami or rising sea levels which are Your emergency signals telling us to get our act together and make radical changes in our economic and financial systems before it is too late. This includes deepening our compassion and developing a keener sense of solidarity with *all* Your children, from the Dogon farmer in Mali fighting ever more severe droughts to the villager in coastal Bangladesh whose whole village has been washed away by rising sea levels.

We bless You for the incredible marvel of this planet, including its weather systems and their sometimes incomprehensible manifestations, knowing that "infinite Mind creates and governs all, from mental molecule to infinity," that everything has its place in the perfection of Your ultimate plan for this planet and the universe.

So may I learn to say "Yes thank you" to any weather condition, whether it foils my vacation plans or enables the perfect vacation, for somewhere, at a level I may not comprehend, *all* is on schedule!

Day 364

A Blessing to Overcome Apathy

Who has never been challenged by apathy in her or his life – be it one's own apathy where action is needed, or the apathy of whole systems resisting change.

I bless myself in my refusal to accept apathy in the many forms it takes, overt or hidden.

I bless myself in challenging my own apathy in any area, be it overcoming a specific bad habit, indulgence in any area such as food, sex, "TV-itis," superficial reading or absorbing information that does not enrich or uplift me, procrastinating the need to exercise or meditate... the list is endless.

I bless myself in challenging collective apathy in innumerable fields, be it racism, the growing power of specific economic groups, the pressure to conform in so many areas.

May I love myself enough to come from a keen, even stubborn sense of what is right for me, of what it means to really be true to my most authentic self, and live it with passion, whatever the cost may be.

Day 365

The Last Word on Blessing: Walk Your Talk

I could think of no more appropriate way to conclude this book than with this powerful text by Andrew Harvey, the creator of the concept of spiritual activism. Andrew is one of the great mystics of today who has inspired thousands all round the world to turn their spirituality into the real power behind their lives rather than icing on the cake. He has also been a real source of inspiration to me, in part because he is a man of passion, and I do not believe anything of lasting value can be achieved without passion. It is all too easy to make (create, utter, send out) a nice blessing for the environment and hop into one's car or an airplane for a trip that is really not necessary or that could be made in another manner. I have slightly reworded it to conform to the form of the blessings used throughout this book.

O beloved,

May I not pray for the poor

Without working tirelessly to end the systems that thrive on poverty.

May I not pray for the animals without working hard to end the systems that are slaughtering them.

May I not pray for justice and compassion and the coming of your kingdom without being willing to give my life to make them real.

May I be saved from the subtle and lethal hypocrisy that would make me believe I love you when I risk nothing to make this love real in your world.

A Brief Post Scriptum

My Final Prayer for You, Dear Reader

Among the Moba of North Togo, if things were going well, the traditional way of replying to a person who asked someone how they were was, "My heart is covered with honey."

So, dear friend, my deepest desire is that the practice of blessing will bring you such a deep, quiet joy that if one day we meet in some corner of the globe, be it on a warm day in Verhoyansk, Siberia, Kaolack, Senegal, La Forclaz, Switzerland or a Zen monastery in Montana, and I ask you: "How are things getting along?" your face will break into the most beautiful smile and you will reply, "My heart is covered with honey."

Pierre Pradervand

pierre@vivreautrement.ch

www.gentleartofblessing.org

https://www.facebook.com/ppradervand/

www.vivreautrement.ch (French website)

Chronological List of Blessings

32. For the Fount of Goodness We Are
33. A Taxi Driver's Blessing
34. A Blessing for Parents
35. The Beatitudes Revisited
36. A Scottish Blessing
37. A Blessing for Single Mothers
38. For Seeing the Perfection in My Life
39. Addiction to Drugs, Alcohol and Violence Healed testimony
40. For the Healing of Being a Control Freak
41. For the Militants of ISIL
42. Inspired by the Prophet Muhammad
43. Standing Strong
44. A Blessing for Inmates in Prison and Their Guards, Part I
45. A Blessing for Inmates in Prison and Their Guards, Part II
46. Putting First Things First
47. Blessing My Food
48. An Irish Blessing for Times of Sorrow
49. A Blessing on Service
50. For Unselfed Being
51. Harmony Restored in a Polygamous Household testimony
52. For Inner Peace
53. A Buddhist Blessing
54. A Blessing for Abundance
55. On Stewardship of My Life
56. A Blessing by Steve Jobs
57. A Blessing for Financial Speculators
58. Native American Blessings: Holding on to Good
59. For an "Anonymous" Clerk or Cleaning Woman
60. A Blessing Psalm
61. A Blessing by Peace Pilgrim
62. Seeing Through the Eyes of Love
63. A Blessing for Silence
64. Gives Away Hundreds of Copies of The Gentle Art of Blessing
65. Waiting in a Café

231. For the Happiness of Humankind
232. Impossible Work Situation Resolved testimony
233. For Miracles
234. Native American Blessings
235. A Blessing on Following My Own Path
236. A Blessing for Humility
237. An Ojibwa Blessing
238. Celtic and Irish Blessings
239. Love's Protection
240. A Blessing for You My Friend
241. A Blessing to Simply Trust Divine Love
242. A Blessing Affirming Divine Guidance of Our Lives
243. For Children of Separated or Divorced Parents, or When a Parent Just Disappears
244. God Be Me
245. Harmony Restored Before Concert testimony
246. A Blessing by Laurel Burch
247. Seeing the Day with Fresh Eyes
248. Lakota Instructions for Living
249. Blessing for Earth-Healers
250. A Franciscan Blessing
251. A Blessing to be a Tool of Love's Healing Touch
252. For Those Consumed by Anger, Hatred or Resentment
253. A Blessing for Every Day
254. For Children Who Have Temper Tantrums
255. A Blessing for Awareness of the Divine Presence
256. A Blessing for Friends (Marianne Williamson)
257. A Blessing for Joy
258. Blessing Brings Deep Peace after a Theft testimony
259. A Blessing to See God Everywhere
260. For Learning to Love Well
261. A Blessing to See Everyone's Innocence
262. A Blessing for Child Soldiers
263. A Simple Blessing

362. Saved from Tuareg Rebels by Blessing testimony
363. A Blessing for the Weather
364. A Blessing to Overcome Apathy
365. The Last Word on Blessing: Walk Your Talk

Alphabetical topics index

General Themes:

Body and Health blessings

Blessing my body, 10
For those experiencing constant physical pain, 107
For those condemned by medical diagnosis, 128
For someone undergoing a surgical operation, 137
Blessing for an illness, 190
To overcome the plague of alcoholism, 192
To heal the challenge of insomnia, 193
To heal the belief of incurable disease, 197
For a person suffering from a serious disease, 282
For someone trying to kick substance abuse, 306
When struggling with substance abuse, 348

Celtic, Irish and Scottish blessings

Blessings by John O'Donohue, 8, 66, 100
Scottish blessing, 36
Blessing in times of sorrow, 48
Traditional Irish blessing, 118, 154
Blessings by Eileen Caddy, 145, 320
Scottish, Irish and Celtic, 162, 238
Blessing for a home, 171

Children, blessings for

Street children I and II, 30, 31, 181
Bullying, 114

Earth and Environment blessings

Homeless and Migrants, blessings for

Jobs, blessings for

Native American blessings

Those in prisons, blessings for

Relationships, blessings for

Individual blessings in alphabetical order

O-BOOKS

SPIRITUALITY

O is a symbol of the world, of oneness and unity; this eye represents knowledge and insight. We publish titles on general spirituality and living a spiritual life. We aim to inform and help you on your own journey in this life.

If you have enjoyed this book, why not tell other readers by posting a review on your preferred book site? Recent bestsellers from O-Books are:

Heart of Tantric Sex
Diana Richardson
Revealing Eastern secrets of deep love and intimacy to Western couples.
Paperback: 978-1-90381-637-0 ebook: 978-1-84694-637-0

Crystal Prescriptions
The A-Z guide to over 1,200 symptoms and their healing crystals
Judy Hall
The first in the popular series of six books, this handy little guide is packed as tight as a pill-bottle with crystal remedies for ailments.
Paperback: 978-1-90504-740-6 ebook: 978-1-84694-629-5

Take Me To Truth
Undoing the Ego
Nouk Sanchez, Tomas Vieira
The best-selling step-by-step book on shedding the Ego, using the
teachings of *A Course In Miracles*.
Paperback: 978-1-84694-050-7 ebook: 978-1-84694-654-7

The 7 Myths about Love...Actually!
The journey from your HEAD to the HEART of your SOUL
Mike George
Smashes all the myths about LOVE.
Paperback: 978-1-84694-288-4 ebook: 978-1-84694-682-0

The Holy Spirit's Interpretation of the New Testament
A course in Understanding and Acceptance
Regina Dawn Akers
Following on from the strength of *A Course In Miracles*, NTI
teaches us how to experience the love and oneness of God.
Paperback: 978-1-84694-085-9 ebook: 978-1-78099-083-5

The Message of A Course In Miracles
A translation of the text in plain language
Elizabeth A. Cronkhite
A translation of *A Course in Miracles* into plain, everyday
language for anyone seeking inner peace. The companion
volume, *Practicing A Course In Miracles*, offers practical lessons
and mentoring.
Paperback: 978-1-84694-319-5 ebook: 978-1-84694-642-4

Rising in Love

My Wild and Crazy Ride to Here and Now, with Amma, the
Hugging Saint
Ram Das Batchelder
Rising in Love conveys an author's extraordinary journey of
spiritual awakening with the Guru, Amma.
Paperback: 978-1-78279-687-9 ebook: 978-1-78279-686-2

Thinker's Guide to God

Peter Vardy
An introduction to key issues in the philosophy of religion.
Paperback: 978-1-90381-622-6

Your Simple Path

Find happiness in every step
Ian Tucker
A guide to helping us reconnect with what is really important in
our lives.
Paperback: 978-1-78279-349-6 ebook: 978-1-78279-348-9

365 Days of Wisdom

Daily Messages To Inspire You Through The Year
Dadi Janki
Daily messages which cool the mind, warm the heart and guide
you along your journey.
Paperback: 978-1-84694-863-3 ebook: 978-1-84694-864-0

Body of Wisdom

Women's Spiritual Power and How it Serves
Hilary Hart
Bringing together the dreams and experiences of women across
the world with today's most visionary spiritual teachers.
Paperback: 978-1-78099-696-7 ebook: 978-1-78099-695-0

Dying to Be Free
From Enforced Secrecy to Near Death to True Transformation
Hannah Robinson
After an unexpected accident and near-death experience, Hannah Robinson found herself radically transforming her life, while a remarkable new insight altered her relationship with her father, a practising Catholic priest.
Paperback: 978-1-78535-254-6 ebook: 978-1-78535-255-3

The Ecology of the Soul
A Manual of Peace, Power and Personal Growth for Real People in the Real World
Aidan Walker
Balance your own inner Ecology of the Soul to regain your natural state of peace, power and wellbeing.
Paperback: 978-1-78279-850-7 ebook: 978-1-78279-849-1

Not I, Not other than I
The Life and Teachings of Russel Williams
Steve Taylor, Russel Williams
The miraculous life and inspiring teachings of one of the World's greatest living Sages.
Paperback: 978-1-78279-729-6 ebook: 978-1-78279-728-9

On the Other Side of Love
A Woman's Unconventional Journey Towards Wisdom
Muriel Maufroy
When life has lost all meaning, what do you do?
Paperback: 978-1-78535-281-2 ebook: 978-1-78535-282-9

Readers of ebooks can buy or view any of these bestsellers by clicking on the live link in the title. Most titles are published in paperback and as an ebook. Paperbacks are available in traditional bookshops. Both print and ebook formats are available online.

Find more titles and sign up to our readers' newsletter at
http://www.johnhuntpublishing.com/mind-body-spirit

Follow us on Facebook at https://www.facebook.com/OBooks/
and Twitter at https://twitter.com/obooks